# The Challenge of Strategic Management

*David Faulkner*
*and Gerry Johnson*

Cranfield
School of Management

KOGAN
PAGE

First published in 1992

Reprinted 1992, 1996

Kogan Page Ltd
120 Pentonville Road
London N1 9JN

© David Faulkner and Gerry Johnson, 1992

**British Library Cataloguing in Publication Data**
A CIP record of this book is available from the British Library.

ISBN 0 7494 0766 2  ✓

Typeset by Books Unlimited (Nottm) – Sutton-in-Ashfield, Notts. NG17 1AL
Printed and bound in Great Britain by Biddles Ltd, Guildford and Kings Lynn

# CONTENTS

## PART 3 –Making Strategies Happen

# LIST OF FIGURES

# LIST OF TABLES

# THE CRANFIELD MANAGEMENT RESEARCH SERIES

The Cranfield Management Research Series represents an exciting joint initiative between the Cranfield School of Management and Kogan Page.

As one of Europe's leading post-graduate business schools, Cranfield is renowned for its applied research activities, which cover a wide range of issues relating to the practice of management.

Each title in the Series is based on current research and authored by Cranfield faculty or their associates. Many of the research projects have been undertaken with the sponsorship and active assistance of organisations from the industrial, commercial or public sectors. The aim of the Series is to make the findings of direct relevance to managers through texts which are academically sound, accessible and practical.

For managers and academics alike, the Cranfield Management Research Series will provide access to up-to-date management thinking from some of Europe's leading academics and practitioners. The series represents both Cranfield's and Kogan Page's commitment to furthering the improvement of management practice in all types of organisations.

## THE SERIES EDITORS

**Frank Fishwick**
*Reader in Managerial Economics*
*Director of Admissions at Cranfield School of Management*

Frank joined Cranfield from Aston University in 1966, having previously worked in textiles, electronics and local government (town and country planning). Recent research and consultancy interests have been focused on business concentration, competition policy and the book publishing industry. He has been directing a series of research studies for the Commission of the European Communities, working in collaboration with business economists in France and Germany. Frank is permanent economic adviser to the Publishers Association in the UK and is a regular consultant to other public and private sector organisations in the UK, continental Europe and the US.

**Gerry Johnson**
*Professor of Strategic Management*
*Director of the Centre for Strategic Management and Organisational Change*
*Director of Research at Cranfield School of Management*

After graduating from University College London, Gerry worked for several years in management positions in Unilever and Reed International before becoming a Management Consultant. Since 1976, he has taught at Aston University Management Centre, Manchester Business School, and from 1988 at Cranfield School of Management. His research work is primarily concerned with processes of strategic decision making and strategic change in organisations. He also works as a consultant on issues of strategy formulation change at a senior level with a number of UK and international firms.

**Shaun Tyson**
*Professor of Human Resource Management*
*Director of the Human Resource Research Centre*
*Dean of the Faculty of Management and Administration at Cranfield School of Management*

Shaun studied at London University and spent eleven years in senior positions in industry within engineering and electronic companies.

For four years he was a lecturer in personnel management at the Civil Service College, and joined Cranfield in 1979. He has acted as a consultant and researched widely into human resource strategies, policies and the evaluation of the function. He has published eight books.

# CONTRIBUTORS

**Siobhan Alderson** is a research officer at Cranfield School of Management. Her main research interest areas are international management competence and business ethics. She is part of a Cranfield team conducting in-depth research into European top management competence development and has published and presented papers on this research.

**Andy Bailey** is a research officer in strategic management at Cranfield School of Management. He is a psychologist by training and previously undertook research in the area of cognitive styles and decision making at the Occupational Research Centre, Hatfield Polytechnic. His current research interests include the processes of strategy development and strategic change.

**Cliff Bowman** BA MBA, Lecturer in Strategic Management. After graduating, Cliff joined Shell UK in a marketing function, before moving to the UK Civil Aviation Authority as an economist. Since 1979, he has been engaged in management development. He has undertaken consultancy and management development work for a wide range of private and public sector organisations. Books he has published include *Strategic Management* (Macmillan, 1987) and *Management* (Heinemann, 1987).

Current research interests are centred on the process of structural reorganisation following shifts in strategy, and the mapping of management teams' perceptions of their organisation's strategies.

**David Faulkner** Bsc (Econ) MA, HIMC, Lecturer in Strategic Management. Prior to joining Cranfield David had a long career in strategic management consultancy first with McKinsey and subsequently with Arthur D Little. He also has experience as an entrepreneur, having built up and run his own leisure goods company.

David is an Oxford-trained economist by background. His particular interests in the strategy field include issues of strategy formulation and, in particular, the development of cross-border strategic alliances, a field in which he is engaged in extensive research. He also continues to be an active management consultant, working with senior executives on issues of business and corporate strategy.

**Gerry Johnson** BA (London) PhD (Aston) Professor of Strategic Management, Director of the Centre for Strategic Management and Organisational Change and Director of Research at Cranfield School of Management. After Graduating from University College London, Gerry worked for several years in management positions at Unilever and Reed International before becoming a Managent Consultant. Since 1976, he has taught at Aston University Management Centre, Manchester Business School, and from 1988 at Cranfield

School of Management. Professor Johnson is author of *Strategic Change in the Management Process* (Blackwells, 1987), co-author of *Exploring Corporate Strategy* (Prentice Hall, 1984, 1988) and editor of *Business Strategy and Retailing* (Wiley, 1987). He is also author of the *Strategic Management Journal*. His research work is primarily concerned with processes of strategic decision making and strategic change in organisations. He also works as a consultant on issues of strategy formulation and strategic change at senior level with a number of UK international firms.

**Andrew Kakabadse** Bsc MA Phd AAPSW MBPS Professor of Management Development. Professor Kakabadse worked in the health and social services and from there undertook various consultancy assignments concerned with local government reorganisation and large capital projects in developing countries. He has consulted and lectured in the UK, Europe, US, SE Asia, Gulf States and Australia, and holds positions on the boards of a number of companies. His current area of interest focuses on improving performance of top executives' and top executive teams' excellence in consultancy practice, and the politics of decision making. He recently completed a major work study of chief executives and has published 11 books and over 50 articles including the best selling book *Politics of Management* (Gower, 1983), and *The Wealth Creators* (Kogan Page, 1991).

**David Pitt-Watson** BA MA MBA, Visiting Professor. David Pitt-Watson is a Director of Braxton Associates, a leading strategy consulting firm. He joined Braxton eleven years ago to help establish its operations in Europe. Since then he has been responsible for helping formulate the strategies of many large and successful international companies, from Britain, continental Europe, the US and Japan. His experience covers a vast range of private manufacturing and service industries as well as public sector organisations. Prior to joining Braxton, David worked for McKinsey & Co, and for 3i Group. He holds a BA from Oxford University, and an MBA from the Swanford Business School.

**Susan Segal-Horn** BA MA MBIM, Lecturer in Strategic Management. Susan Segal-Horn is a regular speaker at international conferences and her research focuses on strategy in the service industries, particularly international growth and globalisation. She is currently carrying out research and consultancy on the future of the European food industry post-1992. She is also Visiting Associate Professor of Corporate Strategy at the Graduate School, University of Notre Dame. In 1985 she was awarded the Sloan Fellowship at London Business School.

**Murray Steele** Bsc Msc MBA, Senior lecturer in Business Policy. Murray Steele graduated on the 1976/77 Cranfield MBA Programme. He qualified as a mechanical engineer at Glasgow University in 1970, followed by a period as a Research Engineer. Prior to coming to Cranfield he worked in various management positions in the engineering industry. These included project and production manager for a small printing company; industrial engineer in a large engineering organisation, and works manager of a small engineering sub-contract in the automobile industry.

Murray consults on strategic change with the boards of a variety of UK companies and is also chairman of a hotel company.

**John Ward** is a Professor in Information Systems at Cranfield School of Management. He studied Natural Sciences at Cambridge and is a fellow of the Chartered Institute of Management Acountants. Before joining Cranfield in 1984, he worked in industry for 15 years, latterly as Systems Development Manager at Kodak. His particular interest is the use of IS/IT as a strategic weapon and the integration of IS/IT strategies with business strategies. He has researched and published extensively on these subjects. He is the co-author of the book *Strategic Planning for Information Systems* (John Wiley, 1990) and acts as a consultant to a number of major organisations.

PART ONE

# INTRODUCTION

# 1

# INTRODUCTION

*David Faulkner and Gerry Johnson*

In business schools throughout the world the strategy course has often become the cornerstone of the MBA syllabus or executive programmes. Yet twenty five years ago the words strategic management were hardly used. Courses were called business policy, and books were written about corporate or long-range planning. Since the end of the 1970s courses have been revised, authors have sought titles for books with combinations of words to link with 'strategic management', and research in business schools has been reorientated to focus on issues of strategic management. But what is strategic management, and why has there been so much attention given to it in the last decade or so?

Strategy is concerned with the long-term direction and scope of an organisation. It is also crucially concerned with how that organisation positions itself with regard to the environment, and in particular to its competitors. Strategy derives from the military vocabulary as a term. It is concerned with establishing competitive advantage, ideally sustainable over time, not by tactical manoeuvering, but by taking an overall long-term perspective. Managers working in organisations are familiar with the term strategy, and with discussing strategy, but many find it extraordinarily difficult to manage its implementation, often due to perceptual and organisational limitations within themselves and the firm.

Why then strategic management and not strategic planning, the older and more familiar term? Strategic planning became associated with an activity carried out somewhat apart from the line management of the enterprise, and reviewed only at periodic well defined intervals. It was also associated with long-term planning which was inclined to take a definitive view of the future, and to extrapolate trend lines for the key business variables in order to arrive at this view. Economic turbulence was insufficiently considered, and the reality that much strategy is formulated and implemented in the act of managing the enterprise was ignored. Precise forecasts ending with derived financials were constructed, the only weakness of which was that the future almost invariably turned out differently. Strategic management, then, puts the activity back where it belongs, with the line manager, and emphasises that its key difference from day to day management is, that it is concerned with the issues affecting the fundamentals of the business. But this is a major difference.

The purpose of this book is to use some of the research carried out at Cranfield School of Management to show, not only why strategic management is a challenge, but also how it can be understood better, and how some of the key strategic issues can be coped with more effectively. All the papers in this book are based on research carried out by their authors.

## THE CHALLENGE OF STRATEGIC MANAGEMENT

Figure 1 provides a very simple framework for thinking about the management of strategy. Strategy, it is suggested, is a function of managers' decisions, which seek to relate three key factors: the environment in which the organisation operates, the resources it has at its disposal, and the expectations and objectives of the various groups with a stake in its survival.

The simplicity of the figure conceals the complexity of reality. The manager faces a high degree of uncertainty. The business environment may be difficult to understand historically, but to predict its future shape is even more difficult. An illustration of the impossibility of predicting the future accurately is seen in the number of recent world events with major consequences, that were quite unforeseen by even the more perceptive commentators. It is difficult to find anyone who envisaged with any accuracy of timing at all, the dissolution of the Soviet Union, the reunification of Germany, the Gulf War, the development of democracy in Latin America, the crushing of the Democratic movement in China or the move of most advanced countries towards right wing policies based on a market forces ideology. Not only is the future unpredictable, but the expression 'long-term' has different meanings for different industries. For a retailer it may be three years, but for an oil company perhaps twenty-five. In either case the future is unknown. In relatively stable conditions unexpected things happen, and increasingly few business environments are stable.

The text books on strategic planning in the 1960s and 1970s suggested that the first step in determining long-term strategy was to establish clear objectives: theoretically this makes sense. However, in practice managers know that the sometimes conflicting influences and expectations of the various stakeholders can make the clear establishment of agreed objectives, let alone the problem of achieving them very difficult. Shareholders may have different expectations from managers, who in turn may have different expectations from City analysts, workers, the community and so on. Even the managers may not have a homogeneous set of expectations amongst themselves. The manager of strategy has to find ways of reconciling these potential conflicts, as the notion of clear and precise objectives and expectations is seldom met in the real world.

The resource capability of the organisation may also not be totally clear. What managers see as historic strengths may be weaknesses and inflexibilities in a changing environment. Moreover, to realise some of the

**Figure 1.1** The management of strategy

stakeholders' expectations may require the acquisition of additional resources, which can only be obtained at increased risk.

Even if the manager is clear about the environment, the stakeholders' expectations, and the resources at the firm's disposal, this is not to say that these three factors are congruent; they may be pulling in different directions. The forces in the environment may demand that the firm change its product mix, the shareholders may demand short-term returns, but the resources available may be insufficient to provide the necessary new product investment.

## DEVELOPING A STRATEGIC MANAGEMENT PERSPECTIVE

The first challenge to be met is the sheer complexity of the task. Typically, managers are trained in operational decision-making and management, but not strategic management. Consider the difference: operational management is concerned with short-term and commonly routinised managerial issues; strategic management means managing complexity in ambiguous longer-term, non-routine contexts, with issues that may be organisation-wide and fundamental to the survival of the organisation. Operational management is normally concerned with functionally specific tasks, any one of which is unlikely to imperil the organisation's future. Strategic management is concerned with positioning the organisation in the context of a changing environment and the expectations of influence groups, the very antithesis of operational management. Yet operationally trained managers are expected to convert into becoming strategic managers on promotion often without any further training, when they reach senior positions in the organisation.

Senior managers often find difficulty in making the transition from operational to strategic mode, and, seeking security, revert to their former functional perspectives. The former accountant still tends to see problems in accounting terms, the marketing manager in marketing terms, and the organisation faces internal tensions due to the partial views of its senior managers. Of course senior managers need to retain their skills as functional specialists, but the definition of a successful senior executive lies in his or her ability to see matters strategically as well.

## COPING WITH CHANGE

A further problem facing the strategic manager is that of coping with change. Figure 1.1 is basically concerned with formulating strategy. Yet most managers who have been involved in the strategic management process will say that the major difficulty is in *implementation* and effecting strategic change. There are several problems here.

First, managing change is essentially about managing, not concepts or ideas, but people. Strategy is often taught as though it were basically conceptual in nature, and concerned mainly with ideas about the future of the business. To be effective, however, strategy must take effect in action and behavioural change. Here we have another challenge. The strategic manager must be capable of handling complex ideas about the future of the business, and detailed aspects of the behaviour of people in the organisation simultaneously.

A further problem is that to cope with environmental complexity, managers often develop simpler 'models of reality' in which they make assumptions about the nature of their organisation and its place in the world. Indeed, they probably have to make such assumptions in order to make the task manageable, and to work effectively together. However these assumptions, sometimes called *recipes* or *paradigms*, can provide a significant constraint on change. So changing strategies may not simply mean adopting different ideas, it may also mean changing the behaviour of people, and even their basic beliefs and assumptions.

## THE BOOK IN OUTLINE

In its concern with the challenge of strategic management, this book addresses a number of themes from different perspectives. In Chapter 2, Murray Steele sets the scene with a discussion of some of the changes in the environment and the business scene likely to take place in the medium-term, and suggests some implications for firms' strategy. The next two chapters deal with the basics of business unit strategy. In Chapter 3 David Pitt-Watson takes strategy back to basics, and relates it to its formative influence in classical economic theory, proposing the thesis that the key to strategic success lies more in being able to provide a better product or service at low cost, than in seeking novel opportunities in the industry structure. In Chapter 4 Cliff Bowman builds on this theory in his critique of the popular concepts of generic strategies using management perceptions, and in Chapter 5 he draws together the themes of the previous two chapters through the development of a practical model for charting competitive strategy. Susan Segal-Horn outlines a way of identifying strategic opportunities through the concept of strategic groups and strategic space in Chapter 6, and in Chapter 7 David Faulkner, in his review of strategic alliances, discusses the possibility of increasing a firm's market strength through a strategy of cooperation rather than competition in relation to chosen competitors.

The problems involved in making strategy happen become the focus of the following chapters. In Chapter 8 Andy Bailey and Gerry Johnson explore different explanations of how strategies come about in organisations, and show how any one style is unlikely to so dominate a company that other styles are totally absent. In Chapter 9 Cliff Bowman and Gerry Johnson consider the varied ways in which managers understand strategies in their firms, and show how surfacing this can aid strategic decision-making and implementation, and in Chapter 10 Gerry Johnson considers strategy development in a cultural context, illustrating in particular the various blockages to change that can exist which inhibit the effective implementation of strategy. In Chapter 11 John Ward relates the area of management information to the management of strategy, and illustrates how modern computer-based information systems can facilitate both the development and the implementation of strategies. In the final chapter Siobhan Alderson and Andrew Kakabadse consider top team building as a prime requirement for the effective implementation of strategy. All the chapters in the book are based on research carried out at Cranfield School of Management by the contributors.

2

# THE CHANGING BUSINESS ENVIRONMENT

*Murray Steele*

## THE IMPACT OF DEMOGRAPHIC CHANGES ON BUSINESS

Any lecture or discussion on business strategy would, fairly shortly after its commencement, begin to consider the impact of the external environment on an organisation. Figure 2.1 shows the various external factors influencing any organisation – economic, political, social, ecological, legal and technological. Similarly any strategic planning exercise would have in its early stages a thorough review of the environment the organisation was likely to face over the life of the plan.

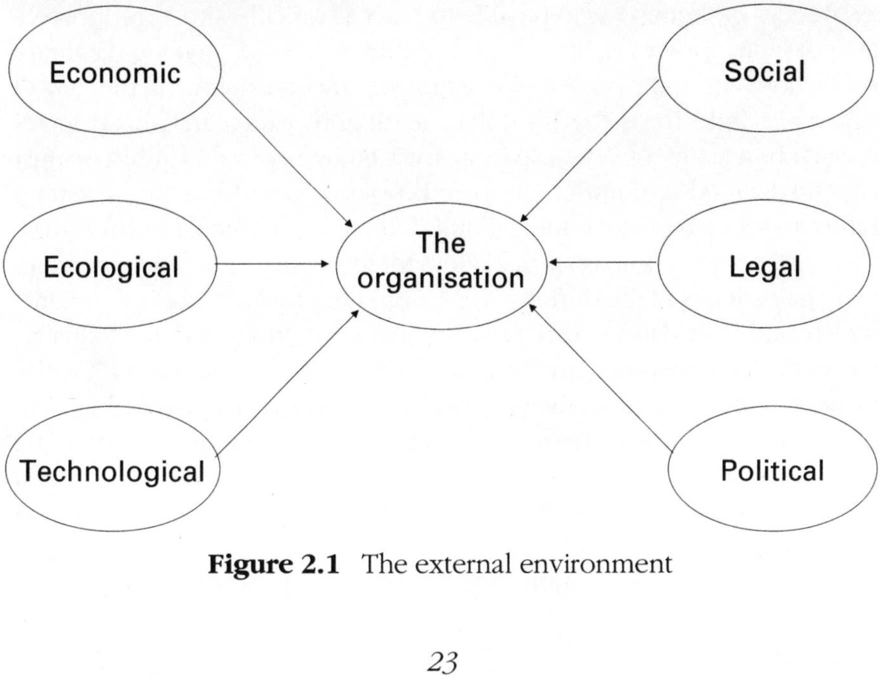


**Figure 2.1** The external environment

However reviews of likely future environmental scenarios are fraught with difficulties. How do you predict the future? Many companies plan strategically on a five year cycle. Consider the following economic statistics which affect the UK, comparing 1992 with five years ago.

**Table 2.1** UK economic indicators

| | 1987 | 1992 | 1997 |
|---|---|---|---|
| Price of Oil, $ per barrel | 18.34 | 17.50 | ? |
| Inflation Rate (%) | 4.0 | 4.1 | ? |
| Base Interest Rate (%) | 10.0 | 10.5 | ? |
| US$/£ Exchange Rate | 1.64 | 1.71 | ? |

There may appear to be little difference between some of the data for 1992 and 1987. However, the statistics, as usual, are capable of disguising many facts. Wide variations have existed between 1987 and 1992. Oil prices have been as high as $33 per barrel as a result of the Gulf War. UK inflation peaked at almost 11 per cent in 1990 before declining. Similarly between 1987 and 1992 base interest rates went as high as 15 per cent. The US$/£ exchange rate has operated in a band between $1.51 and $2.10 to the pound.

How are we to predict what these important economic indicators will be in five years time (1997)? It may be possible to argue that, as these factors are so significant and hence beyond the influence of any business organisation, the best that can be hoped for is to achieve a high degree of awareness of them so as to be able to react as quickly and appropriately as possible. However it is not feasible to avoid making accurate predictions in some cases. For example, the currency of the world aerospace industry is the US dollar, ie all aeroplanes are priced in US dollars, hence any business strategy for a company in this industry must contain detailed assumptions and predictions of their domestic currency's future movement against the US dollar. It can be particularly frustrating for an aerospace company's management to see the operational productivity gains it has made during a year wiped out by currency movements which are beyond its control. Similarly in the world automobile industry, currency relationships can be a principal factor in decisions, eg the location of new plants. In the mid-1980s when Jaguar was exporting 65 to 70 per cent of its output to the United States, a one cent movement in the £/$ exchange rate affected Jaguar's profits by £3.5 million. This had a significant impact on the company's expansion plans which were funded mainly from US revenues.

The degree of uncertainty shown by the economic and political examples given above are typical of the uncertainty that exists in predicting many of the environmental influences affecting organisations. Environmental forces do not act only in a singular sense. They also interrelate with and impact on each other, thus creating secondary effects. For example

1. How do political changes affect the economic and social dimensions? An incoming Labour government in the UK would probably shift the national emphasis from economic to social factors, from cuts in taxation to higher spending on public services, thus possibly placing a higher burden of corporation tax on businesses.
2. What impact will technological developments have on social trends? The increased use of technology may hasten the general drive to reduce working hours thus making it more difficult for organisations to attract employees with the appropriate skills.

What, then, can we be certain of in our considerations of the future environment?

Some trends which have reasonable degrees of certainty attached to them *are* discernible. For example, it has been a strong trend for some time – but will be given additional impetus by a series of recent unsavoury and well publicised cases (Guinness, BCCI, Blue Arrow and Maxwell) – that the legal scrutiny of business will increase. This trend will also be accelerated by the loosening of economic and political boundaries in Europe in 1993, thus exposing British business to the full blast of EC legislation.

The pace of technological development, particularly in data processing and information management, shows no sign of relenting. Woe betide any executive who has a fear or dislike of working at a computer terminal. The introduction of user-friendly executive information systems has meant that, in many, but not all, cases, the personal computer on the chief executive's desk has changed from being merely an adornment to being a practical tool of management in regular use.

It is hard to see many arguments against concluding that ecological or 'green' factors are here to stay as major influences in the environment of business. The term 'green' can be applied across a broad range of activities. At a design centre exhibition in London in 1989 a series of ordinary household products were displayed and assessed as to their 'green-ness.' If they were considered ecologically sound by the Design Centre, they were stamped with a large label, in green colouring, of the word 'green.' If they were considered ecologically detrimental, they were stamped with a large 'red' label. Many of the items on display considered to be 'red' surprised visitors to the exhibition. Examples of 'red' products were: bottles of perfume with excessive packaging relative to the volume of their contents; refrigerators which emitted chemicals, now known to be harmful; lawn mowers with insufficient protection for the user. The impact of the exhibition was to bring home to the visitor that ecology or 'green' meant far more than deforestation of tropical rainforests, and indeed could be considered to be happening all around them.

The final area to be considered is social, and here there is one factor where the future can be predicted with a reasonable degree of accuracy. The demographics of national populations, barring unpredictable events of a catastrophic nature, can be predicted well into the future with reasonable degrees of certainty. The remainder of this chapter will be devoted to describing the demographic changes which will take place in the United Kingdom and Europe and the far-reaching impact they will have on business organisations and their management.

As an example of the impact demographic changes will have, consider the European brewing industry. The principal consumers of beer are men between the ages of 20 to 29 years. It is estimated that they drink 70 per cent more than men in the 45 to 54 age range. They are wooed, through aggressive brand marketing campaigns, by the brewers to drink their products. However, across Europe, population numbers in this age range are reducing significantly. Table 2.2 shows the changes in the major European countries from 1987 to the year 2000. The reduction in the combined total for men and women is also shown for comparison.

**Table 2.2** European population changes 1987–2000 (projected)

| Number of people aged between 20 and 29 years (000s) | *Men only* | | | *Men and women* | | |
|---|---|---|---|---|---|---|
| | 1987 Actual | 2000 Forecast | Change (%) | 1987 Actual | 2000 Forecast | Change (%) |
| Belgium | 793.2 | 645.7 | −18.6 | 1556.4 | 1263.5 | −18.8 |
| France | 4269.9 | 3988.2 | −6.6 | 8504.6 | 7815.4 | −8.1 |
| Italy | 4647.4 | 4062.6 | −12.6 | 9175.8 | 7949.4 | −13.4 |
| Holland | 1285.7 | 996.1 | −22.2 | 2520.4 | 1952.9 | −22.5 |
| Spain | 3202.1 | 3299.9 | +3.1 | 6314.5 | 6426.3 | +1.8 |
| UK | 4643.1 | 3716.7 | −20.0 | 9175.6 | 7247.9 | −20.9 |
| West Germany | 5251.0 | 3241.8 | −38.3 | 10239.0 | 6358.4 | −37.9 |

*Source:* OECD

The European beer market has reached a state of maturity. The major national markets show no growth or slight decline in sales. Only the southern European countries 'sunbelt' show any growth in consumption patterns and they are relatively small markets for beer compared to the northern European countries. Plateaued sales and the effect of this reduction in major potential consumers will hit the industry hard. The intensity of competition will increase as brewers fight harder to woo consumer loyalty to their brands. Segmentation of the market will increase as brewers seek to create their own niches which they can defend. Smaller brewers are more likely to be swallowed up by the larger ones as rationalisation moves take place to bring supply more in line with demand. All of these processes will be accelerated by the reduction in the number of potential customers.

The effect of these changes will be felt particularly in Germany which has the highest consumption rate of beer in the world at 143 litres per capita per annum. The number of males between the age of 20 and 29 – the principal drinking age – will drop by 2 million or 38.3 per cent from 1987 to the year 2000. West Germany, as it was, is the most fragmented beer market in Europe with 1200 breweries, the five largest brewers have a combined market share of 28 per cent, and over 5000 brands. This reduction in the number of consumers must lead to a quickening pace of concentration in the German industry as smaller brewers find it much tougher to survive.

The root cause of these demographic changes are twofold. First, the general decline across Europe in birth rates, and second, the increased longevity of people over the age of 65. For a national population to remain static, each woman must give birth to an average of 2.1 children. Below this rate, the population starts to decline. Table 2.3 shows the birth rate across the major European countries from 1960 to 1990.

West Germany, Sweden and Denmark's birth rates fell below replenishment rate as long ago as 1970. The impact is obvious. For example, since 1970 to 1990 West German deaths have exceeded births by 1.5 million, and prior to unification the West German population was predicted to fall from 63.6 million in 1990 to 51.4 million in the year 2025 – a drop of 12.2 million.

In 1990, only Ireland and Sweden are *not* in a situation of net population decline. Some countries have had staggering reductions in their birth rates, for example Spain, Portugal and Italy – all 'sunbelt' European countries. Spain is typical of the three. It fell below replenishment rate in 1981, and in only nine years has seen its birth rate collapse to 1.30 children per woman. Over the last 20 years these three countries

**Table 2.3** Annual birth rate per woman for the principal European countries, 1960–1990

| | 1990 | 1985 | 1980 | 1975 | 1970 | 1965 | 1960 |
|---|---|---|---|---|---|---|---|
| UK | 1.84 | 1.80 | 1.89 | 1.81 | 2.45 | 2.87 | 2.71 |
| France | 1.80 | 1.82 | 1.95 | 1.93 | 2.48 | 2.83 | 2.73 |
| Germany, FDR | 1.44 | 1.28 | 1.45 | 1.45 | 2.02 | 2.51 | 2.37 |
| Germany, GDR | 1.56 | 1.74 | 1.94 | 1.54 | 2.19 | 2.48 | 2.35 |
| Italy | 1.29 | 1.41 | 1.69 | 2.21 | 2.43 | 2.67 | 2.41 |
| Holland | 1.62 | 1.51 | 1.60 | 1.66 | 2.57 | 3.04 | 3.12 |
| Belgium | 1.59 | 1.51 | 1.69 | 1.74 | 2.25 | 2.71 | 2.54 |
| Spain | 1.30 | 1.63 | 2.22 | 2.79 | 2.84 | 2.94 | 2.86 |
| Ireland | 2.17 | 2.50 | 3.23 | 3.40 | 3.87 | 4.03 | 3.76 |
| Sweden | 2.14 | 1.73 | 1.68 | 1.78 | 1.94 | 2.41 | 2.13 |
| Denmark | 1.67 | 1.45 | 1.55 | 1.92 | 1.95 | 2.61 | 2.54 |
| Portugal | 1.48 | 1.70 | 2.19 | 2.52 | 2.76 | 3.08 | 3.01 |

*Source:* Council of Europe

have had economic growth higher than the European average – in Spain and Portugal this is linked mainly to a dramatic growth in tourism. This economic growth has created more opportunities for women to have careers, thus causing them to reappraise their traditional role as mothers. Simultaneously, greater economic prosperity, including increased pension provision and state security benefits, has reduced the traditional need for large families to care for parents in their old age.

During the 1980s the UK birth rate appears to have stabilised between 1.80 and 1.84, although it did fall as low as 1.77 in 1984. Most European countries have instituted financial inducements for women to increase the number of children they give birth to, but without success.

Over the same time period as birth rates have been falling, life expectancy has been rising. The net effect is to create a situation in all European countries where people aged 65+ are an increasing proportion of the total population. Figure 2.2 shows the growth in over 65s as a percentage of the total population for Europe and its four most populated countries.

The economic impact of these combined effects is predictable. A smaller economically active workforce will have to support a larger 65+ population than at present. The impact on companies and individuals is clear: unless assumptions about pension provisions are challenged, individuals are going to have to pay more of their earnings to support pension schemes. For example, in Italy the state pension scheme already

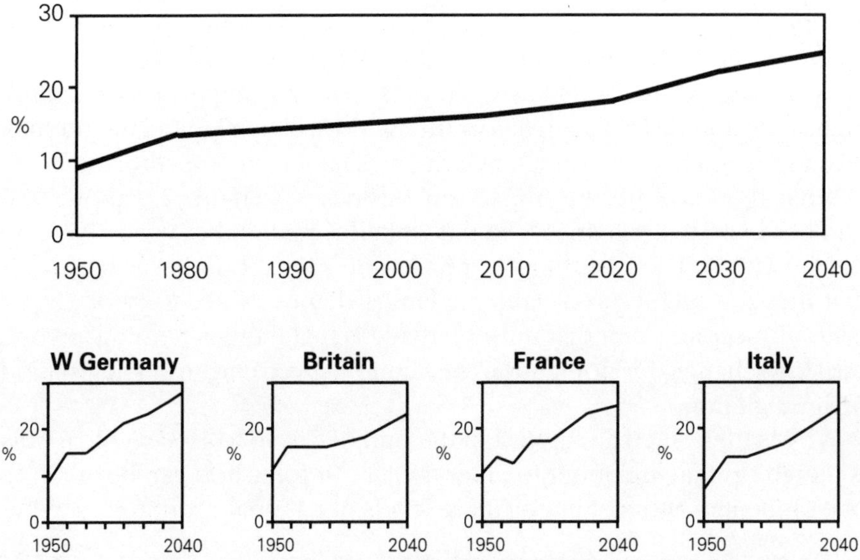


**Figure 2.2** Percentage of EC population aged 65 or over

shows signs of what may lie ahead for all European countries. In 1987, the Italian state pension fund had a deficit of $895 million despite an injection of $24.7 billion by the Italian government. The Bank of Italy estimates that individual social security contributions need to rise from 26 per cent of wages in 1987 to 57 per cent in 2010 to prevent the Italian pension fund collapsing. To maintain personal standards of living Italians will have to earn more, thus increasing the overheads of their companies. This may also explain why Italy has a thriving black economy where many individuals have second and even third jobs which are not registered through the state taxation system.

Social tension between young and old may increase. The young economically active sections of populations will be working to support state pension schemes for the over 65s who, in many cases, are already wealthy. For example in the UK, the over 55s have two thirds of the country's total savings. In France, the over 55s are 25 per cent of the population but receive 55 per cent of welfare payments.

Germany faces the most difficult situation in Europe. Whereas the approximately 16 million East Germans will compensate for the population decline West Germany would have suffered pre-unification, their national age profiles are similar. By 2025 the over 65s will be 22.1 per cent of the combined German population, up from 14.9 per cent in 1990. The average working age adult in Germany will see his or her annual contribution to the state pension scheme rise, in real terms, from just under $3000 in 1990 to $5000 in the year 2030. The impact on one of the highest cost industrial societies in the world will be significant and may give increased hope to some of Germany's national competitors.

What then will be the impact on businesses? Figure 2.3 shows the number of 16 to 19 year olds in the United Kingdom between 1971 and the year 2000. The first thing that has to be said about these statistics is that they are highly predictable, having a degree of accuracy of ±2 per cent; the second point that must be made is that there is nothing anyone can do to change this population distribution, given current UK legislation on immigration.

Why is there such an interest in the number of 16 to 19 year olds? This is the group that are about to enter the labour force and can be taken as one of the indicators of likely future levels of national economic activity.

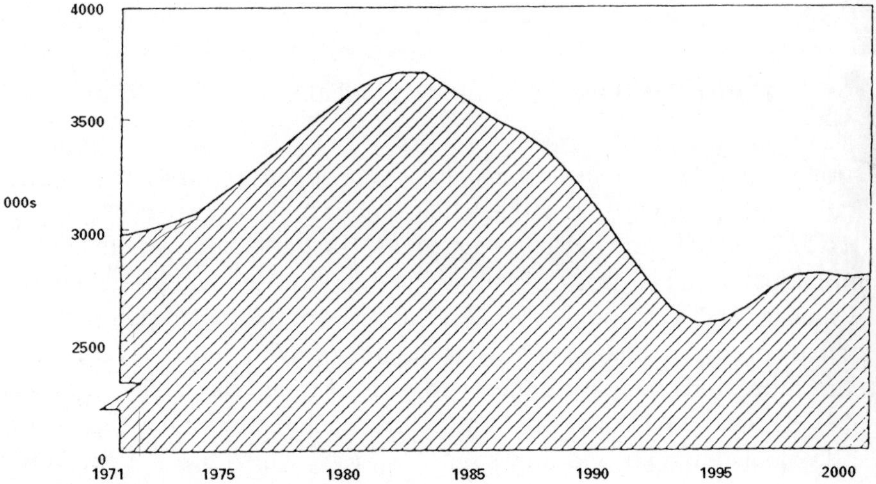


*Source:* OPCS
*Note:* 1985 based population projections

**Figure 2.3** Changes in the population aged 16 – 19 years in Great Britain

Between 1984 and 1994 the number of teenagers in Britain will drop by 1.2 million. This has already had an impact on many UK businesses. In 1988 a large financial institution wished to employ 1400 school leavers, equivalent to the total leaving school, in the town of its headquarters in the South of England. The National Health Service in the area also wished to recruit a similar number. The financial institution only managed to recruit 400, after lowering its educational entry requirements and raising starting salaries by 24 per cent. The impact on the salary expectations of existing employees by this increase in starting salaries was not reported.

Prior to the recession many towns in the South of England had the equivalent of full employment, and companies were seeking to move northwards where there was a more readily available pool of labour. The recession has dampened this effect, but increases in economic activity will see a return to this problem.

In 1988 it was reported that the National Health Service in 1993 would need to attract 62 per cent of all suitably qualified female school leavers as student nurses. This example shows one of the problems facing managers as a result of the demographic changes. The word *female* is highlighted because it represents a mindset that nurses must be female. This is not the case and the number of male nurses will continue to grow. This mindset is typical of many that managers will have no alternative but to challenge in the coming years as a result of demographic changes, which are both predictable and unchangeable. However, recent research has shown that while a substantial majority of managers are aware of the demographic effect, they believe that its full impact is still some years away, when, as we can see in Figure 2.3, we are more than three quarters of the way into it.

A major impact this drop in the teenage population will have on managers is a fundamental shift in the implicit relationship which exists when an offer of employment is being made. Currently the understanding is that the prospective employee is grateful to the prospective employer for the opportunity to work. In the not too distant future, probably by the mid-1990s, given a return to reasonable rates of economic growth, this implicit understanding will reverse. The employer will become grateful to the prospective young employee for accepting their offer of employment. In addition this scarcity of young people will force employers to take a much keener interest in the ongoing education and training development of their young employees, reversing a trend to dispense with or ignore this activity (unlike our major national competitors – Germany and Japan).

One company which has recognised the long-term impact these changes will have, and has taken appropriate action, is the Rover group, which has taken a long-term view of its human resource requirements. Two particular actions stand out. First, it has established a Rover Room in schools within a certain radius of its main plants. The rooms are fully equipped by Rover, from computers to scissors, and pupils from the ages of 6 to 18 can work in these rooms, thus becoming familiar with the company, even from an early age. Second, one-third of the company's annual graduate intake has had previous work experience of the company during their vacation, thus giving them a greater knowledge of the company and their prospects.

Despite this substantial drop in the number of teenagers, the UK labour force is predicted to grow by over 900,000 from 1987 to 1995. The growth, however, is not in the traditional sector, ie 16 to 24 years of age; it is in the age brackets 25 to 34 and 45 to 59. Figure 2.4 shows this effect.

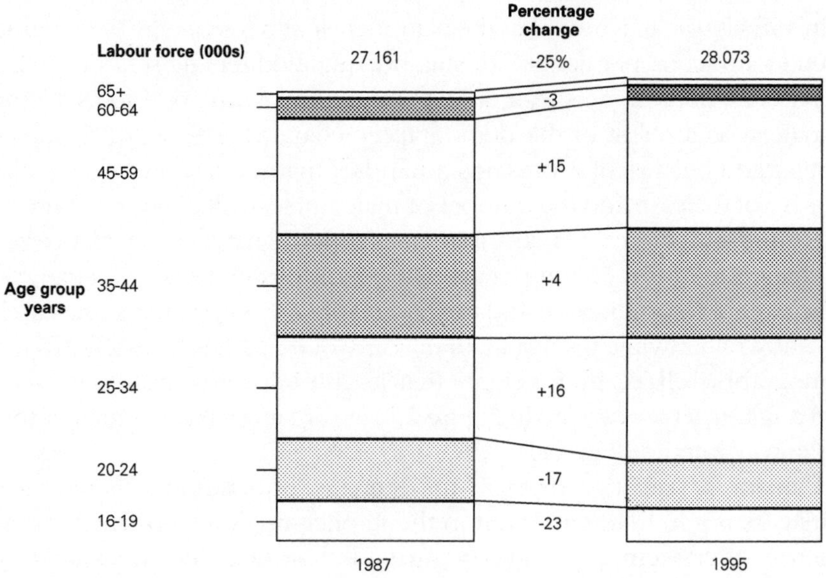


**Figure 2.4** The British labour force

The growth in the 25 to 34 section of the working population is enhanced by women returning to work after the birth of their children, ie combining the role of motherhood with a career. This trend will become an increasingly important one in the future as businesses come to rely more and more on women as a vital part of their workforce. The implication for businesses and their managers is that this is a section of the working population with special needs which must be catered for. Unfortunately this is not happening. A recent survey by showed that only very small numbers of companies, typically large ones, made any special provisions for mothers returning to work. Only 2 per cent of the organisations in the survey offered work place nurseries and 1 per cent offered childcare allowances. The Department of Employment estimates that by the year

2000, 90 per cent of all new recruits to the labour force will be women. In future, companies wishing to attract mothers to work will have to offer a variety of inducements such as flexible contracts, job sharing, school term time contracts only, childcare facilities or allowances, the opportunity to work from home, and so on.

The growth in the 45 to 59 group is the effect of the post-war baby boom working its way through the population. This group is also experiencing a substantial growth in its personal wealth. As well as reaching a stage in life where income exceeds their expenditure due to children leaving home and mortgage payments reduce as a proportion of their total expenditure, this group also benefits from inheritance from their parents who were the first UK generation to be able to buy, in substantial numbers, their own properties. In 1990 it was estimated that £7.5 billion was inherited by families from their parents and that 67 per cent of homes were owned by their inhabitants. The United Kingdom is unique in this sense in Europe. Much of the wealth of Britain is tied up in domestic property; no other European country has the same levels of property ownership. The recession will undoubtedly slow down this inheritance effect as properties are currently harder to sell, but it will accelerate when the housing market recovers.

The impact on managers will be significant, for instance there is the recent example of the chief accountant of a medium-sized company, whose best cost accounts clerk unexpectedly announced her resignation. This person was a model employee. She was diligent, highly accurate, had a near perfect attendance and punctuality record and was very effective in her job. However her mother had recently died leaving her a cottage which she had been able to sell for £150,000. The lady, who was aged 47, had travelled very little during her life, and decided to spend £30,000 on a six month, round-the-world trip. She informed the chief accountant that when she returned from her trip she would decide whether or not to return to employment. However, the fact that the interest she would earn on the remainder of her inheritance was equivalent to a substantial proportion of her current salary meant that if she did in fact return to work, it would be for reasons other than financial. What could the chief accountant have done to prevent this situation? Clearly the answer is nothing. Such scenarios will become a much more frequent occurrence during the 1990s.

What, then, should managers be doing to prevent their organisations suffering from the worst effects of this major demographic change? The first and obvious answer is that managers must become aware of the impact these effects will have on their organisation. Unfortunately many are not. It is interesting to consider the sequence of events which led to the demographic effect becoming an identifiable issue in public discussion. In March 1988 a survey was published in the Sunday Times whose basic conclusion was that if you were over 40 years of age your prospects of changing jobs were greatly reduced. The author of the survey had analysed the appointments sections of the quality press over a six month period, looking particularly at the specified age range for applicants. Four months later, the National Economic Development Office (NEDO) published a report, entitled 'Young People and the Labour Market, A challenge for the Nineties', which included Figure 2.3. The Director General of the CBI was moved to say that: 'the demographic changes will have a greater impact on British business than the reduction in European barriers to trade in 1992'. In actual fact the trend identified in Figure 2.3 had been discernible for a long time, but few managers had been aware of it.

The survey mentioned above concluded that whilst many managers were aware of a 'demographic effect', their response to it would be a traditional one, ie if shortages of the appropriate human resources exist, offer increased rates of pay. This may have been a successful method in the past, but it will not work in the coming years. This environmental change is not one that will be reversed in the future; they are once and for all changes.

A clear implication for managers is that the combined effect of lower numbers of teenagers and wealthier 45 to 59 year olds means that employees will be able to afford to be more selective about their places of employment. Employee turnover rates will rise and managers will spend increasing amounts of their time on personnel recruitment. The businesses that attract and retain staff will be those organisational cultures that provide employees with high levels of individual satisfaction. This will be particularly relevant to the 45 to 59 year olds, who increasingly will wish to come to work for reasons other than financial ones. Organisations will have to offer individuals interesting and challenging work which fits their personal aspirations and fulfillment needs. Skill development partnerships between the individual and the employer will have to become the norm, unlike the present situation where they seem to be divorced in many organisations, as witnessed by the classic comment; 'We don't train our people, because if we do they might leave and someone else will benefit'. In blunt terms, managers will have to work harder at retaining people than they do at present. Organisations are going to have to create cultures which will appeal to people. All organisational mechanisms which lead individual employees to have reduced levels of self-esteem or self-respect will have to be identified and possibly removed. The appropriateness of symbols of formality and status will have to be reconsidered, eg segregated eating and toilet facilities for different grades of managers, or the wearing of formal business dress when this is unneccessary.

Individual managers values and beliefs are also going to be challenged in ways which have not occurred before. Their view of their own roles may well have to change, and may involve a shift from being 'policemen' to being 'coaches'; from trying to catch people out in culpable situations to getting the best from them, probably in a team situation. Their view of certain sections of the population, such as women, ethnic minorities and the elderly must also change. Many male managers find it uncomfortable to manage increasing numbers of women. Their stereotypes, from experience, are rooted in traditional models of male to male relationships at work. They find it difficult to adjust their language, for example, in a situation where they are managing a mixed male and female workforce.

A good example of a company which has recognised the impact of these effects is B & Q, the DIY retailer. When B & Q opened its new store in Macclesfield, its advertising campaign to recruit staff specified that applicants would have to be over the age of fifty. They were inundated with responses. When the store opened the average age of the staff was 54, with only the store manager and his assistant under 50. The older staff took a little longer to train than the younger ones which the company had recruited traditionally, but they offered compensatory benefits. They had a clearer idea of what customer service meant than younger staff and because of their age many of them had done the DIY jobs which customers entered the store to purchase materials for. Reports of older sales staff requesting younger and stronger customers to shift heavy items did not deter the customers. B & Q's Macclesfield store easily surpassed its sales target in the critical first 13 week sales period after opening.

## IMPACT ON EXTERNAL ASPECTS OF BUSINESS

So far in this chapter, the focus has been on impacts which are internal to organisations as a result of demographic changes. Let us now turn to issues more related to *external* aspects of business.

Europe's population is predicted to peak at 320 million in the year 2000 and decline to 300 million in 2040. This will have a fundamental impact on business assumptions. With such a drop in population, the assumption that organisations will display continual sales growth cannot go unchallenged. The size of many markets must shrink as a result of a reduced number of potential consumers. For example the European car industry must take the view that by the year 2020, the reduced number of European car buyers, (levels of ownership which will have risen throughout the 1990s), and longer-life cars, means that the market will be smaller. By this time the manufacturers will have diverted their attention to export markets, possibly Eastern Europe, which may have attained individual levels of disposable income sufficient to buy Western European cars. Perhaps more relevant business growth objectives will be continual increases in profit with only intermittent sales growth.

Many businesses will also have to reconsider their strategic focus. The people with the higher levels of disposable income will be older, and may not appreciate marketing methods geared to younger people. A simple example of this is the growth in sales of bigger fitting denim jeans to customers who are over 55, but who still retain a youthful attitude, having been regular purchasers of jeans when they were younger. The mindset that has been challenged is that the manufacturers of jeans made only tight-fitting jeans because they considered that to be fashionable. Similarly financial services companies are clearly targeting the older customer with new products and channels of distribution specifically designed for them, because they are the largest segment of the market.

The ability to identify and develop market segments quicker than competitors will be crucial. To do this successfully, much of the conventional wisdom about competitive marketing strategies will have to be challenged and some of it possibly discarded. An inevitable outcome of these changes is that companies will have to cope with delivering their products or services, cost effectively, to a greater number of smaller and changing 'niche' markets than they do at present.

For those individuals entering the profession of management in 1992, and looking forward to a career spanning 40 years or so, the changes in the demographic profile of Europe will have the most profound and lasting impact on their management beliefs and the competences they need to acquire to be effective managers. Similarly, existing managers are going to have to reappraise much of their managerial approach. It is going to be very different, in terms of managing people, than any previous period in business history.

PART TWO

# DEVELOPING STRATEGIES

# 3

# BUSINESS STRATEGY AND ECONOMICS

*David Pitt-Watson*

## INTRODUCTION

In the early 1950s, the British would boast about the strength of their motorcycle industry. Twenty years later it was almost dead on its feet, with productivity levels which were a fraction of those of the Japanese competitors. In 1975, the average worker in the British motorcycle industry produced 14 bikes. At the same time, the average worker at Honda produced 106 bikes *and* 21 cars![1]

The story of the British motorcycle industry is one of tragic strategic and economic failure.

**Table 3.1** British and Japanese motorcycle industries: productivity comparison

| | *Motorcycle output* | *Motorcycle output per man year* |
|---|---|---|
| **Britain** | | |
| Small Heath factory 1975 | 10,500 | 10 |
| Wolverhampton factory 1975 | 18,000 | 18 |
| Meriden factory 1972/3 | 28,000 | 14 |
| **Japan** | | |
| Honda | 2,000,000 | 106 bikes plus 21 cars |

Here is another, rather different example. Twenty years ago the UK Monopolies Commission prevented either Beecham Pharmaceuticals or the Boots Company from taking over a rather modest organisation which 'developed, manufactured and sold pharmaceuticals, fine chemicals, foods, surgical instruments, hospital equipment, agricultural and garden chemicals'. The modest organisation was called Glaxo. Today it describes itself as 'an integrated research based group of companies whose purpose is the discovery and development, manufacturing and marketing of safe, effective medicines of the highest quality'. Glaxo is now worth more than Beecham and Boots combined. In real terms its sales have multiplied threefold, its profits nearly sevenfold.[2]

It is a dramatic story of strategic and economic success.

## *Why this chapter?*

Business strategists offer advice on what makes companies successful. They ought to be the natural source of advice on what went right at Glaxo, and what went wrong for the motorcycle industry. In reaching their conclusions strategists borrow from all sorts of academic disciplines; from organisational psychology, from production engineering, from project planning, even from biology. But perhaps the most important discipline on which their theories have been founded is economics.

So, to evaluate the work of the strategists, we first need to understand the economic principles and evidence on which their theories are based.

Most of the recommendations made by those who have become known as strategy gurus are intuitively appealing. In particular, those who have based their advice on economic principles have created a whole new vocabulary, which has become part and parcel of the way we conduct business today. You will have heard some of the terms they have developed: cash cows, stars, five forces, activities, value chains.

Implicitly or explicitly, the theories of the economic based business strategists have radically influenced the conduct of business in the English speaking world. The *first objective* of this chapter will be to describe some of the more important ways in which their thinking has shaped company strategies.

Although the strategists' theories are intuitively appealing, often they have limited justification either in theory or in practice for the approaches they suggest. Further, if their approaches are interpreted too simplistically, they can lead to the wrong decisions being taken. Because of this, the *second objective* of this article is to point out these pitfalls, to help ensure that in the future organisations are less likely to fall into these traps.

But the *third objective* for this chapter is to discover what we can learn from economics about how to generate successful business strategies.

After all, economics is about the conduct of trade and industry. So the observations of the economists should tell us a lot about how to plan and manage business. Economics should help to tell us what the British motorcycle industry did wrong and Glaxo did right. It should help us learn from the successes and failures of others.

## HOW STRATEGISTS HAVE USED ECONOMICS: CLASSICAL APPROACHES

According to economists there are two basic ways to explain the different levels of profit amongst different businesses. Either it is

1. because the markets in which the business competes have characteristics which make them intrinsically more profitable; or
2. because the business's competitive position (in terms of cost or product qualities) is strong relative to others in the market.

It is important to distinguish between these influences.

If it is the market which determines profitability, then the most important strategic choice is deciding in which market to compete. The companies which have the ability to identify the most attractive markets, will be most successful. It is a bit like prospecting for gold: if you have chosen the right spot, you might hit the motherlode. If you haven't, it won't make an awful lot of difference how hard you dig, there will always be slim pickings.

If, on the other hand, it is a competitive position relative to others within a market which determines profitability, then this suggests that managers should spend less time on identifying markets which appear attractive, and should devote their attentions to outperforming competitors. Let's look at how strategists have interpreted these observations.

### *Choosing profitable markets/Looking for greener grass*

In the 1960s and 70s the main thrust of economic research suggested that it was the market which was the main influence on profitability. In particular, economists believed that the most profitable markets were those where there were few producers, and high barriers to any new competitor coming in. As a result, competitors were able to raise their prices, and, providing that nobody broke ranks, they would be very profitable. However, the profit was only earned at the expense of the customer who had to pay the higher prices which suppliers were able to charge.[3]

Of course this extra profitability would only be achievable if your customers didn't object to the price rises. If you had a concentrated group of customers, then they would be likely to be tough negotiators in squeezing prices and hence profitability. Equally, if you had a very concentrated group of suppliers or a strong trade union they would have the ability to raise their prices if they felt your company was particularly profitable and could afford to pay them more.[4]

Therefore the definition of profitable companies would be those where the industry in which they competed had a concentrated group of competitors, where there were high barriers to entry into the industry, and where there were many fragmented buyers and suppliers. The extra profits were generated, not because of lower cost or higher added value, but because companies were able to raise prices to a higher level than if they had numerous undisciplined competitors, or strong consolidated customers and suppliers.

Some of these observations have passed into the received wisdom on strategy. Some writers, notably Michael Porter of Harvard Business School, have suggested that 'industry analysis' is likely to be the most important element in determining whether a strategy will be successful or not since 'studies have repeatedly shown that average industry profitability is by far the most important influence on firm profitability'.[5]

According to Porter there are five forces which influence industry profitability; these are 'competitive rivalry; barriers to entry; threat of substitutes; the power of buyers and the power of suppliers'. Porter is more sophisticated than the economists of the 1960s. However, his view echoes their notion that concentration, barriers to entry and lack of any countervailing power from buyers and suppliers will allow monopoly profits to be earned. According to his theory, if you are in an industry where the barriers to entry and the threat of substitutes is low, where buyers and suppliers are fragmented, and where competitive rivalry is muted, then not only will that make you more profitable, it will also 'determine the ultimate profit potential of the industry'.[6]

Implicitly or explicitly, the view that one market is intrinsically more profitable than another has gained wide acceptance in the business community. Over the past ten years, many western chemical companies have decided to move from commodity to specialty products, because they believe it is more difficult for new competitors to enter these markets. Many acquisitions are made with the view that more concentration in the industry would lead to higher prices. Many companies complain that it is impossible to make significant profits because big buyers force prices down. Are they right? If so, what difference does it make to strategy formulation?

It is certainly true that if you know the profitability of an industry to be high, it is a good indication that each of the firms within the industry will be making high profits. This might suggest that if you see an industry where lots of companies are making money then it might make sense to join in. There are, however, a number of problems with this:

- By the time you have entered the market the profits may already have fallen.
- If you go where others are making money, your activity will tend to bring profits down as you invest to gain market share.
- If profits are high then it could be because there are significant barriers to new entrants so it will be very costly to invest in the market which looked so profitable.

The position is one of stalemate: the market is profitable for existing competitors, but it is very difficult for a new competitor to share in their success.

To be useful, managers need some guide to what makes markets profitable, other than the fact that they are profitable already. If it were possible to predict profitability by measuring concentration, barriers to entry and so forth, then companies could direct their resources towards those markets which have the right characteristics. The problem is that when researchers have tried to predict whether or not a market will be profitable by looking at the level of growth, the concentration of companies and so on, then the accuracy of the prediction falls dramatically. In economists jargon 'data [on industry profitability] can yield interesting stylized facts to guide general theorising . . . even if they cannot be supported by a full blown structural estimation'.[7] In other words, it is possible to predict that all businesses within an industry will tend to be more or less profitable. Indeed, researchers have found that they are able to predict about 40 per cent of the difference in company profitability from knowing what industry they are in. What they *can't* tell accurately is what made that industry profitable in the first place.

So while choice of market may be important in determining company profits, it is difficult and impractical to try to decide which markets will be attractive and to use this as a starting point for strategising. Even Porter agrees that to predict industry profitability you would need to look at 44 variables, and he is unable to tell how each should be measured and how important it will be in the overall calculation of market profitability.

This is not to say that we should ignore industry analysis. It is important to understand the trends in an industry; the changing basis of supply, demand and competition. However, it is simply not practical to decide on a strategy by trying to choose a market on the basis of its intrinsically greater attractiveness. Otherwise the British motorcycle industry could have solved its strategic problems by getting out of the (apparently unattractive) motorcycle industry, and investing in the (apparently attractive) drugs industry. If the motorcycle industry had adopted such a solution, not only would it have been bizarre from a practical point of view, it would also fail to explain why Honda was so successful in motorcycles, which strategists would have predicted was an unattractive market!

It is wildly simplistic to suggest that specialties are better than commodities, that consolidated industries are more profitable than fragmented ones, or that industries with many buyers are better than those with fewer, concentrated ones. Those companies which implicitly or explicitly build strategies on these assumptions will find themselves skating on very thin ice.

The evidence would suggest that despite the enormous amount of economic research which has been done in this area, those companies that begin strategising by trying to pick attractive markets are unlikely to find this to be a successful starting point.

## *Competitive position: the search for the Holy Grail*

An alternative approach to finding an attractive market is to find an attractive competitive position within a market. The aim is to find a particular formula for facing up to competitors which will lead to higher profitability.

Again, the strategists have a number of suggestions as to the formula a company should adopt. The first popular theory of this nature came from the Boston Consulting Group. Their work was heavily influenced by evidence from production engineers, who demonstrated that as organisations became more experienced in the production of a product or service, their cost of production fell, and fell by a predictable amount. So organisations with lots of experience would have lower costs and therefore higher profits than those with less experience. The strategic implications were clear: go for growth, become the biggest in your market place. The bigger and more experienced you are the lower will be your costs, and therefore the higher your profits. This theory came to be known as 'the experience curve'.

The experience curve theory proved to be very influential. Much of the building of capacity in the chemical and petrochemical industry in the 1970s came about as the result of firms jockeying to gain scale and experience and so obtain lower costs than their competitors.

Even more influential was an idea which derived from the experience curve, known as the growth share matrix. It was based on three observations. First, the experience curve; that businesses which have a high share of their market relative to competitors will be profitable because they have greater experience. Second, that companies will require more cash for investment if they are to hold share in growing markets relative to the cash requirement in mature markets. Third, that products follow a life cycle of growth, maturity and decline, and that it is comparatively easy to gain market share in the period of growth, and difficult to gain share when the product matures.

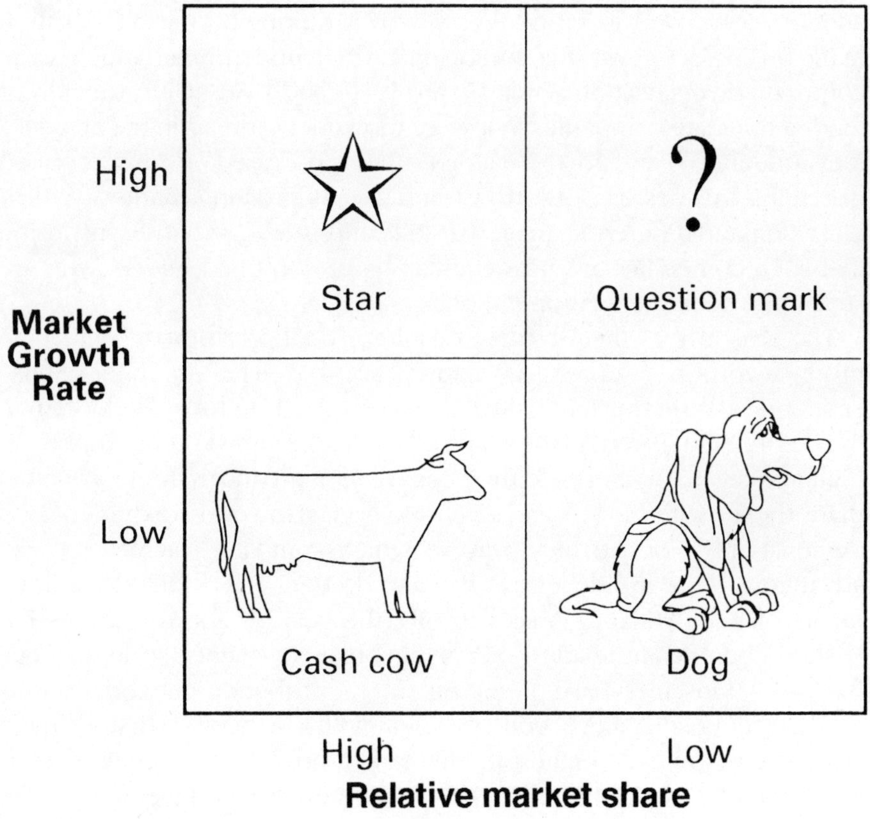


**Figure 3.1** The growth share matrix

This suggests that their are four generic types of business as illustrated in the matrix in Figure 3.1 'Cash Cows', where a company has high relative share in a low growth market. These should be managed to generate a lot of cash, though not at the expense of market share. 'Stars', where a company has high relative share in high growth market. These would be profitable, but would require investment. The priority for these businesses should be to ensure that they hold this high share of the market, and so mature into cash cows in the future. Businesses with low relative share in low growth markets had few prospects and were known as 'Dogs'. With little hope of gaining share these should be managed for cash, even if this meant liquidating the business. Businesses with low relative market share and high growth posed a management problem. They were known as 'Question Marks'. They should only be backed selectively, if there was the real prospect of gaining share before the market matured.

The Boston Consulting Group then went on to suggest that companies should try to balance their portfolio of businesses. So if your company had a lot of 'cash cows', it should diversify by acquiring promising 'question mark' businesses. It was this sort of logic which underpinned much of the corporate diversification activity in the 1970s and 1980s. Unfortunately, it tended to create companies that were too widely spread in the activities they undertook and in the markets they addressed. It also required managing businesses both in fast and slowly growing markets, which often demand different managerial skills. It is therefore hardly surprising that such companies are now the targets of corporate raiders who are seeking to demerge their operations.

The reason that the Boston Consulting Group's approach failed to produce corporate success is because it was based on a number of false economic assumptions. Initially there seemed to be a lot of evidence that the theory held water. As the graph in Figure 3.2 shows, companies with high market share *relative* to their competition are much more profitable than those with a low relative position. However, experience is demonstrably not the only way in which companies achieve a cost advantage: there are dozens of ways to do this. These include endowments of nature (Saudi Arabia in oil), the cost of labour (various Far Eastern countries in textiles), advantageous investments, scale, patents, training, an installed base of equipment, a distribution network, brands and market positions. A second problem with the theory is that even if it is important to be the biggest in the market, how do you decide what is your market? Does BMW have to be the biggest car producer if it is to be successful? Third, the theory suggests that there can be only one leader in a market. If the only profitable position is to be leader because this gives you the lowest cost, what do you do with businesses which aren't leaders?

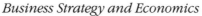

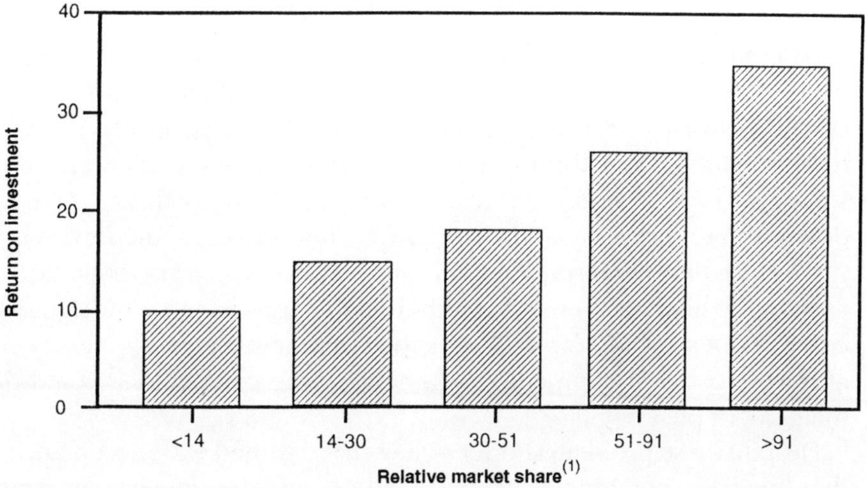


*Notes:*

(1) The graph shows the rates of return achieved by different businesses against their share of the market compared to their three largest competitors added together. (For example, those whose market share was between 51 and 91 per cent relative to their three largest competitors had an average return on investment of 26 per cent.) It shows that companies with a high share relative to competitors tend to be more profitable.

*Source: PIMS*

**Figure 3.2** Effect of relative market share on profitability

The theory would suggest that ultimately companies which were not leaders should be liquidated leaving only one competitor in each market. Fourth, the theory says that companies should try to balance their cash requirement by investing in 'portfolios' of businesses. But if your company generates too much or too little cash, you can always return it to your shareholders or ask them for further finance. There is little reason to get involved in businesses about which you know little, just because you can't find a home for all your cash. Finally, low cost is not the only characteristic companies need in order to be profitable. It's possible to establish a strong competitive position by meeting customer needs better, even if it costs more. It is this which seems to lie at the heart of BMW's or Rolls Royce's success, yet neither would claim to be low cost relative to General Motors or Toyota.

It was this final observation which led Porter to propose an alternative approach to choosing a 'generic strategy'. He reckoned businesses have to make a choice; *either* they should be cost leader, *or* they should focus on differentiating their product, and so make a profit from the price premium which customers are willing to pay.

However, this approach is impossible to sustain if you try to explain what companies actually do, with the sort of precision which would be needed to choose a strategy. For example, General Motors and Toyota certainly have lower costs than BMW, but they don't have lower costs than Lada or Skoda. Does this mean that they have chosen a 'differentiation' strategy? The answer is of course that they are trying both to keep costs down *and* to differentiate their product. They aim to be the lowest cost *for the customers they serve.* BMW or Rolls Royce would also try to be low cost for the markets they serve. Although their products are much higher cost than General Motors or Toyota they can meet *their* customers needs at lower cost than competitors – otherwise the competitors would run them out of business.

Despite these problems Porter's views have gained wide acceptance in the business community. Many readers will be familiar with the syndrome. Some companies try to produce myriads of different products, each tailored precisely to an individual customer's needs, producing enormous costs in scheduling, production downtime and stocking, which are never properly recouped in prices. Others focus on a narrower and narrower market segment, in the hope that this will protect them from the lower costs of their competitors – this was the strategy of the British motorcycle industry in the 1950s and 1960s. Still others have concentrated only on being the lowest cost, forgetting that customers want other things apart from low prices. If customers always wanted lower prices, then Lada and Skoda would have been tremendous success stories. They were not.

Other strategists have also tried to develop recommendations by combining the elements of analysis used in choosing markets with the analysis of competitive positioning. For example, General Electric and McKinsey & Co believed that by calculating competitive position (based on such factors as scale, growth, market share, profitability, technology and image, etc) and market attractiveness (based on market size and growth, purchasing power of buyers and suppliers etc), they could recommend the best strategy for a business. But again, their approach suffered from many of the faults of earlier attempts to define generic strategies. What constituted a market; how do you decide on the relative importance of the different measures of attractiveness and position; and finally, where is the evidence that any of these theories have led to success? Strategists' attempts to suggest that there is some universal formula, based on the characteristics of the market, or the experience of the firm, or the choice of generic strategy, are ultimately unconvincing.

So, strategists who have based their theories on economic analysis have had limited success. But the question remains, can economics help in deciding the best strategy for a business?

## ECONOMICS AND BUSINESS STRATEGY: A REAPPRAISAL

At a very basic level, there are two agents involved in any transaction; a consumer and a producer.

The consumer tries to maximise his or her 'welfare' by purchasing goods which give greatest value relative to the price charged for them. The producer tries to maximise profits by charging the highest price which can be achieved. In a free market there are only two ways for producers to achieve their goal of higher profit. Either they can produce goods and services which deliver better value to customers than those offered by competitors and so increase volumes or prices, or they can reduce their costs which will again enhance margins.

There is one critical mechanism which keeps the system in balance, and that is competition. If the price becomes *too* high relative to the cost of producing the goods in question, other producers will enter the market to capture a slice of the high profits and consequently this will drive the price down. If the price is too low, production will stop because profits are not high enough, and prices will therefore be driven up. It is this process which Adam Smith described as the 'invisible hand'. In simple business terms this means that for companies to be successful they need to provide goods and services that customers want and do so better and/or at lower costs than their competitors. Companies are not restricted in the markets and products they can participate in. They should try to compete in all the products, services and markets where they are able to achieve these goals of meeting customer needs better and at lower cost, since this will give them the competitive advantage which they need to be profitable. Of course this is just plain commonsense. After all, if a company didn't meet customer requirements better than its competitors, then it would never make a sale; the customer would buy from the competition. Indeed it is almost impossible to conceive of a customer who knowingly buys from a supplier whose mix of product, price and service delivers less overall value than the competitors', unless of course the customer simply doesn't know about all the competitors' offerings. So meeting customer needs is essential to achieving sales.

Further, if a company can't meet the same customer needs at an equal or lower cost than its competition then it is unlikely to make a profit in the long term. Customers will pay the same price for the same product or service. So if their products are similar, a company with high costs will make a lower margin than a company with low costs. This means that the low-cost company can either lower prices or spend its extra profit in producing additional product qualities in order to squeeze out the high-cost producer.

Of course, if it were true that some markets were intrinsically more attractive than others it might still make sense to be the high-cost producer in the attractive market, rather than a low-cost producer in an unattractive one. However, as we discussed, it is very difficult to predict what characteristics make markets attractive. Choosing an attractive market, therefore, seems an unlikely starting point for building a strategy. If the economists' observations are correct, it suggests a new starting point for strategy. It begins with two simple principles. These are, that for a company to be successful, it must:

1. provide a mix of product features and services to its customers which they value;
2. provide a better set of features and services, and/or provide them at a lower cost than competitors.

Because, if a company can meet customer needs better and at lower cost, then it should be profitable.

Strategic management is the understanding, planning and above all the execution of business policies based on these principles. It involves companies taking coherent actions to direct their efforts towards those areas where customer value and competitive advantage can be achieved.

This is not to say that it is easy to decide unquestioningly and methodically how and where a company should focus its efforts. To do so involves answering a number of complex questions about customer requirements, competitive response and relative cost position. Nor does it imply that the only successful companies are those which determine their strategy in a methodical fashion. In fact most businesses decide their strategy through a combination of planning, political, evolutionary, cultural and visionary forces. But economic theory and common sense tells us that they will only be successful if they result in a business meeting customer requirements better than its competitors, otherwise the business is unlikely to make any sales. And if it doesn't meet customer requirements at lower cost than its competitors, it is unlikely to make much profit.

Economic theory is quite clear about what a business must do to be successful. The question is whether it is possible to use this economic logic to construct a methodical approach to deciding the best strategy for a company to pursue. If so, then business strategy can be deeply rooted in the most basic principles of economics, and is therefore less likely to suffer from following policies which turn out to be fads or fallacies.

In the rest of this article we will look at some of the issues which need to be addressed if a company is to decide upon its strategy in this logical and methodical fashion.

## A METHODICAL APPROACH

It is all very well for economists to say that successful businesses meet customer needs better and at lower cost. But how can businesses choose which customer needs to meet and which cost and value-adding activities to undertake?

Like so many complex questions, this can only be answered by breaking it down into a series of simpler, more manageable issues, which can be resolved methodically. One such breakdown is shown in Figure 3.3. The logic is straightforward. If a company wishes to meet customer needs better, it first has to know what customer needs are; how customers value different products and service qualities, how needs differ amongst different customers, whether there is more than one customer (for example both a distributor and an end user) whose needs have to be met, and so on. A similar breakdown can be made of how a company can achieve low costs; what are a company's costs, how do they differ from those of competitors, what implications does this have for market focus? Let us look at some of the considerations which need to be borne in mind when addressing these questions.

### *Meeting customer needs*

Meeting customer needs is the foundation of any successful free market enterprise. It is therefore surprising that so few companies understand fully the criteria by which their existing and potential customers choose to purchase their product or service, and how they decide who to purchase it from. Of course, to a greater or lesser degree, every company understands its customer requirements implicitly, otherwise it wouldn't make any sales. But without an explicit objective understanding it is impossible to begin a methodical process of building a strategy, just as it is impossible to build an accounting system without any information about costs. I'm sure many readers of this chapter will recognise the syndrome in their own companies: one group of managers insisting that customers need technical excellence, another group insisting that the price must be lower, still others concerned about delivery promises, and

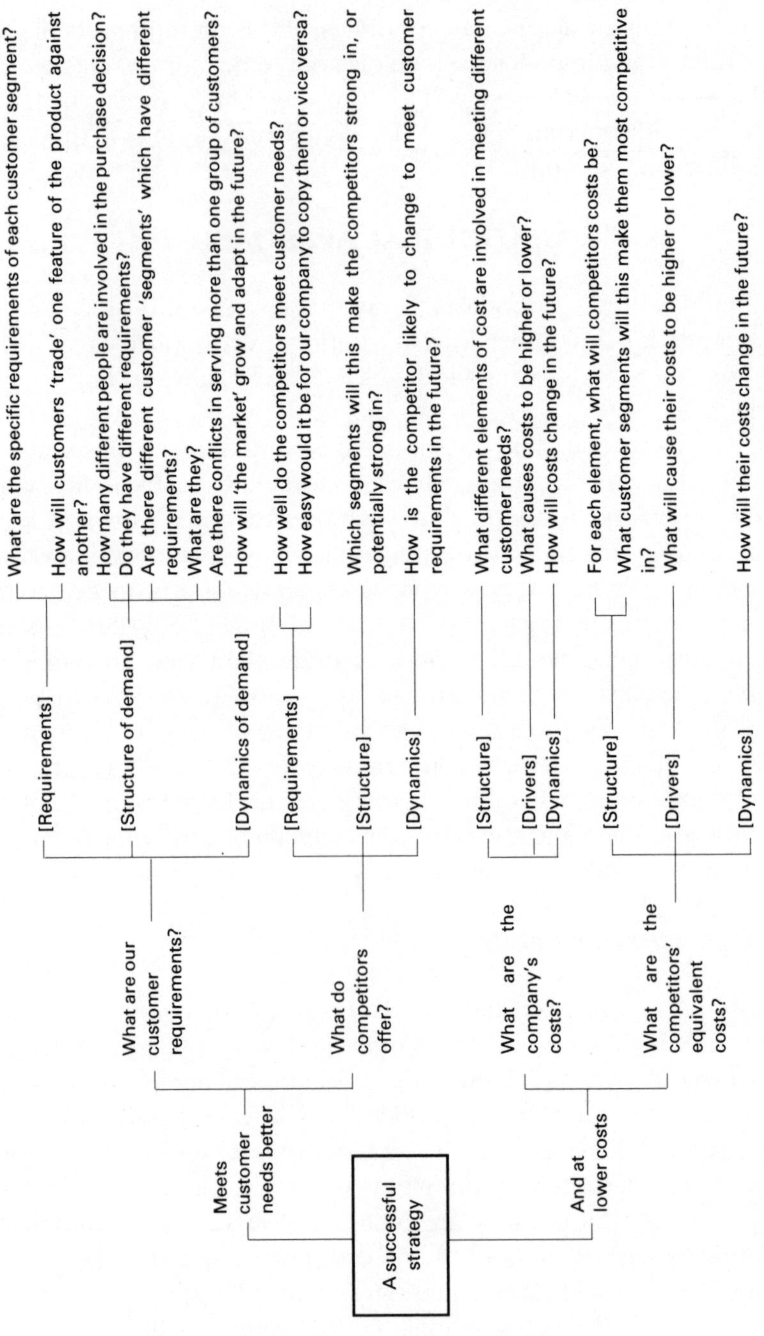


*Source:* Braxton Associates

**Figure3.3** Strategic issues

each group supporting its own contention with anecdotes. Yet no one has bothered to gather the systematic information that would resolve the issue, namely, asking the customers what it is that they want.

Here is an example of a European business which suffered from precisely that problem. The business was part of a sophisticated multinational company, one of the 50 largest in the country. It made plant and equipment for the chemical industry where it had an 80 per cent market share in its domestic market. It had recently been attacked by a German competitor which was offering much lower prices. The sales force reported back that the Germans were offering lower prices, and recommended that a major price cut was required, which would have wiped out all company profit. The company was therefore gearing up for a major price war, but before doing so, it commissioned some market research, the results of which are shown in Figure 3.4. Far from being the most important consideration, price was only the fourth criterion to be considered by customers when they made a purchase. Product availability and delivery reliability were much more important. So a more effective way of meeting the competitive challenge was to improve these aspects of service to customers. The company did this and within 18 months the German competitor was forced to close its sales office.

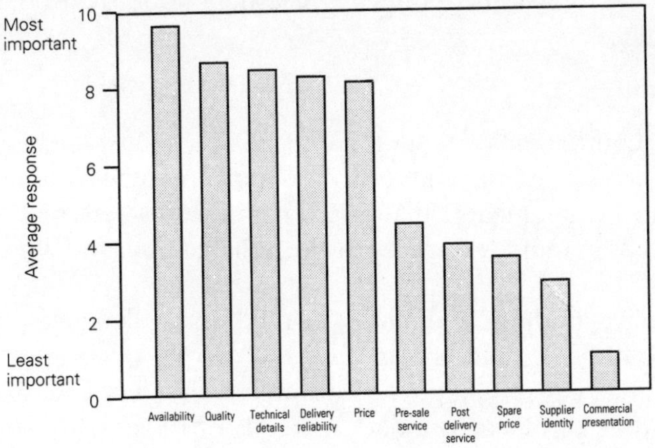


**Figure 3.4** Customer purchase criteria

It would be nice if it was always that simple. However, purchase decisions are often very complex. In this chapter we don't have space to address all these complexities in depth, however, we will mention a few.

### *Trade-offs*

Usually there are several different qualities a customer requires in any purchase. For example in the case of the chemical equipment company, they want delivery availability, but they also want technical performance, reliability, price and so on. Before producers can decide which of these to concentrate on improving, they need to know how customers will value any incremental improvement. For example, if availability is increased from a week to 48 hours, how much more will customers value that service? How much more will they pay? It is possible that although customers value availability, they find a week to be a perfectly acceptable delivery time, and won't pay any extra for the improvement.

A simple ordering of customer preferences can give a guide to those areas where improvement will have the greatest effect on sales, and is far more concrete than the gut-feeling on which so many business decisions rest. However, to decide on the specific operating improvements which should be implemented often requires more detailed knowledge of how customers will trade off one quality against another. There are complex techniques, such as conjoint analysis, which can help resolve these issues in detail. But for most businesses, the best way to get a grip on how potential customers value different aspects of a product or service is quite simple. Ask them! Ask them directly. Ask them honestly. And ask them systematically.

### *Segmentation*

Customer requirements are not identical. Each customer will have different purchase criteria. Within any group of potential customers, there are likely to be 'segments'; that is groups of customers with different considerations in mind when they decide what to buy, and who to buy it from.

Strategically, finding segments with differing demands allows a producer to target a different product and service offering at different customers, thus generating greater customer value. For example, Volvo has targeted its products to meet the needs of those who want a safe reliable car, whereas Ferrari has focused on those who require speed and acceleration. Neither would be able to meet the needs of family saloon car buyers better or cheaper than GM, Ford or Toyota, yet by carefully focusing on a specific market segment they can meet the needs of their particular customer segment at a competitive cost.

Creative segmentation is particularly important for companies which have a low market share relative to competition, and where it is difficult to find a clear competitive advantage in the mass market. In many industries it is common to find several smaller competitors who have differentiated their products to fit the needs of a particular market segment. For example, in large computers, Cray have concentrated on 'super-computers' for the scientific market, Sun on workstations and so on. However, determining a segment is not a panacea. Unless there is a structural advantage which can be achieved from segmentation, the gain is likely to be short-term, since the competition will simply copy any segment based strategy. We will look at this question when we come to discuss the issue of relative costs.

*Different customers*

Often there are several people involved in a buying decision, for example, different members of a family may be involved in a purchase. Equally there may be wholesalers and retailers, as well as the final customer, whose needs have to be met. So determining customer needs may involve considering several different agents, not just a single end user. For example, a packaged goods manufacturer which thinks only of the needs of the shopper, but fails to provide the appropriate markups, delivery and service to the retailers is unlikely to last for long. This means that the product or service offered has to contain a very large number of characteristics, which are mutually compatible, and which will appeal to all customer requirements.

*Customer conflicts*

It is scarcely surprising therefore that conflicts arise when businesses attempt to sell to more than one customer. For example Toyota felt that it was unable to offer a 'top of the range' car using the Toyota name, and had to establish the Lexus brand. Many companies in the British building trade have difficulty in selling both to builders merchants and directly to builders. Some packaged goods companies refuse to manufacture 'own-label' products for fear of undermining their brand franchise. Where such conflicts do exist they again open up competitive opportunities to exploit the image and channel conflicts which arise from trying to meet different customer needs.

*Dynamics*

It is of course impossible to plan a strategy without some understanding of the likely level of future demand. For some products/services/markets, this can be done quite easily by looking to the past (eg demand for beer in the UK). However, demands change. Although demand for beer is about constant, British drinkers today consume vastly more lager and less bitter than they did 20 years ago. Equally, needs get satisfied. For example, the market in Britain for video recorders is now declining because most of the people who want to buy one have done so already, and so sales are restricted to replacements. Furthermore, different goods will be more or less sensitive to swings in the economic cycle. For example, the demand for building products is disproportionately high when the economy is growing, to meet the demands for new infrastructure. When economic activity is flat, little new infrastructure is needed so demand falls away sharply.

There are no magic solutions in deciding what will be the level of demand in the future. However, a lot can be gained from considering not only what growth has taken place in the past, but what has driven that growth. For example, if one product is substituting for another (lager for beer) it should be possible to draw up some realistic scenario of how that substitution will continue in the future. If a product is penetrating a given set of customers (video recorders) it should be possible to predict when the penetration will come to an end. If a product is used in capital investment rather than as a consumable (building products) it should be possible to predict how demand will be affected by economic cycles, and so on.

Having determined customer needs, and understood their likely growth in the future, the art of the strategist is to match the scale of a business' operations and the products and services it offers to these demands. A business should try to compete in every product and service, if it can do so better and at lower cost than other companies. So a second, critical factor in building a strategy is to understand the performance and capability of competitors.

## *Meeting customer needs better*

The key element which distinguishes strategy from marketing is the explicit consideration of competitive advantage. Just as it is critical to know what customer purchase criteria are, it is equally important to understand how well one company meets those needs relative to those of its competitors. After all, it is the interaction of customer needs with competitor offering that determines who will make the sale.

Therefore, to build a systematic strategy not only requires a knowledge of customer purchase criteria, but also an understanding of how well a company 'rates' in terms of its ability to meet these purchase considerations *relative* to its competitors. Those competitors which meet customer needs better will make the sale, and will tend to gain market share. Those which fail to, will tend to lose share.

Since there are many different segments, each with different requirements, this means that companies which are good at satisfying the needs of one group of customers may be poor at satisfying those of another. If one customer group is growing faster, then the competitor which targets that group will also grow. Therefore by tailoring the products and services it offers, a company can engineer the growth it will achieve from the combination of market dynamics and share gain. If it meets customer needs better, then it will grow relative to its competitors. If it does not grow, then it is likely that something is very wrong in its assessment of needs and performance.

### *Meeting needs at lower cost*

A company should try to meet customers requirements as well as it can. However, a strategy based solely on meeting needs is unlikely to be successful if competitors can imitate the product/service offering. For example in the computer industry in the 1960s and 1970s IBM was responsible for very few new technical developments, but was able to copy the advances made by competitors and introduce them successfully through its own distribution network.

For a competitive position to be sustainable in the long term, it must be based on a fundamental advantage in cost or skills. It is therefore critical for a company to understand what its costs and skills are, relative to competition. The starting point for any comparison of competitors costs is to understand the costs for one's own company. In some cases, the components of the cost structure are very clear and easy to compare. For example, Figure 3.5 shows the relative costs of production plants for certain bulk chemicals in East and West Europe. The East Europeans have a significant advantage, at least in the short term, thanks to their lower costs for labour, power and other feedstocks. It suggests that they will be very successful in this market, provided that their cost advantage remains.

However, for other companies with more complex and subtle production procedures, it is impossible to undertake such a straightforward appraisal. In these cases, it is necessary to consider a company in terms of all the different 'activities' it performs, and to compare its skills and costs in each of these.

Activities are things which organisations do which create value and incur cost. They might include the purchase of materials, different steps in manufacture, different design and research activities, sales and

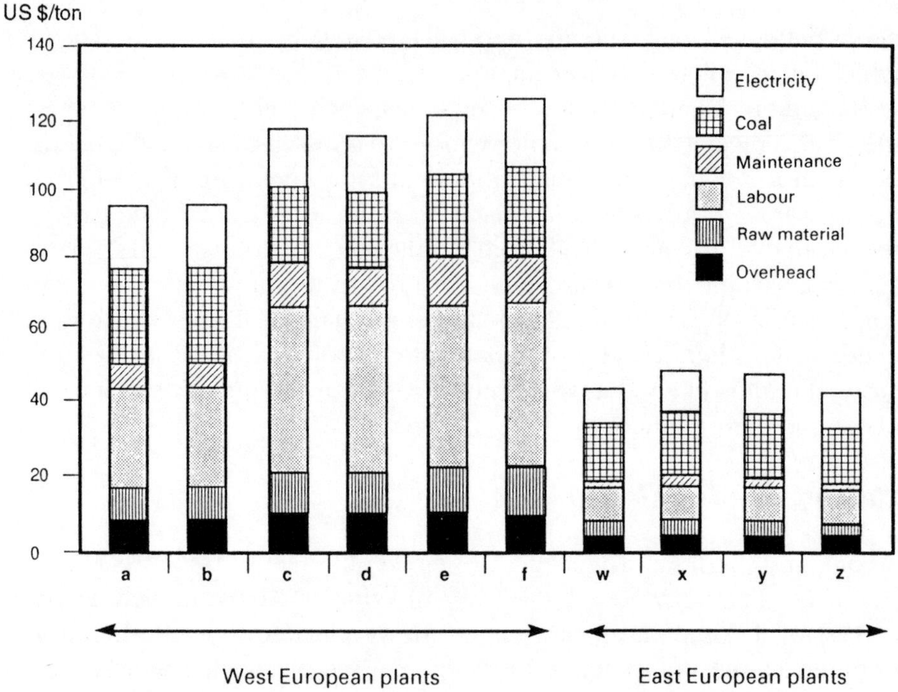


**Figure 3.5** Production cost: plant comparison 1991

distribution networks and so on. Since costs are incurred at the activity level, it is necessary to understand a company's relative capability by activity, if its cost position is to be compared with the competition, rather than simply making an appraisal of the products and services it offers.

Ultimately it is possible to break down a business into a very large number of different activities. However, for strategic purposes we need only to break down the activities to a degree where they allow value, cost and capability comparisons to be made between the company and its competitor. For example an engineering company might simply want to consider its purchasing, research, manufacturing and sales activities separately. Or it may consider that there are numerous types of research skills in different areas of technology, each of which can give the company a competitive advantage, and each of which needs to be considered separately. In some 'high tech' businesses, the definition of these research activities may be very complex.

If the activities have been well enough defined, it should be possible to look at each of them and assess how the company's costs and skills will compare with its competition. There are numerous reasons why companies' costs differ. In the case of the East and West European chemical producers, it was related to the cost of labour, energy and feedstock, however, there are numerous other reasons for cost differences:

- The scale of operation often leads to savings in purchasing, in manufacturing and in fixed selling and administration costs.
- Investment in equipment can often reduce unit costs and/or produce higher quality.
- Brand names give a huge cost advantage to an existing producer against a new entrant.
- Technological expertise is enormously costly to replicate, as are sales and distribution networks.
- For some companies, taxes and subsidies make a significant difference to their costs.
- Sometimes it is distribution costs which determine a company's cost position relative to others.

Cost and skills advantages can also arise from the integration of different activities. For example, it is more efficient to produce rolled steel at a single pass than to concentrate production in one location and steel rolling elsewhere. In a hospital, a skilled surgeon is unlikely to be able to work effectively unless other clinical services are available on site. In both cases integration of activities will assist the cost and quality of the product and service they produce. However, businesses must also beware that they do not over-integrate and try to maintain too many activities where they don't have a sure cost position.

Any structural skill or cost difference which is difficult for a competitor to replicate can be the basis of a competitive advantage, if it results in a business being able to serve customer needs better and at lower cost. Since these skill differences arise at the level of activities, rather than at the level of products or markets, it makes sense for businesses to concentrate their efforts on those activities in which they can gain and sustain a cost or skill advantage rather than embark on a market-lead diversification where they have no such advantage. Honda, for example, became remarkably skilled at the manufacture of petrol engines as a result of its success in motor bikes. It has therefore diversified its activities to cover not only bikes but cars, outboard motors and lawnmowers, all linked to its skill in engine manufacture.

If a business does not have an activity structure which will allow it to meet customer needs better, and at lower cost, it will not be able to gain and sustain a competitive advantage. Without a competitive advantage it will not be able to achieve high profitability. So, just as any methodical strategy needs to be based on understanding customer needs and competitors' offerings, it also needs to involve an understanding of costs relative to competitors. This may require considerable time, just as understanding detailed customer requirements may involve complex techniques, skill and technical expertise. However, a 'first cut' at competitive costs can often be readily assessed by comparing a company with its competitors, activity by activity; by assessing the cost drivers (scale, technology, labour, etc) which impact on the cost of the activity; and thus calculating which companies are able to meet needs at lower costs. Companies that have the potential to achieve a strong cost position, will tend to be profitable and will merit investment and expansion, to build on their advantage. For companies which do not, the prospects are less rosy.

However, costs do not remain static. Year by year good companies improve their cost position. And companies can often find radical ways to change their relative cost structure. So if the initial cost position for a business looks poor, the management should not despair. But they do need to find some way to meet customer needs better and/or at lower cost; this may be based on focusing on a particularly activity, or undertaking an activity in a different way from competitors. It is often linked to focusing on a particular new customer segment where the company can build a competitive advantage.

Equally, companies which currently have a cost advantage should not become complacent. Day by day, month by month, year by year, their competitors will be trying to reduce their costs, to find and target new customers needs and segments and to focus and improve their activities. It is this process which is the most beneficial result of competition. A leader will not remain a leader unless it is constantly adapting to meet these challenges, to improve customer performance and cost. Remember also that there is a close link between a business's ability to improve its costs, and its success in serving its market. For example, if scale is an important factor in driving costs, then the company which grows the fastest will achieve the greater scale, which will improve its costs and profitability, which in turn will give it the finance to grow. A company which fails to grow will tend to lose its scale advantage relative to competitors and will set in train a vicious circle of decline. Such was the fate of the British motorcycle industry.

> The Japanese emphasis on market share objectives has led in the longer term, not only to high unit output volumes, but also to improved productivity, lower costs and higher profitability. And conversely the loss of share by the British has been a vital factor in bringing about the low

productivity and lack of profitability that has come to characterise the industry.

(Dresser, Goold, Hedley)

## CONCLUSIONS

This chapter has three objectives. First, to describe how economic principles have been interpreted by strategy writers and how they have influenced companies' desires to diversify, to gain share, to acquire new businesses and so on. Second, to assess how far these recommendations have led to better management practice. The conclusion on this point is not positive. The recommendations of many of the strategy consultancies and academics have limited scientific foundation. There is little evidence to suggest that their application in corporations throughout the Western World has resulted or should have resulted in business success, although it is true to say that the strategists did try to fill a gap in helping businesses decide on the direction they should take. Without them business strategy would have been determined through other disciplines: marketing, finance and by the overwhelming power of the leadership and cultural influences within organisations. Nevertheless, if businesses wish to build a strategy they should beware of doing so on the basis of industry analysis and competitive choice, since there is little scientific or theoretical evidence to suggests that this will prove successful. It should therefore be a matter of some concern to academics and business people alike, that the curriculum of management schools and the approaches taken in many strategy books are so heavily geared towards the teaching of such theories.

The third objective was to discover what economies can contribute to strategy. Strategy economics is alive and well. It is based not on the studies of market structure undertaken in the 1960s and 1970s, or on the studies of competitive performance undertaken in the 1980s, although it is consistent with the results of that work. It is based on fundamental economic principles which would have been recognised by Adam Smith and David Ricardo. That is, that for a business to be successful it must meet customer needs better than competition. Otherwise it will not make a sale, because, in economists' jargon, it will not help consumers maximise their welfare. And if it is to be profitable, it must meet customer needs at a lower cost than competition, because, in a competitive market, prices will be set close to producers costs. So if a company's costs are high relative to competitors it will have slim margins.

Further, this simple economic framework provides a practical foundation from which businesses can start methodically to decide on their strategy. It is not a simple process. Questions of customer needs and competitive costs can be difficult to answer, both from the point of view of the data needed and the analysis required. But there are techniques for addressing these issues, some of which we have touched upon in this chapter, which should be amongst the skills of any manager who is trying to lead a process of strategy determination.

There are of course many other disciplines needed to implement a strategy successfully. For example, managers need to have the project management and planning skills to set a strategy process going, otherwise they will lack the data and the analysis to derive a strategy and the system to implement it. They need to understand how organisational, political, cultural and other factors tend to influence strategic choice, otherwise their economic analysis is unlikely to have much impact. But at the end of the day the success of their business will depend on how well, and at what cost, it can meet customer needs relative to competition. It was the failure to keep up with competitors improvements in these areas over a period of 20 years which ultimately lead to the demise of the British motorcycle industry. It was the achievement of these goals throughout the late 1970s and 1980s which led to Glaxo's success.

Meeting customer needs better and at lower cost. These are the criteria which decide commercial success. The contention of this article is that they should also be the principles upon which businesses should plan their strategy.

## References

1. Dresser, Goold, Hedley (1975) *Strategy Alternatives for the Motorcycle Industry*, HMSO, London.
2. Glaxo Annual Reports.
3. Scherer/Ross (1990) *Industrial Structure and Economic Performance*, 3rd edition, Houghton Mifflin.
4. Galbraith, J K (1952) *American Capitalism: The Concept of Countervailing Power*, Houghton Mifflin.
5. Porter, M E and Montgomery, C A (1991) Strategy: Seeking and Delivering Competitive Advantage, *Harvard Business Review*.
6. Porter, M E (1980) *Competitive Strategy*, The Free Press, Macmillan, New York.

7. Schmalensee, R (1985) Do Markets Differ Much? *American Economic Review*, June.

4

# INTERPRETING COMPETITIVE STRATEGY

*Cliff Bowman*

This chapter explores Porter's generic strategies using the perceptions practicing managers have of their firm's strategic priorities. The following chapter builds on the empirical findings presented here, and develops a conceptual framework for exploring issues and options in competitive strategy. This framework emerges from the insights into competitive strategy derived from managers perceptions.

## INTRODUCTION

Empirical investigations into Porter's[1] generic strategies have been somewhat inconclusive. Such studies have illustrated, *inter alia*, some of the problems of researching Porter's ideas, in particular the way in which the generic strategies are interpreted. This chapter begins by setting out some of the differing interpretations of the generic strategy concepts that can be found in the strategy literature and discusses the problems and confusions that have resulted from these differing interpretations.

Next, a relatively neglected perspective, the perceptions of practicing managers, is brought into the debate. This takes the form of an empirical investigation of managerial perceptions of strategic priorities derived from Porter's generic strategies. By inspecting the structure of the data derived from this survey a set of strategic thrusts is revealed that provide a useful comment on Porter's strategies and an extension to our understanding of competitive strategy. (NB: Because of the technical nature of this analysis the detail of the approach used has been included as an appendix to the chapter.) The implications of these findings are explored at the end of the chapter.

## INTERPRETING THE GENERIC STRATEGIES: 'COST-LEADERSHIP'

Porter suggests that there are three 'generic strategies' (cost-leadership, differentiation and focus) that firms can pursue to achieve competitive advantage. The *focus* strategy requires the firm to apply either cost leadership or differentiation to a narrow segment of the market to gain advantage. Firms that do not pursue these strategies, or who flip unsuccessfully between them, run the risk of being 'stuck-in-the-middle' and performing at or below the industry average.

It is evident from the literature that there are important differences in the way in which researchers have interpreted Porter's cost-leadership strategy. Moreover, as we shall see, Porter himself offers differing interpretations of this strategy.

There are four main problem areas that result from the differing interpretations:

1. confusing cost-leadership with serving particular market segments;
2. confusing inputs with outputs;
3. confusing cost-leadership with competing on price; and
4. confusing cost-leadership with a low cost strategy.

### *Cost-leadership and market segmentation*

Porter argues that, for cost-leadership to yield superior profits, the firm must combine lowest costs with average prices. However, successful cost-leaders that he chooses to exemplify his theory could be regarded as competing in price sensitive market segments (eg Hyundai[2]; La Quinta[3]; and Harnischfeger[4].)

If this were the case, then Hyundai would be charging average prices for the particular segment they serve (which might include Proton and Lada as direct competitors). The question would then be: are Hyundai the lowest cost of the car producers *serving this segment* (as opposed to car producers serving higher priced segments)? It is not clear from Porter's use of this example that this is the inference he is making. In the context of his exposition, he is arguing that Hyundai is a low *price* car producer, which is targeting a price sensitive segment of the market.

The means of achieving the lowest cost position (eg a 'conveyorised assembly line') often require a high degree of stability and standardisation in the product or service being offered. Again, these may well be requirements of particular segments which find a 'standard, no frills product' acceptable.[5] There is no reason why a cost-leadership strategy could not be pursued in any market segment (price sensitive or otherwise), but the point of reference must be other firms serving the segment.

### *Cost-leadership as a competitive strategy: confusing inputs with outputs*

Mathur[6] suggests that 'competitive strategy is primarily concerned with the positioning of the firm's outputs (or offerings), not of inputs'. If the cost-leader does charge 'average' prices, and offers 'average' product quality it is difficult to see how the firm would achieve anything more than 'average' market share. So as far as the customer is concerned, then, the cost leadership strategy is invisible.

If this is indeed the result of this competitive strategy then the firm pursuing it would be unlikely to be able to exploit available scale and experience advantages to a greater extent than its rivals, thus severely reducing the likelihood that cost-leadership would be achieved. In other words, if we interpret Porter strictly, how does the cost-leader achieve the sales volumes required if it cannot compete through product differentiation, and chooses not to compete on price?

However, if the low cost position *is* translated into lower prices, then the firm should increase its market share, but it may well not improve the firm's relative profitability. For now, the cost-leader is no longer charging average prices, and therefore there is no guarantee that its low cost position would lead to above average profits.

### *Lowest cost or lower prices?*

The connection between cost-leadership and competing on price is made in empirical and theoretical studies of the generic strategy concepts. In Dess and Davis'[7] study statements associated with the three generic strategies (cost-leadership, differentiation and focus) were tested with two different groups: managers and 'experts' in strategic management. The experts were required to read Porter and then to rate a list of 21 statements of 'competitive methods' according to its importance for each generic strategy. The experts rated 'competitive pricing' as being strongly associated with cost-leadership (a mean rating of 4.86, with 5 as the maximum).

Skivington and Daft[8] suggest that 'low cost strategic decisions are often found in markets where commodity-like products and price sensitive buyers collectively pressure firms to engage in price competition'. And in

Miller and Friesen's[9] empirical investigation of the generic strategies they refer to cost-leaders offering lower prices, and pricing 'aggressively' to build market share. Miller makes a strong connection between the cost-leadership strategy and low prices to satisfy price sensitive customers:

> 'Users of the [cost-leadership] strategy are likely to confront the least environmental unpredictability and change. They seek out customers who care more about price than about image or novelty.'[10]

McNamee and McHugh's[11] attempt to test out Porter's concepts in the clothing industry refers to 'low price' strategies rather than cost leadership. Karnani[12] infers that, for cost-leadership to be attained, the firm must compete on price, and Govindarajan,[13] citing Porter, maintains that 'a strategy of low cost signifies an attempt to sell an essentially undifferentiated product at lower-than-average market price.'

### *Cost-leadership or low cost?*

Throughout Govindarajan's article he refers to Porter's 'low cost' strategy (*not* 'cost-leadership' or 'lowest cost'). This illustrates a lack of precision in the interpretation of Porter that contributes to the confusion surrounding the generic strategy concepts. In a similar vein Miller and Friesen[14] found a number of 'cost leaders' within the same industry (consumer durables), and Dess and Davis[15] are prepared to conclude that a cluster of four firms in the same industry are 'cost leaders'. These writers are presumably referring to low cost orientated firms rather than 'cost-leaders'.

To conclude, there appears to be some confusion surrounding the strategy of cost-leadership. It is not clear whether cost-leadership is necessarily associated with competing on price, and there is evidence that some investigators are using the term loosely to imply a 'cost control' orientation. Finally, a strong connection is made in the literature (by Porter and others) between cost-leadership and serving price sensitive, commodity-like market segments. Thus the choice of generic competitive strategy appears to being confused with the selection of a target market segment.

## INTERPRETING 'DIFFERENTIATION'

Similarly to cost leadership, differentiation has been variously interpreted. Three main points of difficulty can be identified in the literature:

1. Do differentiators reap advantage through premium pricing, or through increased market share?;
2. Over whom are differentiators premium pricing?; and
3. Are there two (or more) types of generic differentiation strategy?

### *Premium prices or market share gains?*

Porter argues that differentiators achieve superior profits through their ability to premium price. He states that 'the ultimate test of differentiation is: do you command a premium price?'. However, Hill[16] suggests that an aim of differentiation is 'to capture more of the market at the same price'; Hill does not, then, automatically associate differentiation with premium pricing.

Porter himself relaxes the connection between a differentiation strategy and a premium pricing in his video case examples.[17] Citing American Airlines as his example of a broad scope differentiator, he suggests that their superior performance results, not from the ability to premium price, but from their ability to increase market share.

### *Premium pricing over whom?*

Central to Porter's theoretical schema is the concept of the 'industry'. Indeed, the generic strategies are derived, and their advantages are explained in the context of a discernible industry structure. However, there are problems in defining the boundaries of an industry, and hence difficulties in deciding over whom a firm is premium pricing.

For instance, Murray[18] cites Southlands 7-11 stores as exemplifying product differentiation based on convenience, 'but this is only when they are compared with food retailers targeting other market segments (eg supermarkets). When they are compared with other firms competing in their own niche (ie other convenience stores), it becomes clear that 7-11 stores strive for cost-leadership.' As more than one firm in an industry can pursue differentiation, we may see several firms, all serving similar customers, all 'premium pricing'. But how does a firm achieve superior performance if all its rivals are 'premium pricing' to the same extent? Over whom are these firms charging premium prices?

### *Different types of differentiation?*

Miller makes a distinction between innovative differentiation and marketing differentiation. Innovative differentiation 'strives to create the most up-to-date and attractive products by leading competitors in quality, efficiency, design innovations, or style'[19] Marketing differentiation attempts to create a unique image for a product through marketing practices. It would seem that this distinction is particularly important in addressing the problems of pursuing both differentiation and cost-leadership simultaneously, which could, according to Porter, lead to the firm being 'stuck-in-the-middle'.

## INTERPRETING 'STUCK-IN-THE-MIDDLE'

Porter maintains that 'a firm that engages in each generic strategy but fails to achieve any of them is 'stuck in the middle'. It possesses no competitive advantage . . . . Becoming stuck in the middle is often a manifestation of a firm's unwillingness to make choices about how to compete. It tries for competitive advantage through every means and achieves none, because achieving different types of competitive advantage usually requires inconsistent actions'.[20]

An innovative differentiation strategy may well require a flexible, highly responsive, integrated organisation, with decentralised decision-making, product/project teams, and a culture which values initiative. To deliver a lowest cost strategy may require a very different type of organisation, more akin to a 'machine bureaucracy'.[21] Thus an argument against trying to pursue cost-leadership and innovative differentiation simultaneously would centre on the tensions and contradictions that may result in trying to cope with the differing organisational requirements of each strategic thrust.

However, Miller's marketing differentiation strategy may not be incompatible with a cost-leadership strategy. Here the route to differentiation is located primarily in marketing activities. If necessary (indeed, it may be desirable) these activities could be subcontracted to an agency, leaving the business to concentrate primary on a cost-leadership strategy.

In addressing the issue of achieving both sources of advantage Murray argues that:

> . . . the exogenous preconditions for a viable cost leadership strategy stem principally from the industry's structural characteristics [vertical integration confers benefits, process innovations can still be realised, learning effects can still be realised, optimal scale exceeds 50 per cent of the market]. The preconditions for product differentiation stem primarily from customer tastes. Because these two sets of exogenous factors are independent, the possibility of a firm pursuing cost-leadership and product differentiation simultaneously is not precluded.[22]

Karnani argues that 'a firm cannot afford to emphasise one dimension at the cost of neglecting the other. Moreover, the relative contribution to successful performance of the two ways of gaining competitive advantage depends on certain characteristics of the specific industry one is considering'.[23]

Hill argues that 'the immediate effect of differentiation will be to increase unit costs. However, if costs fall with increasing volume, the long-run effect may be to reduce unit costs'.[24]

Cronshaw, Davis and Kay[25] point out some of the differing interpretations of the 'stuck-in-the-middle' concept. It has been used, as in the discussion above, to refer to not making a choice between the two generic strategies. It has, however, also been used (by Porter and others) to refer to market positioning (opting for a 'middle market' position), and to a general lack of clarity in strategy.

The link between industry, or segment situation and the choice of generic strategy explored by Murray is shared by Hambrick:

> It is simply not accurate to say that all generic strategies are equally viable within an industry . . . any broadly 'generic' strategy is really a composite of numerous variations, not all of which are equally suited to a given situation.[26]

Porter's concepts of 'parity' and 'proximity' are relevant to this discussion: 'a cost leader must achieve parity or proximity in the bases of differentiation relative to its competitors to be an above average performer. . .', and 'a differentiator . . . aims at cost partity or proximity relative to its competitors . . . ' Murray concludes from this that 'this implies that a cost leader that competes against a product differentiator must also be a product differentiator, and vice versa'.

To summarise this review of the literature, a number of issues concerning the interpretation of Porter's generic strategies have emerged:

- Is cost leadership associated with competing on price? If it is, then it is not clear that the combination of a low price/low cost strategy will lead to superior profit performance.
- Do differentiators premium price? Or can they achieve superior performance by increasing market share?
- Are there two differentiation strategies: innovative differentiation, and marketing differentiation?
- How is competition to be defined? Over whom do the firm premium price, or achieve lowest costs? Indeed, is the selection of one of Porter's generic strategies more a decision about *where* to compete than about *how* to compete?

- Can firms pursue cost leadership and differentiation simultaneously?

So far, the discussion has centred on interpretations of the generic strategies made by academics. As the aim of Porter's work is to inform strategy making processes in business organisations, an important addition to our understanding of the generic strategies would be the interpretations of these concepts made by practicing managers.

## MANAGERIAL PERCEPTIONS OF THE GENERIC STRATEGIES

Managers' views about competitive strategy are derived from their experiences. Some managers will have encountered prescriptive theories about strategy during management development programmes. Others will have formed their views from their experiences in particular functions, organisations and industries. For example, the activities of a successful competitor may well shape a manager's perceptions as to what constitutes good competitive strategy.

Managers create 'knowledge structures', based on these past experiences, which they use to interpret the world.[27] These knowledge structures enable the manager to take decisions even when faced with complex, multi-faceted problems and large amounts of information. However, an unfortunate by-product of simplified cognitive representations is that managers may act upon 'impoverished views of the world'.[28] Therefore in interpreting the competitive strategy of their business, managers may be using simplified conceptions of strategy derived from their past experiences. These may be shared within groups of managers (eg managers within the same function, organisation, or industry) and can result in managers from such groupings sharing similar perceptions of strategy.[29]

Where managers have been exposed to prescriptive theories about strategy, these would be interpreted (and evaluated) by the managers on the basis of their past experiences, therefore a manager may reject a prescription if it contradicted his strongly held beliefs. Alternatively, if a manager held no particularly strong opinions about competitive strategy, exposure to a well argued theory may be readily incorporated into the manager's world view.

Dess and Davis[30] used managers' perceptions in their empirical investigation of Porter's generic strategies. As part of their study, they compared managerial perceptions of competitive strategy with those of academics (or 'experts'). Using factor analysis (a statistical technique that helps to identify the underlying structure of a set of data) Dess and Davis compare the factors derived from the managers' responses to a 'competitive methods' questionnaire, with competitive methods identified by 'experts' as pertaining to each of Porter's three generic strategies. The comparisons reveal a marked lack of agreement between the 'experts' and the managers, although Dess and Davis do not interpret the results in this way. Of the 21 competitive methods used, only four are rated by *both* groups as being important to a differentiation strategy; four are commonly rated as pertaining to 'low cost'; and only one method is commonly rated as pertaining to 'focus'. Thus only 43 per cent of the competitive methods used in the study were uniformly allocated by both managers and experts.

Differences between the experts and the managers include 'competitive pricing' (rated by experts only as pertaining to cost-leadership); and new product development (rated by experts, but not by managers), as pertaining to differentiation. These important differences between the perceptions of academics and managers would suggest that, even when both groups are presented with a limited set of competitive methods, their interpretations of how these methods combine into overall competitive strategies are clearly not the same. Therefore in advancing our understanding of competitive strategy the perspectives of practicing managers may provide a useful contribution. The rest of the paper reports on an empirical investigation into managers' perceptions of a set of strategic priorities derived from Porter's generic strategies which adds an alternative perspective on competitive strategy. Because of the technical nature of the research, the explanation of the methodology and the detailed results have been placed in the Appendix to this chapter.

## EXPLORING MANAGERS' PERCEPTIONS OF COMPETITIVE STRATEGY

In order to explore how managers perceive the competitive strategy of their business, a questionnaire was developed based on Porter's two generic strategies: *cost-leadership* and *differentiation*. The statements used in the questionnaire can be found in Table 4.1 (the derivation of the questionnaire is explained in the Appendix).

The managers' responses were aggregated and analysed using factor analysis (see Appendix). If managers understood the strategy of their firm in line with the two generic strategies proposed by Porter, the statements would group into just two factors; one factor grouping the cost-leadership statements together, the other grouping the differentiation statements together. However, the results reveal that managers group the statements into *four*, not two, strategic thrusts. The four thrusts that emerge from the factor analysis can be summarised as follows:

- Factor 1: Cost-control
- Factor 2: Uniqueness
- Factor 3: Compete on price
- Factor 4: Product/Service development

**Table 4.1** Statements derived from Porter's generic strategies

| | |
|---|---|
| C1 | 'We place considerable emphasis on the control of operating costs' |
| C2 | 'There is constant pressure here to cut overhead costs' |
| C3 | 'We make extensive efforts to secure the lowest cost sources of supply' |
| C4 | 'We try hard to maintain the maximum feasible utilisation of our capacity/resources' |
| C5' | 'We emphasise competitive prices in our marketing communications' |
| C6 | 'We carefully monitor operations to help us keep costs under control' |
| C7 | 'As our customers are very price sensitive, we devote considerable time and effort into improving efficiency' |
| C8 | 'We aim to be the lowest cost producer in our industry' |
| C9 | 'Because we offer very similar products/services to the competition, we try to maintain competitive prices' |
| D1 | 'We emphasise our distinctive products or image in our marketing communications' |
| D2 | 'We regularly develop new products/services, or significantly change the line of products/services we offer' |
| D3 | 'We try to offer unique products/services enabling us to charge premium prices' |
| D4 | 'We give new products/service development top priority' |
| D5 | 'Our line of products/services seldom change in a substantive manner' [this would be rated low if a differentaition strategy is pursued] |
| D6 | 'Information about sales performance is considered to be more important than cost control information' |
| D7 | 'We aim to offer superior products/services to those of our competitors' |

## *Factor 1: 'cost-control'*

The cost-control factor is focused internally on priorities associated with cost reduction and efficiency.

Factor 1 pursued alone by a firm would not confer a competitive advantage perceptible by the buyer: cost-control *per se* is invisible to consumers. Cost advantages, however, can be translated into either lower prices or higher perceived value (by adding product features whilst not raising the price) which *would* confer competitive advantage.

Cost-control activities that were not converted into either of these forms of competitive advantage would lead to superior profits if the firm was able to achieve a lower than average cost level as a result, whilst achieving average prices for the industry. However, the risks of pursuing cost-control only are that the firm may be out-manoeuvered by a competitor. The profit advantages may prove to be short-term if competitors move to cut price, and/or add perceived value. This risk is exacerbated if the cost-control strategy is a result of an excessively internally orientated management group. An internal focus may reduce the management group's ability to sense changes in the firm's competitive environment.

### *Factor 2: 'uniqueness'*

Miller's 'marketing differentiation'[31] would correspond to Factor 2. Here new product development is *not* stressed as a means towards achieving uniqueness, but distinctive products or distinctive image, conveyed through marketing communications, *is* important.

Offering products or services that are perceived to be superior to those offered by the competition should improve market share. Increases in share can lead through to improved profit performance if the firm takes advantage of, for example, scale economies (eg spreading overheads), and/or experience curve benefits. However, the one statement in the questionnaire that refers to premium pricing (D3) is associated with this factor (see Table 4.1). Firms pursuing uniqueness may, therefore, choose not to reap the benefits of their superior competitive offerings in the form of market share increases; they may choose instead to premium price. However, the statement 'Information about sales performance is considered to be more important than cost control information' is also associated with this factor, which might suggest that these priorities are also orientated towards increasing market share.

### *Factor 3: compete on price*

This factor includes the need to be the lowest *cost* producer. This could be interpreted at face value: competing on price requires the firm to be the lowest cost producer. However, this outcome could merely reflect a different interpretation of the statement. In spite of this statement being the one that is most obviously derived from Porter, the fact that it is correlated with statements concerned with competing on price would suggest that managers may be interpreting it as aiming to be the lowest *price* producer in the industry (ie lowest cost to the consumer). This would appear to be the case because if the statement were interpreted as intended it would clearly be associated with the statements included in Factor 1. Managers appear, then, to be confusing lowest cost with lower prices in much the same way as the researchers cited earlier.

Firms may proactively opt for a strategy of competing on price (to squeeze out competitors, for example), or they may find themselves left with this as the only option. If there has been little effort put into improving the perceived value of the products offered, a firm may find itself falling behind its competitors. Faced with falling market share the management may cut prices. However, unless the firm has a very low (relative) cost base the squeeze on margins that may result from price cutting could be crippling.

Unfortunately, if the firm has fallen behind the competition with respect to the perceived value of its products, it may also be lacking in a positive drive to control costs. In short, it may generally lack strategic direction. The absence of strategic purpose that led to the problem with relative perceived value may not be compensated by a strong sustained drive to cut costs, so we may find a poorly managed firm being forced to compete on price, recognising that they have to be lowest cost, but without the emphasis on cost control that would be required to achieve the lowest cost position (ie Factor 3 not combined with a strong Factor 1 thrust).

Miller and Friesen's empirical study[32] revealed four 'failure' clusters of firms. In explaining some of these clusters they surmise a vicious circle of failure: ' . . . poor product quality can erode market share, requiring a subsequent reduction in prices'.

### *Factor 4: 'product/service development'*

In addition to the statements associated with new product/service development, the statement about sales information being important (D6) has a negative loading on this factor. This may mean that firms that engage in product/service innovation are not particularly orientated towards sales performance (and, by implication, market share may well not be perceived as a priority). The only other statement that has a notable loading on this factor is statement D3 (unique products/premium prices). This could mean that the advantages to be gained from innovation would be reaped through price premiums rather than through increases in market share.

Product/service innovation may be undertaken for a variety of reasons. New product development may be a continual priority where the industry 'rules of the game' dictate this (a failure to develop new products/services would lead to competitive disadvantage). Alternatively, where product innovation is used aggressively to gain a competitive advantage it would be linked to the pursuit of superior/unique/distinctive products or services.

## SUMMARISING THE FINDINGS

When presented with a set of statements derived from Porter's Generic Strategies managers group the statements into four strategic thrusts. Two of these thrusts are associated with competitive strategies that are visible to the consumer; first, competing on price, and second, offering superior or 'unique' products/services. The other two thrusts could be viewed as internal competences, insofar as they may not be perceived by the consumer: cost control; and product/service development. Managers, then, distinguish between cost control, and competing on price, whereas in the studies cited earlier (and in Porter's work) these two thrusts are often confused.

Firms could conceivably pursue all or none of these four thrusts. They may act deliberately to combine thrusts in order to derive strategies for sustainable advantage, or they may well reactively find themselves pursuing realised strategies that are only concerned with one of these thrusts. Firms that do not display strong orientations to either competing on price, or to striving to offer unique products/services, are likely to achieve average or below average market shares. Firms that do not combine either of these 'output' thrusts with a strong cost control orientation are unlikely to realise the profit advantages that could accrue from their relatively advantageous market share position. If product innovation is a feature of the industry then firms would need to combine three thrusts to gain advantage:

- uniqueness;
- cost control; and
- product/service development.

A firm that was able to combine all four thrusts would probably outperform the competition, and would be able to develop a formidable basis for sustainable advantage (this firm would be able to compete on price, as well as offering innovative, superior products; a strong cost control orientation would enable the firm to take full advantage of available scale and experience effects).

Firms may find themselves reactively competing on price if they have not pursued a strong 'uniqueness' thrust in the past: their products may be perceived as inferior, and price cuts may be seen as the only way of maintaining a presence in the market.

## CONCLUSIONS

The differing interpretations of Porter's generic strategies to be found in the literature reveal a degree of confusion surrounding these concepts. This, in itself, is worrying as Porter's ideas have become embedded in mainstream thinking and teaching in strategic management. Part of the appeal of the generic strategy concepts probably lies in their apparent simplicity (indeed, Porter is able to explain them in just five pages in 'Competitive Strategy'), but evidently Porter's brevity has fathered confusion rather than clarity.

The outcome of the second part of this chapter suggests that the statements derived from the generic strategies are grouped by managers' responses into four, not two, factors:

- Competing on price;
- Offering unique products/services;
- Cost control;
- Product/service development.

The first two of these factors are associated with competitive behaviour visible to the customer. The second two factors can be viewed as internal competences which may or may not lead through to observable changes in the offerings of the firm. Managers clearly distinguish, then, between internal activities and external competitive market positioning.

As the four factors are not correlated with each other, each of these four strategic thrusts may be pursued independently. However, we might expect that particular combinations of these thrusts would lead to different performance outcomes. A strong cost control thrust is essential if the firm is choosing to compete on price, and it would lead to superior profitability if it is combined with the drive to offer superior products or services. In this sense, strategies for sustainable competitive advantage must combine appropriate internal competences with external competitive positioning.

In the following chapter the four strategic thrusts are used to develop a conceptual framework for discussing issues in competitive strategy. The distinction managers make between 'outputs' that are observable (eg superior products, and/or lower prices) and internal competences (cost control, and new product development) is central to this conceptual framework.

## APPENDIX

This appendix briefly sets out the approach used in the study, and presents the results in detail.

### *Methodology*

Because of the similarities between Dess and Davis'[33] study and this one, their approach has been adopted and developed.

To explore managerial interpretations of Porter's generic strategies a questionnaire was constructed using statements that pertain to either cost-leadership or differentiation. The focus strategy was excluded from the investigation, insofar as it refers, not to choice of target market, but to the selection of a competitive strategy to compete in that market (firms adopting a focus strategy still have to select between cost-leadership and differentiation). These statements were derived from Porter, standard policy textbooks and from research into the generic strategy concepts.[33,34,35]

An original list of 40 statements was tested with a panel of experts in strategic management. They were asked to classify each statement as pertaining to either cost-leadership, differentiation, both strategies, or neither. From this evaluation the statements were reduced to 25 that were classified unanimously as relating to either cost-leadership or differentiation.

The respondents were asked to rate whether the statements applied to their firm. (1 = 'This statement does not apply to our firm'; 5 = 'This statement accurately describes the situation in our firm'). The instructions continued: 'the numbers 2 to 4 enable you to indicate intermediate positions in between these two extremes'. The instructions stressed that 'we are interested in your firm's CURRENT STRATEGY; the statements refer to what your firm is doing NOW, not what you think it might be doing in the future'.

The questionnaire was then extensively tested with practicing managers. In this testing phase the aim was to eliminate statements that were essentially duplications of other statements, and to reword ambiguous statements. The result of the pilot testing and development was a 16 statement questionnaire (see Table 4.1).

The questionnaire was then administered to 1716 managers from 168 different strategic business units (SBUs). The managers were from the top management teams of their SBU, or were from functions reporting directly to the top team. The SBUs cover a very wide spectrum of business activity, including manufacturing and services, and with sizes ranging from small partnerships to multinational enterprises. The responses were collected over a two year period (1989–1991).

In this study we are interested in discovering, *inter alia*, whether managers interpret the competitive strategy of their firm in line with Porter's generic strategies. If managers perceive of strategy in Porteresque terms then we would expect statements derived from Porter's cost-leadership strategy to be correlated with each other. In other words, if managers conceive of strategy in these terms, whether or not they saw their firm as pursuing cost-leadership would be reflected in the correlations between 'cost-leadership' type statements (ie if a manager saw his firm as *not* pursuing cost-leadership, he would rate all these statements low (1); if he *did* see his firm as pursuing cost-leadership, he would rate them all high (5)). Similarly, if managers perceive strategy in Porteresque terms the statements associated with differentiation would be correlated together.

Factors are derived from the correlation matrix which reveal, in this case, which statements tend to be associated with each other. If managers did, indeed, interpret the competitive strategy of their firm in line with Porter's concepts we would expect the data to reveal two factors: one grouping all the cost-leadership statements together, and the other grouping the differentiation statements together.

In order to judge how many factors best represent the underlying structure of a data set it is usual to inspect the eigenvalues. Eigenvalues greater than 1·0 indicate that the factor explains more of the variance in the data than a single variable. This yardstick has been used frequently in interpreting factor analyses[35], particularly when one is trying to establish how many factors best represent the data.

## *Results*

The eigenvalues are presented in Table 4.2.

These values would suggest that four factors, rather than two, best represent the underlying structure of the data (ie four factors have eigenvalues > 1). Consequently, a factor analysis specifying a four factor solution was carried out. The rotated (Varimax) factor loadings are presented in Table 4.3.

*Factor 1*

Factor 1 has four statements with loadings > 0·50. These four statements are associated with cost control (control of operating costs, control of overheads, monitoring operations to control costs, and securing low cost supplies).

*Factor 2*

Factor 2 has four statements with loadings > 0·50. These are: aiming to offer superior products/services; trying to offer unique products/services and premium pricing; emphasising distinctive products/image in marketing communications; sales performance information is more important than cost control information.

*Factor 3*

The four statements loading strongly on to this factor are: we offer similar products/services, therefore we try to maintain competitive prices; we emphasise competitive prices in our marketing communications; customers are price sensitive, therefore we put effort into improving efficiency; we aim to be the lowest cost producer in our industry.

*Factor 4*

Three statements load onto this factor: we regularly develop new products/services; we give new product/service development top priority; our line of products/services seldom change (negative loading).

**Table 4.2** Eigen values

| 1 | 2 | 3 | 4 | 5 | 6 | 7 | 8 |
|---|---|---|---|---|---|---|---|
| 3.664 | 2.462 | 1.480 | 1.141 | 0.880 | 0.804 | 0.763 | 0.704 |
| **9** | **10** | **11** | **12** | **13** | **14** | **15** | **16** |
| 0.622 | 0.604 | 0.578 | 0.563 | 0.546 | 0.449 | 0.431 | 0.328 |

**Table 4.3** Rotated factor loadings

| *Statement* | *Cost control* (1) | *Uniqueness* (2) | *Compete on price* (3) | *Product/service Development* (4) |
|---|---|---|---|---|
| C1 | 0.824 | 0.041 | 0.126 | 0.008 |
| C6 | 0.794 | 0.071 | 0.118 | 0.022 |
| C2 | 0.731 | – 0.038 | 0.095 | 0.020 |
| C3 | 0.533 | 0.133 | 0.276 | – 0.013 |
| D7 | 0.184 | 0.721 | 0.029 | 0.082 |
| D3 | 0.114 | 0.675 | – 0.225 | 0.317 |
| D1 | 0.074 | 0.663 | 0.102 | 0.129 |
| D6 | – 0.409 | 0.503 | 0.115 | – 0.213 |
| C9 | 0.032 | – 0.096 | 0.795 | – 0.155 |
| C5 | 0.101 | 0.146 | 0.705 | 0.079 |
| C7 | 0.328 | 0.067 | 0.614 | 0.088 |
| C8 | 0.278 | – 0.023 | 0.549 | 0.052 |
| D5 | 0.006 | 0.050 | 0.103 | – 0.822 |
| D2 | – 0.024 | 0.311 | 0.122 | 0.747 |
| D4 | 0.085 | 0.465 | 0.139 | 0.573 |
| C4 | 0.473 | 0.214 | 0.215 | – 0.014 |

Per cent of total variance explained

| 1 | 2 | 3 | 4 |
|---|---|---|---|
| 17.347 | 13.055 | 13.051 | 11.087 |

## References


1. Porter, M (1980) *Competitive Strategy*, The Free Press, Macmillan, New York
2. Porter, M (1987) Michael Porter on 'Competitive Strategy: Reflections and Round Table Discussions', *European Management Journal*, vol 6, no 1, pp 2–9

3. Harvard (1988) Competitive Strategy, video package, Harvard Business School, Boston, MA
4. Porter, 1980 *op cit*
5. Porter, M (1985) *Competitive Advantage*, The Free Press, Macmillan, New York
6. Mathur, S S (1988) 'How Firms Compete: a New Classification of Generic Strategies', *Journal of General Management*, vol 14, no 1, pp 30–60
7. Dess, G G and Davis, P S (1984) Porter's (1980) 'Generic Strategies as Determinants of Strategic Group Membership and Organizational Performance', *Academy of Management Journal*, vol 27, no 3, pp 467–88
8. Skivington, J E and Daft, R L (1991) 'A Study of Organizational "Framework" and "Process" Modalities for the Implementation of Business-Level Strategic Decisions', *Journal of Management Studies*, vol 28, no 1, pp 45–68
9. Miller, D and Friesen, P H (1986a) Porter's (1980) 'Generic Strategies and Performance: an Empirical Examination with American Data. Part 1: Testing Porter', *Organization Studies*, vol 7, no 1, pp 37–55. Miller, D and Friesen, P H (1986b) Porter's (1980) 'Generic Strategies and Performance: an Empirical Examination with American Data. Part 2: Performance Implications', *Organization Studies*, vol 7, no 3, pp 255–61
10. Miller, D (1986) 'Configurations of Strategy and Structure: Towards a Synthesis', *Strategic Management Journal*, vol 7, pp 233–49. Miller, D (1988) 'Relating Porter's Business Strategies to Environment and Structure: Analysis and Performance Implications', *Academy of Management Journal*, vol 31, no 2, pp 280–308
11. McNamee, P and McHugh, M (1989) 'Competitive Strategies in the Clothing Industry', *Long Range Planning*, vol 22, no 4, pp 63–71
12. Karnani, A (1984) 'Generic Competitive Strategies – an Analytical Approach', *Strategic Management Journal*, vol 5, pp 367–80
13. Govindarajan, V (1988) 'A Contingency Approach to Strategy Implementation at the Business Unit Level: Integrating Administrative Mechanisms With Strategy', *Academy of Management Journal*, vol 31, no 4, pp 828–53
14. Miller and Friesen, 1986a *op cit*
15. Mathur, 1988 *op cit*
16. Hill, C W L (1988) 'Differentiation Versus Low Cost or Differentiation and Low Cost: a Contingency Framework'. *Academy of Management Review*, vol 13, no 3, pp 401–12
17. Porter, 1988 *op cit*
18. Murray, A I (1988) 'A Contingency View of Porter's "Generic Strategies"', *Academy of Management Review*, vol 13, no 3, pp 390–400
19. Miller, 1986 *op cit*
20. Porter, 1985 *op cit*

21. Mintzberg, H (1979) *The Structuring of Organizations*, Prentice-Hall, New Jersey, USA
22. Murray, 1988 *op cit*
23. Karnani, 1984 *op cit*
24. Hill, 1988 *op cit*
25. Cronshaw, M, Davis, E and Kay, J (1990) 'On Being Stuck in the Middle or Good Food Costs Less At Sainsburys', Working Paper, Centre for Business Strategy, London School of Business
26. Hambrick, D C (1983a) 'An Empirical Typology of Mature Industrial-Product Environments', *Academy of Management Journal*, vol 26, pp 213–30
27. Gioia, D A and Sims, H P (1986) 'Introduction: Social Cognition in Organisations' in Sims, H P and Gioia, D A (eds), *The Thinking Organization*, Jossey-Bass, San Francisco, California. Walsh, J P (1989) 'Knowledge Structures and the Management of Organizations: a Research Review and Agenda', Working Paper, Amos Tuck School of Business Administration, Dartmouth College, Hanover, NH
28. Weick, K E (1979) 'Cognitive Processes in Organizations' in B Staw (ed), *Research In Organizational Behaviour*, vol 1, pp 41–74, JAI Press, Conn.
29. Beyer, J M (1981) 'Ideologies, Values and Decision Making in Organizations' in Nystrom, P C and Starbuck, W H (eds), *Handbook of Organisational Design*, Oxford University Press, vol 2. Grinyer, P H and Spender, J -C (1979) 'Recipes, Crises, and Adaptation in Mature Businesses', *International Studies of Management and Organization*, vol 9, pp 113–23. Huff, A S (1983) 'Industry Influences on Strategy Reformulation', *Strategic Management Journal*, vol 3, pp 119–31. Johnson, G (1987) *Strategic Change and the Management Process*, Basil Blackwell, Oxford. Prahalad, C K and Bettis, R A (1986) 'The Dominant Logic: A New Linkage Between Diversity and Performance', *Strategic Management Journal*, vol 7, pp 485–501
30. Dess and Davis, 1984 *op cit*
31. Miller, 1986 *op cit*
32. Miller and Friesen, 1986 *op cit*
33. ibid
34. Hill, 1988 *op cit*
35. Murray, 1988 *op cit*

# 5

# CHARTING COMPETITIVE STRATEGY

*Cliff Bowman*

## INTRODUCTION

In this chapter the results of the empirical study of managers' perceptions of competitive strategy is used as the basis for the development of a conceptual framework for discussing and exploring issues in competitive strategy.

## THE CHART

The north-south axis on the chart (Figure 5.1) is 'perceived use-value', ie what buyers perceive as valuable, not what management think is valuable. Perceived use value refers to the feelings of satisfaction experienced by the buyer in purchasing and using the product/service. The east-west axis is relative perceived price. The two axes combined would equate to perceived 'value for money'. (This framework is similar to that used by Kotler in exploring market segmentation.)[1]

Assuming all the firms (represented by '×' in Figure 5.1) are in similar positions in the chart, that is, they are all perceived by buyers to be offering the same products/services, all charging the same price. We would expect all firms to have the same market share.

How can firm A improve market share?

There are two basic options (we will explore other moves later):

1. Offer higher perceived value for the same price as the competition.
2. Offer the same perceived value at a lower price.

These competitive moves could be dubbed the 'better' option, or the

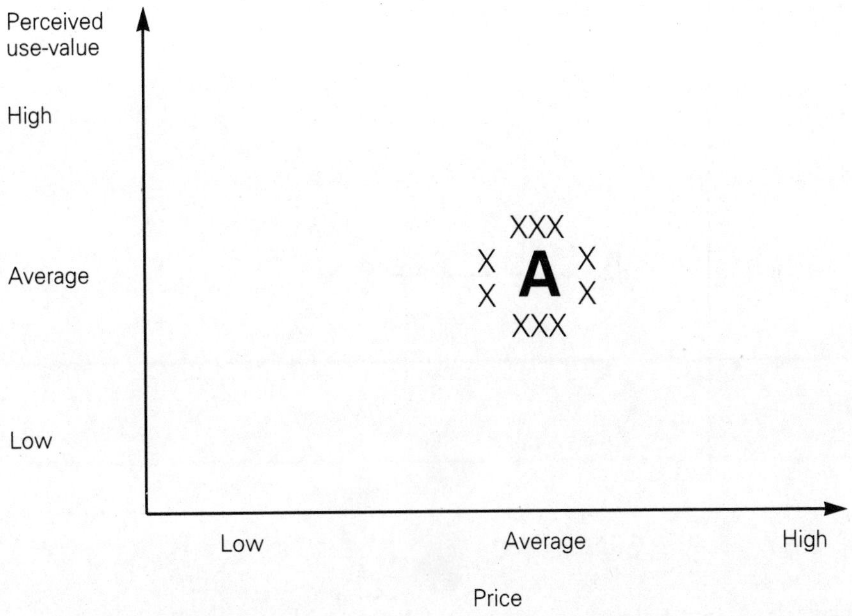


**Figure 5.1** The competitive strategy chart

'cheaper' option and correspond to the two 'output' thrusts identified in the previous chapter ('uniqueness' and 'compete on price').

## *The 'cheaper' option*

If firm A shifts to the left (Figure 5.2), what would the competition do about it? If the price cut pays firm A dividends in market share terms, the competitors will be forced to match the lower prices. This they can do usually – overnight if necessary – so the 'cheaper' option can (and most likely, will) be imitated. In the short term a new average price will rule in this industry, to the left of the original one (Figure 5.3).

Can this option lead to sustainable advantage? Yes it can, but only if firm A has the *lowest costs.* This would enable it to sustain the lower price position longer than the competition, and/or to continually drive prices down until most of the pursuers are shaken off. In other words this competitive move must be combined with a rigorous 'cost control' orientation.

However, this is probably not an attractive option, and if there are other players pursuing the same option life would be very uncomfortable for all

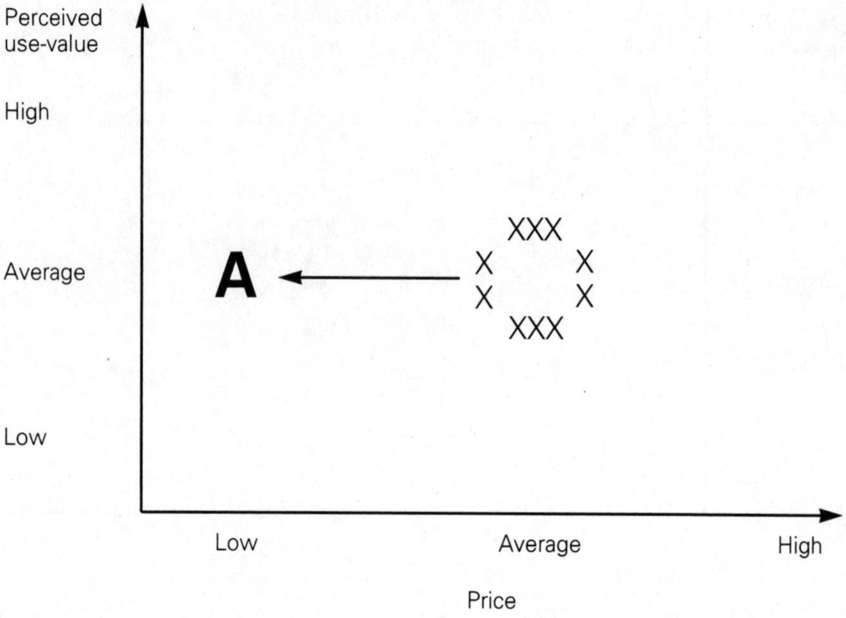


**Figure 5.2** The 'cheaper' option

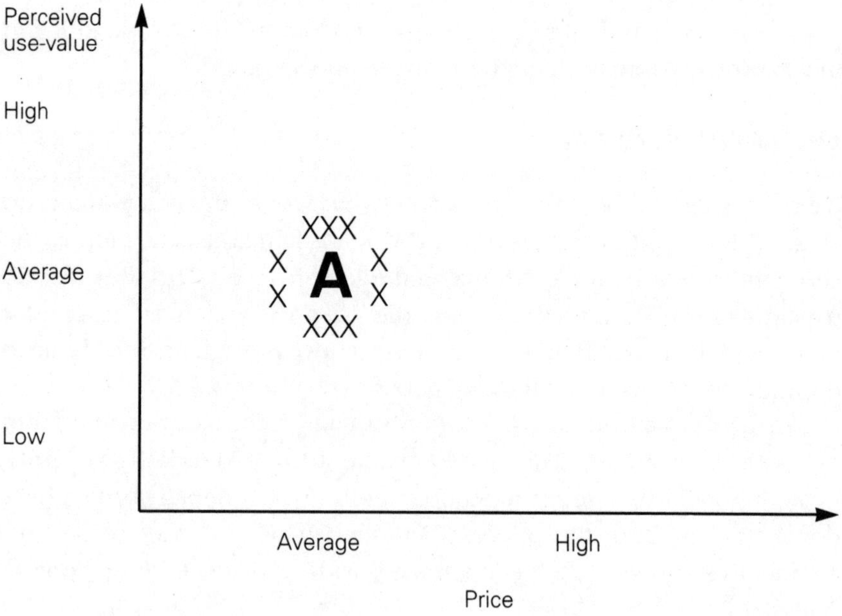


**Figure 5.3** Competitor response to the cheaper option

competitors. Unless firm A does achieve *lowest* costs, they eventually might be squeezed out by *the* lowest cost firm. Even if this does not happen, margins are likely to be cut to the bone for all players. One of the problems of managing this strategy is the need to know the costs of your competitors, and this information is rarely freely available. Furthermore, in many instances firms have difficulty in identifying the costs of particular products or services in their own organisations.

However if, having shaken off its rivals the lowest cost producer can move back east by raising prices, this could be a very profitable strategy, until someone else enters or reenters the market. Entry or reentry may be made more difficult if the incumbent firms have achieved available scale or experience economies, and/or they have created additional entry barriers (eg they may have effective control over the usual channels of distribution).

There are other problems with this strategy. In some markets price and perceived use-value are linked in the buyer's mind; this is usually the case where the buyer lacks experience of the purchase and uses price as a proxy for perceived use-value (eg in consumer durable purchases). The result may be a shift not west, but south-west; the product/service seen as inferior to the higher priced offerings. But perhaps the biggest risk to this strategy is another player pursuing the 'better' option.

### *The 'better' option*

In this instance firm A moves north, offering the buyers better perceived value for the *same* price (Figure 5.4). This could be achieved through branding, product innovation, improved service levels (combining the 'uniqueness' and the 'product/service development' thrusts). However what is critical to this option is the need to understand what buyers value. Often management make the dangerous assumption that they know what buyers want, because they are so experienced in the industry. And, if it is a strongly held and shared assumption within the management team, moving north may not even get on to the agenda as a competitive option. The belief that 'we are already giving the customer what he wants' would rule out any doubts about the product offering or the requirement to investigate customer needs. As a result, faced with a declining share, management groups with these shared beliefs would inevitably resort to the 'cheaper' option as the 'better' option doesn't exist for them.

The 'better' option improves market share so long as a significant proportion of buyers value the extra benefits firm A offers. If *all* the buyers do, then we have a homogeneous, non-segmented market, and

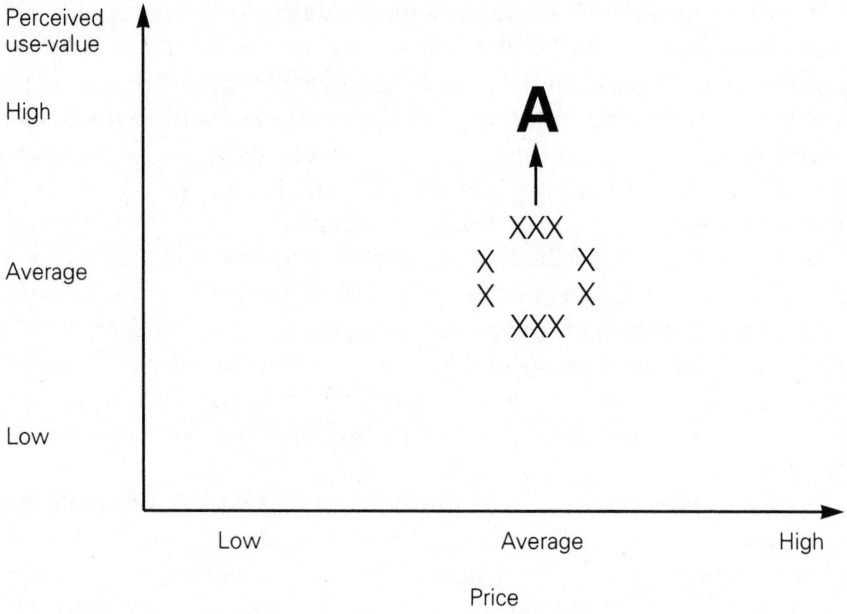


**Figure 5.4** The 'better' option

firm A can sell everything it makes (and more!). However it is more likely that, as an industry moves North, subtle differences in wants emerge, providing opportunities for niche strategies to exploit segments.

What would be the competitors' response to firm A moving north? It depends on the nature of the original improved offer to the buyer. For example, take the banking industry, where a bank moves north by opening for longer hours. This persuades some customers to shift their accounts to bank A, thereby increasing bank A's share of the market. However in a very short space of time, other banks match bank A's opening hours, and maybe market shares settle back to where they were before bank A's move. The net result would be a 'ratcheting up' of acceptable ('average') perceived value in the industry, so a new average results at a higher level of perceived value (Figure 5.5).

Over time competitor moves northward that are imitated have the effect of continually raising the minimum acceptable standards in the industry. In the car industry, anti-corrosion warranties that conferred advantage ten years ago, have become the norm. This means that firms left behind face a competitive *disadvantage*: if they can't follow suit, they are likely to be forced to cut prices as they are perceived to be offering inferior value to the rest of the industry. Here the cut price strategy is a defensive reaction

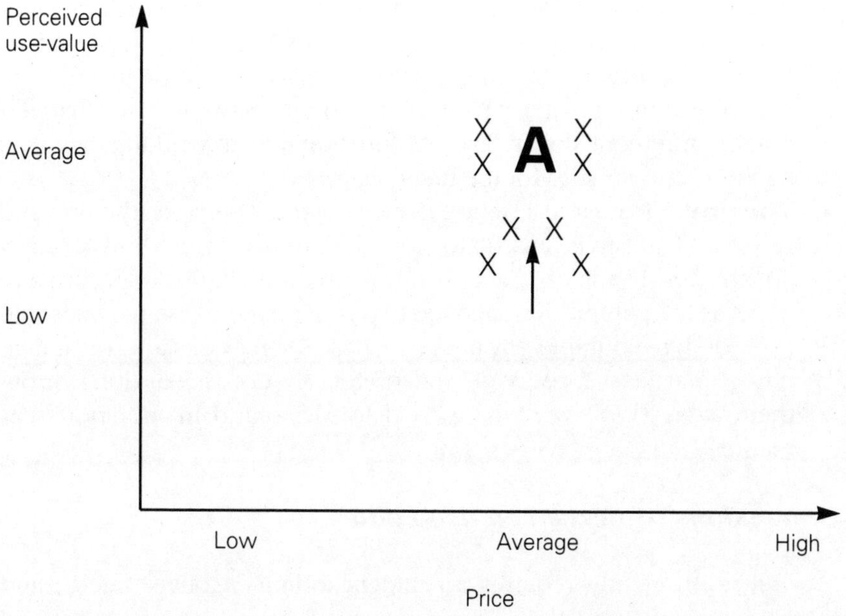


**Figure 5.5** Competitor response to the 'better' option

which may well merely postpone the declining competitive position of the firm.

Some moves north lead to a more sustainable competitive advantage because they are less easy to imitate. Returning to the banking industry, improving customer service, making staff friendlier, more attentive, knowledgeable and helpful is much more difficult to achieve. The bank that gets it right first may be able to stay ahead as their rivals struggle to improve staff performance. Other 'better' strategies involve the firm being *continually* one step ahead, through constant product/service innovation. So, moves north can take a variety of forms:

- **The innovator**: Here the firm aims to maintain a dynamic gap between itself and the competition. Through innovation the firm moves north, but by the time the competition have imitated the move, our 'innovator' has shifted further north through offering additional perceived benefits. The innovator strategy places great demands on the firm, to be at the forefront of research and development, and to be able to rapidly translate developments into marketable products. (Here the firm could be combining the 'uniqueness' thrust with 'product/service development'.)

- **The first imitator**: Why incur all the expense of being the innovator when you can imitate his innovations rapidly? The first imitator needs to be able to keenly sense competitor moves north, and to incorporate the innovations into its own offering without delay. Reverse engineering, procurement skills and cross-functional team working may well be key competencies for the first imitator.
- **The protector**: Here a static gap is maintained between the firm and its rivals. The gap is difficult to close due to strong branding, location advantages, reputation, access to distribution channels, proprietary expertise or patents. In reality no gap is permanently static, but some firms do have durable advantages. These sources of static advantage must be at least preserved, and preferably enhanced: don't throw them away (look what happened to MG brand in the sports car market).

### *Dimensions of perceived use-value*

Moving north clearly requires an understanding of buyer needs, and buyer perceived use-value. There are many dimensions to perceived use-value, and firms will be viewed by buyers as offering different perceived use-value 'packages'. For example, the upper end of the executive car market; BMW, Mercedes, Cadillac and Jaguar all offer high performance, high specification, luxury saloons. Buyers' dimensions of perceived use-value in this purchase decision might include the following:

- car image (does it have 'car park presence'!);
- quality reputation/reliability;
- product features (ABS, CD player, variable suspension etc);
- styling;
- sporting 'pedigree';
- pre- and post-sales service.

To move north in the eyes of a buyer the firm would have to offer a package of perceived use-values that in total exceed the rival offerings. This can be achieved either through being *better on all* these salient dimensions, or to be *as good as* the competition at some of them, and better at one or two of them. Toyota's Lexus recently entered this segment and has gained share from the incumbents. Because Lexus cannot offer 'sporting pedigree', it has compensated for this by being excellent on other dimensions of perceived use-value (eg product features and service). So moving north can be achieved by:

- offering better perceived use-value on *all* salient dimensions;
- offering equivalent perceived-use value on some dimensions, and better perceived use-value on one or two dimensions;
- offering *excellent* perceived use-value on one or two dimensions which more than compensates for below average perceived use-value on other dimensions. Here the total 'package' of perceived use-values offered is greater than that of competitors.

## *Staying put*

Is there an option to stay put, to pursue neither the better nor the cheaper options? The answer is yes, and it will work as long as everyone else stays put too – but the risks are threefold:

1. Clearly, as soon as one firm breaks ranks, the strategy won't work.
2. The 'staying put' option is often linked with the pursuit of 'cost efficiency', which can be dangerous (see next section).
3. A sleepy industry may encourage new, more vigorous firms to enter.

## *Cost efficiency*

The pursuit of cost efficiency is clearly vital to either the better or cheaper options (the 'cost control' thrust identified in Chapter 4). Neither option will improve profit performance unless the firm is an efficient user of resources relative to its competitors. Certainly, these options will improve market share, but in order to translate the share improvements into profit improvements, the management must focus attention on cost efficiency. Efficiency is not, therefore, just important for the 'cheaper' option, it is vital for the 'better' option too.

'Staying put', however, seems to encourage an inward-looking, efficiency-orientated management. The pursuit of cost efficiency becomes an end in itself; it is not combined with a competitive strategy. A strong efficiency orientation can lead to a lack of flexibility in the organisation (as management look to automate, to proceduralise and to standardise work).

The reasons why cost efficiency is an attractive option are clear. First, it avoids management having to look outside the firm. Second, it does not require the consideration, or measurement of, such qualitative and difficult areas like customer satisfaction, changing needs, competitor actions etc. Cost efficiency lends itself to measurement, and there are a range of well understood management 'routines' that can be applied to cut costs. But, on its own, it is not a *competitive* strategy. It plays a role in *sustaining* either the 'better' or the 'cheaper' options.

### *Moving north-east*

Moves north-east that result in modest price premiums (eg 10 per cent) should properly be regarded as being part of the 'better' option. Here the innovator or the protector is rewarded for its uniqueness with either a market share bonus or a price premium (or both). As long as the gap is preserved, the premium can be sustained. However, price premiums greater than 10 per cent may well be moving the firm into serving a different segment of demand.

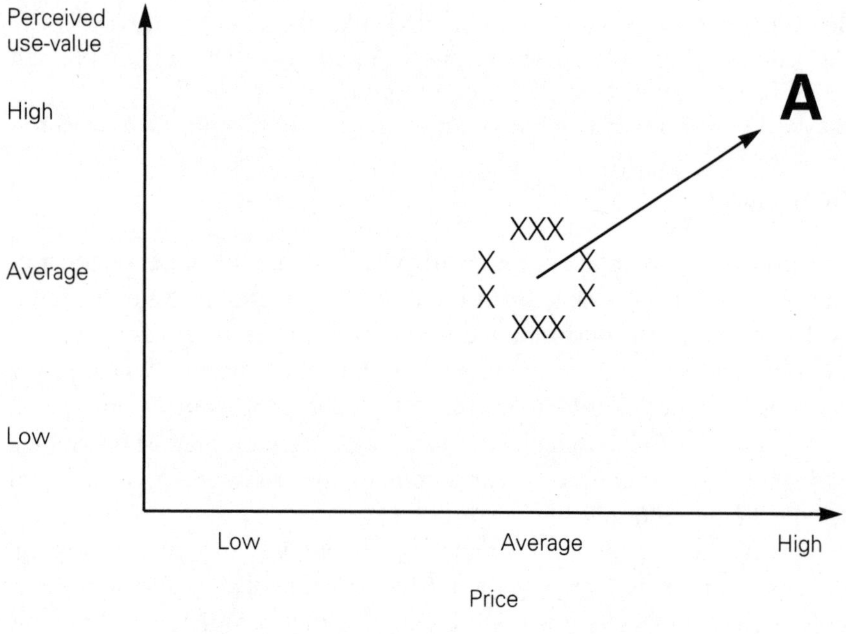


**Figure 5.6** Higher value/higher prices

Assume firm A shifts north-east (Figure 5.6) and it is supplying higher perceived value, and charging significant premium prices (eg greater than 20 per cent). The success of the strategy would depend on two conditions: first, that there is a segment out there that values these attributes, and is willing to pay premium prices to get them. And second, that there is no-one else already up there in the north-east corner. If there *is* someone there, does your offering provide something better at the same prices, or can you offer the same perceived value at lower (relative) prices? In other words, moving north-east forces us to redraw our diagram (see Figure 5.7). We can now assess the effectiveness of this move with respect to the other firms *perceived by the buyers* as offering equivalent products or services. In this sense it is crazy to suggest, for example, that Mercedes has a competitive advantage or disadvantage over Hyundai; they are not perceived by their respective buyer segments as offering competing products. Therefore a move north-east is really a move to serve a different segment, one that is less price sensitive and that is willing to pay for additional levels of perceived use-value.

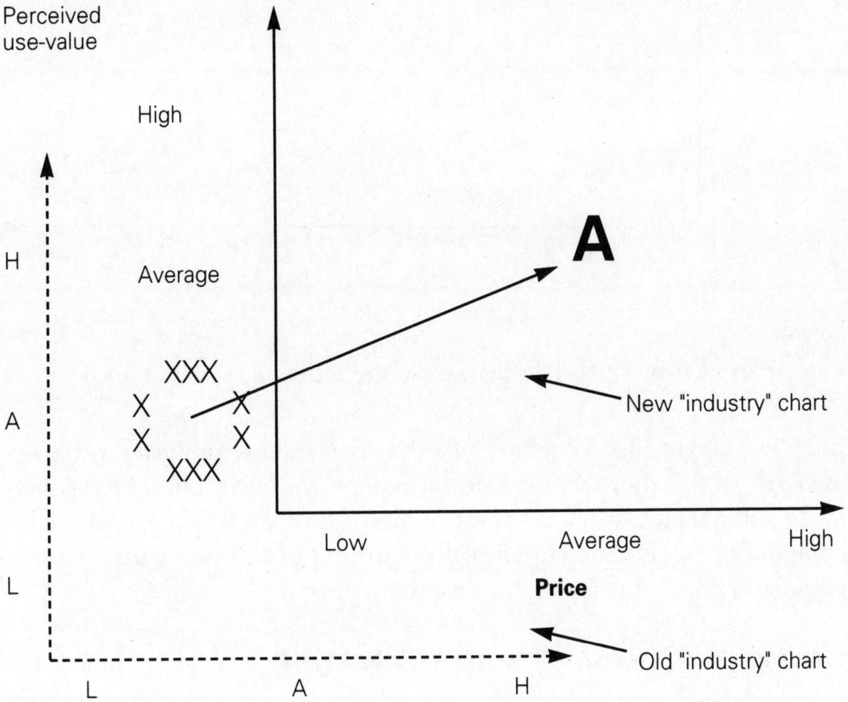


**Figure 5.7** Redrawing the chart – moving 'upmarket'

## *Moving North-west*

Better and cheaper at the same time might appear to be a powerful combination, however there are problems if buyers use price as a proxy measure of quality, ie your buyers would not acknowledge the added value you offer, so that your attempt to move north-west ends up as a shift westwards (Figure 5.8).

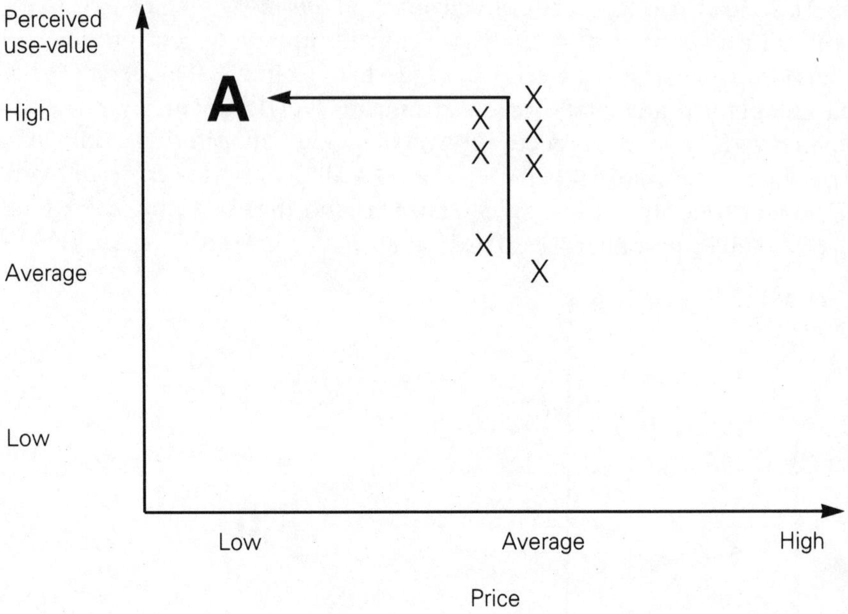


**Figure 5.8** Escaping the pack – the north ⟶ west hook

But it is conceivable that a move north may result in significant increases in share, and if there were scale or experience curve effects available, those volume increases could help to drive unit costs down. So, when the competition finally catch up, firm A could cut prices (see Figure 5.8), or it could add product features to move them even further north.

### *Moving south-west – 'cheap 'n' 'cheerful'*

In the same way that the move north-east required a group of buyers willing to pay for the added perceived value, there may well be buyers who don't require the refinements continually being added into the product/service, or buyers who can't afford to enter the market place with the existing price/value offerings available. If such a group exists, a shift south-west might be viable (Figure 5.9). Stripping out the frills should enable the firm to make profits at the lower price levels. But, just like in the north-east example, we need to redraw the chart to acknowledge that we have shifted 'downmarket'. Here there may well be a very different set

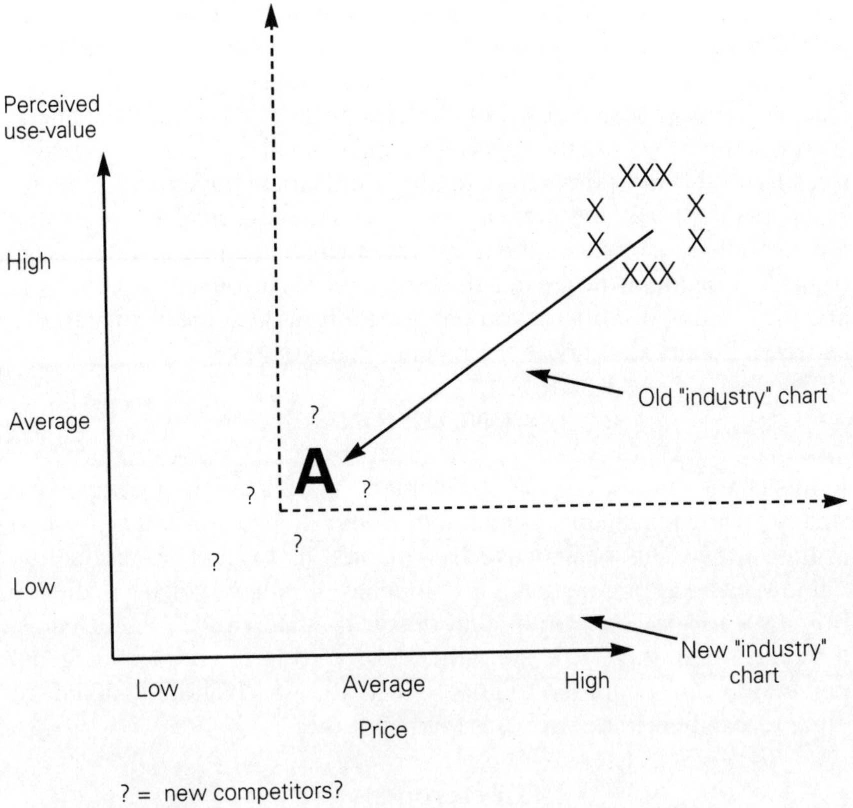


**Figure 5.9** Redrawing the chart – moving 'downmarket'

of players competing for these customers; this is why it is vital to conceive of these 'industries' as trying to satisfy *needs*, not trying to sell a product/service.

## DEFINING THE MARKET AND THE COMPETITION

How do we identify A's competition? A is a competitor with all those providers of products or services *perceived by the buyer* as offering alternative ways of meeting his or her needs. Traditional ways of defining industries may well not be appropriate if the buyer's perspective is taken.

Defining the market is difficult, and poor definition can lead to badly conceived competitive strategies. You don't sell to a market, you sell to a *person*. Everyone is different, their needs are different, and what they perceive as use-value will be different. This atomistic approach may be a viable way of constructing a competitive strategy if the firm can identify its individual target buyers, and the spend of each individual justifies this personalised approach (eg in defence contracting). However this is not feasible for most businesses: they don't know their buyers, and they need plenty of them because the spend per head is small (eg packets of crisps). Because of this most firms have to group individual buyers together and make assumptions about their needs, and what perceived use-value means to them. However, the more you aggregate and generalise away from the individual, the greater are the chances that you may get it wrong, and the more opportunities you provide for firms to come in and target a subset of buyers and service them better than you do.

## CONCLUSIONS

In this chapter we have built on Chapter 4's explanation of competitive strategy using managerial perceptions of the strategic priorities pursued in their firms. This perspective has enabled us to develop a coherent framework for exploring issues in competitive strategy, which has already been used to good effect in strategy debates with top management teams. It would seem, then, that the rather neglected resource of managerial perception can be utilised to good effect, and which should encourage other researchers to develop this field of study.

## References

1. Kotler, P (1988) *Marketing Management: Analysis, Planning, Implementation and Control*, 6th ed, Prentice-Hall, New Jersey, USA

6

# LOOKING FOR OPPORTUNITIES: THE IDEA OF STRATEGIC SPACE

*Susan Segal-Horn**

## INTRODUCTION

Understanding how industries and firms change over time is much more difficult than understanding the structure of an industry or the strategy of a firm at a specific point in time. The analysis of industry structure which is now commonplace within the literature of strategic management, is best known through the framework developed by Porter.[1] However, although Porter does discuss the need for a dynamic analysis of industry structure, ie how industries may change and develop over time, it is the static analysis popularised within the 'five forces' framework which has dominated management thinking. This has provided an effective snapshot, in any given industry, of the current balance of pressure points. Yet major changes in industries and markets, such as the globalisation of markets or the development of regional trading blocs, highlight the need for strategy models which can help understand longer-term industry dynamics. This chapter suggests a framework with which firms can begin to map their strategies against the moving target of changing industry structures.

Although starting from an analysis of existing industry structure, this approach utilises strategic group theory, and in particular the concept of

* The author wishes to acknowledge gratefully the major contribution made to this chapter by Dr John McGee of Templeton College, Oxford, with whom all the work described in this chapter was carried out, and earlier versions of the research findings and the strategic space model were written.

'mobility barriers' (barriers to the movement of a firm's strategy or positioning) to create the concept of 'strategic space'. Strategic space captures areas of potential opportunity within an industry, areas which are not yet available but whose potential under developing conditions becomes feasible. Viable strategic space can change over time. Access to different parts of the space depends upon the effectiveness or otherwise of the mobility barriers within different strategic groups, and of the assets which support those mobility barriers. The industry which is used to illustrate the approach in this chapter is the European food processing industry. The framework, however, is transferable to other industries.

This chapter has two main objectives: first, an appreciation of industry and competitor analysis based on strategic groups; and second, an exploration of the predictive value of strategic group analysis over time, when applied to the evolution of industries and the strategies of firms within those industries.

## STRATEGIC GROUPS AND INDUSTRY ANALYSIS

What is normally meant by the term 'industry' is a set of firms addressing a market.[2] However, defining the boundaries of an industry is not the same as defining *where* and *how* a firm wants to compete. Structural change in an industry often also means changes in how the industry and its boundaries are defined. This will in turn necessitate at least a review of the competitive strategy being pursued by each firm in the industry, in the light of the changed structural conditions. Changed conditions thus challenge the logic of existing strategies and also provide opportunities for redirecting strategies.

Part of this challenge to existing strategies caused by changed conditions is the appropriateness of the investments in core assets which the firm has made to support its existing strategy. The value of these investments may be eroded both by *external* changes (eg shifts in consumer preferences; legislative or regulatory change) or by *internal* changes within an industry or a firm (eg new product or service development; technology change affecting manufacturing, design, channels, etc). Despite the fact that from the 1960s onwards, industries have been characterised by consistently high rates of change in both external and internal factors, the dynamic analysis of industries has not been much explored. To some extent that may be because dynamic analysis is much more complex than static analysis. Part of that complexity is the effect of industry dynamics on the patterns of asset-building and asset accumulation pursued by firms. A useful way of understanding strategic change is to track how firms adjust their core assets over time to cope with external and internal shifts affecting their industry.

Firms can adopt very different competitive strategies within the same industry. The strategic group concept has been defined by McGee and Thomas[3,4] as an analytical device designed as an intermediate term of reference between looking at the industry as a whole and looking at the individual firm. It thus attempts to group firms *within* an industry. The term 'strategic group' is used to denote a cluster of firms within an industry following the same or a similar strategy. A strategic group is therefore a way of making sense of different types of competitors and different bases of competition within an industry, since firms will invest in distinctive sets of assets to support their particular competitive strategy and positioning within their industry. Each strategic group is likely to be affected differently by changed external or internal conditions, because of their particular historic positioning and pattern of asset-building.

In essence, membership of a strategic group rests upon configurations of assets common to group members. These configurations of assets act as 'mobility barriers'. Caves and Porter[5] see mobility barriers as locking strategic group members into specific assets and thereby making it difficult for them to acquire different assets, but at the same time offering considerable protection against imitation from firms outside the group. In this discussion, the term 'assets' is used in the broad sense to cover any factor which generates either an absolute cost to the firm attempting to move from one strategic group to another, or as a cost penalty which a new entrant to the group must bear relative to the incumbents.

**Table 6.1** Potential sources of mobility barriers

| *Market-related strategies* | *Industry supply characteristics* | *Characteristics of firms* |
|---|---|---|
| • Product line | • Economies of scale | • Ownership |
| • User technologies | – production | • Organisation structure |
| • Market segmentation | – marketing | • Control systems |
| • Distribution channels | – administration | • Management skills |
| • Brand names | • Manufacturing process | • Boundaries of firms |
| • Geographic coverage | • R & D capability | – diversification |
| • Selling systems | • Marketing and distribution systems | – vertical integration |
| | | • Firm size |
| | | • Relationships with influence groups |

*Source:* McGee and Thomas[4]

Table 6.1 provides a range of types of assets of firms which are potential sources of mobility barriers. McGee and Thomas[6], suggest that this is a helpful way of understanding the lack of symmetry in competition within an industry, since different strategic groups will be characterised by different mixtures of assets. McGee[7] makes the further point that without such costs attached to the imitation of strategy by other firms, the concept of a strategic group would be meaningless.

## STRATEGIC SPACE AND INDUSTRY DYNAMICS

In most industries there are a relatively small number of strategic groups, representing differences in strategy within that industry. To give an extreme example, in a pure monopoly situation the number of strategic groups in that industry will be just one. In more competitive market places, it is still feasible that any particular strategic group could contain only one firm, although several in any group is more usual. Strategic group analysis offers a 'map' of an industry based on the most significant dimensions of competitive strategy within that industry. Such a map should indicate the positioning of the various strategic groups and reflect the assets on which these positions are based. However, the value of assets may be eroded. The power of mobility barriers may decay and others arise in their place. This building and decaying of asset structures and the mobility barriers which they support, provides the explanation of differences between industry structures over time.

Industry dynamics are the paths by which industry structures evolve. A strategic space is a currently unoccupied location on a strategic group map. It may be unoccupied because it is not feasible, or because the opportunity which it represents has not yet become apparent to firms within the industry. Most importantly, it may be unoccupied for historical, cultural, structural, regulatory, market or technological reasons which, under changed conditions, no longer apply. Thus the pattern of industry dynamics can be understood as the pattern of strategic group change, triggered by internal or external factors, or a combination of both.

The strategic space model is a way of explaining new directions in which investments can be channelled, but does not say anything about the intensity of competition in any one of the spaces. However, if mobility barriers are changing, then they are no longer effectively blocking entry or exit to either new or existing spaces. Barriers to imitation may be weakened (eg because the amount of investment capital or lead time required is reduced), leapfrogged (eg by new types of distribution channels), or simply disappear altogether. The relative profitability of different strategic groups in an industry can no longer be protected by the historic investment in assets already made, since they no longer provide relative competitive advantages. Clearly the ability of firms to adapt will vary and can be understood as representing differences in the mobility 'capacity' of individual firms. Therefore the key to understanding long-term industry dynamics is how firms will adjust their assets over time in order to build and rebuild mobility barriers.

## THE EUROPEAN FOOD PROCESSING INDUSTRY: AN ILLUSTRATION OF STRATEGIC SPACE

This section provides a practical illustration, for one type of industry, of the approach outlined in theory in the previous sections. The discussion draws heavily on research into change in the European food processing industry carried out from 1987 to the present by McGee and Segal-Horn.[8,9,10] Within this section, relevant aspects of the recent history of the food industry will be briefly summarised, so that the evolution of the strategic group structure and the development of the strategic space may be discussed.

### *Industry background*

In its recent history the European food processing industry has passed through a number of distinct phases. Each of these phases has been dominated by different bases of competition, reflecting particular asset structures and the relative power that these asset structures have bestowed upon incumbents. For example, the stages of development of the UK industry have been labelled as follows: a very early period designated by Kaldor[11] as domination by wholesalers; a period of manufacturer domination between 1930–60, culminating in what Foy[12] described as the rise of the scale economy brander; this was then replaced by the power of the retailer, documented by Segal-Horn and McGee[13] as the rise of retailer buying power. Finally, we may be seeing the resurgence of suppliers with the emergence of pan-European consumer segments. For the purposes of this discussion, only the latter three major phases will be addressed.

#### *The scale economy brander*

The food processing industry, as part of the consumer packaged goods industry, was selling to a highly fragmented set of customers in the 1960s and early 1970s. Shops were typically fairly small, retail distribution highly fragmented and controlled for the most part by the food manufacturing companies. Economies of scale were available to the suppliers but not to the customers. Big manufacturers with proprietary technologies sold to small retail outlets. The food companies benefited from mass marketing via national sales forces, national advertising campaigns and sophisticated support services. Powerful brands were created which became household names. These manufacturers' brands were perceived by the customer as custodians of quality and reinforced the strength of the manufacturers. They became the most visible barrier to entry behind which many oligopolies flourished.

*The rise of retailer buying power*

As large retailers replaced small independent shops at varying speeds in the different European national markets, the relative positions of the food manufacturers and the retailers began to be overturned. In the UK there was a specific event which triggered this change: the abolition of Retail Price Maintenance in 1964 which allowed retailers the freedom to discount manufacturers recommended prices for the first time. However, many other general factors also contributed, such as a decline in proprietary technology allowing the entry of efficient smaller food processors, or a virtual revolution in distribution and logistics giving rise to new concepts such as centralised warehousing controlled by the retailers, not the manufacturers. The gradual rise of supermarkets, both as very large units of retail space and as concentrated chains of retail outlets, shifted the balance of power from the manufacturer to the retailer. Competition was now based as often on price as on quality, exacerbated by the rapid develpment of cheaper retailer 'own-label' brands, which removed some of the absolute control of the quality franchise from the manufacturers' brands. National retail accounts supported by centralised purchasing, warehousing and distribution, either directly controlled by the retailer or contracted-out, dramatically reduced the economies of scale of the manufacturers from distribution, and reduced their national sales forces to irrelevant overheads. It was now the *retailer* who controlled the listing of products and their availability to the consumer, via their supermarket shelf space, not the manufacturer rationing his brands to small shopkeepers. Just as retailers began marketing to the consumer, so food companies had to cope with both trade and consumer marketing costs, as well as the rising costs of R&D and technology behind sophisticated new product development. The efficiencies of the retailers undermined the assets and strategies of the manufacturers.

*The springtime of the Eurobrander*

This current phase of the development of the industry is very much a result of technological and market changes, together with the consequences of the formation of the European Single Market. Historically the structure of the European food industry has been extremely fragmented, country market by country market. There have been two main reasons for this. Firstly, the patterns of consumer tastes and preferences had traditionally varied markedly from country to country. Secondly, the structural and regulatory conditions present in each market were highly varied, creating both tariff and non-tariff barriers to cross-border trade. The extent of the cumulative impact of these barriers was discussed in the Cecchini report[14] on the benefits of a single market in Europe, but were most graphically highlighted by the research carried out by the MAC Group of which the following was the concluding statement:

> The existence of trade barriers . . . has served to protect potentially weak domestic companies, and inversely, has encouraged strong companies to expand domestically rather than attempt cross-border expansion. These features of trade barriers have reinforced the relative fragmentation of the EEC food industry. Removal of these barriers should decrease or eliminate these tendencies.[15]

MAC investigated ten product sectors and found over 200 trade barriers. These included such things as packaging and labelling requirements, specific constraints on food additives or basic ingredients, flavouring, rules of inspection, types of containers allowed and so on. MAC estimated that the direct benefits available from removal of specific non-tariff barriers in the European food industry would amount to two to three per cent of industry value-added. EC food directives aimed at 'harmonisation' of major areas of national differences such as food labelling, hygiene standards, additives, composition. sampling, etc. would provide both direct (eg use of less expensive ingredients; reductions in labelling and packaging costs) and indirect benefits (eg broadening of consumer choice; efficiency gains; significant increases in cross-border trade).

These traditional obstacles to cross-border trade are being slowly but steadily dismantled, at the same time that other factors which had always reinforced domestic market boundaries are also weakening. National markets are becoming more responsive to international food products and offerings. Greater access to channels and variety of advertising media encourage manufacturers to try to market similar products in several national markets, to offset the impact of shorter product lifecycles and higher development costs. National laws are less dominant. Distribution networks are being set up Europe-wide. Information systems allow centralised purchasing and distribution to be attempted across European markets. Also, operating across national boundaries gives manufacturers the opportunity to search for countervailing power against strong national retailers. Manufacturing economies of scale begin to seem feasible if market size is no longer purely nationally determined. Rationalisation of production capacity is resulting in fewer more flexible plants, to service a wide product range, responsive to many market segments. This in turn creates greater opportunities for European-wide sourcing.

The structural characteristics of this industry appear once again to be shifting. This shift is perhaps even more fundamental than those preceding it, since this time the evidence, fragmented and inconclusive though it is, appears to be pointing towards a 'European' industry. This is in complete contrast with the historical structure of the industry and with the logic of successful strategies in this industry. Even (or perhaps especially) the multinationals in this industry organised themselves on an individual country market basis. Everything from manufacturing to marketing was constructed and delivered on a local market basis. Strategies were formulated for specific domestic markets to ensure responsiveness to local consumer tastes and preferences and to take advantage of structural differences. Economies of scale across national market boundaries were hard to find. Given the types of shifts described in this section, the establishment of integrated European strategies to replace national strategies, starts to make sense.

Table 6.2 provides a summary of this discussion of the phases of evolution in the European food industry. It also demonstrates the progressive rise and decay of asset structures supporting mobility barriers, as industries move from one phase to the next. The consequences of this next stage of industry evolution for the existing asset structures of firms must now be addressed.

## *Strategic groups and mobility barriers*

The most significant dimensions for explaining competition within the European food industry can be used to construct a two-dimensional strategic group map of the industry. The first dimension is derived from the overwhelming importance of brands within this industry. The PIMS database has shown the relationship between dominant brand, market share and profitability, with only the first and second brands in a market yielding positive return on investment. Retailers own-label brands have

**Table 6.2** Phases of food industry evolution in the European food processing industry

| *Mobility barriers* | *Phases of development* | | |
|---|---|---|---|
| | *(1) 1960–74 The scale economy brander* | *(2) 1974–86(?) The rise of the National retailer* | *(3) 1990–? The Eurobrander* |
| **1** National sales force and distribution | ✓ | ✗ | ✗ |
| **2** Listing muscle | ✓ | ✗ | ✓ |
| **3** Intensive media support at preferential rates | ✓ | ✗ | ✓ |
| **4** Superior product quality | ✓ | ✗ | ? |
| **5** Low-cost processing | ✓ | ✗ | ✓ |
| **6** Sophisticated support services | ✓ | ✓ | ✓ |
| **7** Volume discounts on purchasing | ✓ | ✗ | ✓ |

eroded the returns on all but the strongest manufacturers brands. Although many of the strongest brand names retain a considerable consumer franchise, they have been focused almost exclusively on national markets. Indeed, the MAC report showed that amongst half the 46 European-based food companies investigated, the average representation per product line was in only two or less EC countries.

This leads on to the second significant dimension, the geographic coverage of major brands. If a shift is indeed occurring towards a more integrated industry across Europe, then increasing their geographic spread would be virtually the starting point for such a regional strategy. Both the MAC report[16] and Gogel and Larreche[17] in their Competitive Posture Matrix, compared US, EC and Swiss food companies on the basis of product strength and geographic coverage. Both conclude that US food companies (eg Mars, Kellogg, Philip Morris, Coca-Cola, Heinz) were very strongly placed in both brand strength and geographic coverage compared to European companies (eg Unilever, BSN). Swiss companies such as Nestlé and Jacobs Suchard were more strongly placed in terms of geographic coverage. This meant that the takeover by Philip Morris of Jacobs Suchard in 1990 reinforced the existing brand strength of the American company, as well as extending its European market coverage.

Similar dimensions are used in Figure 6.1 to construct a strategic group

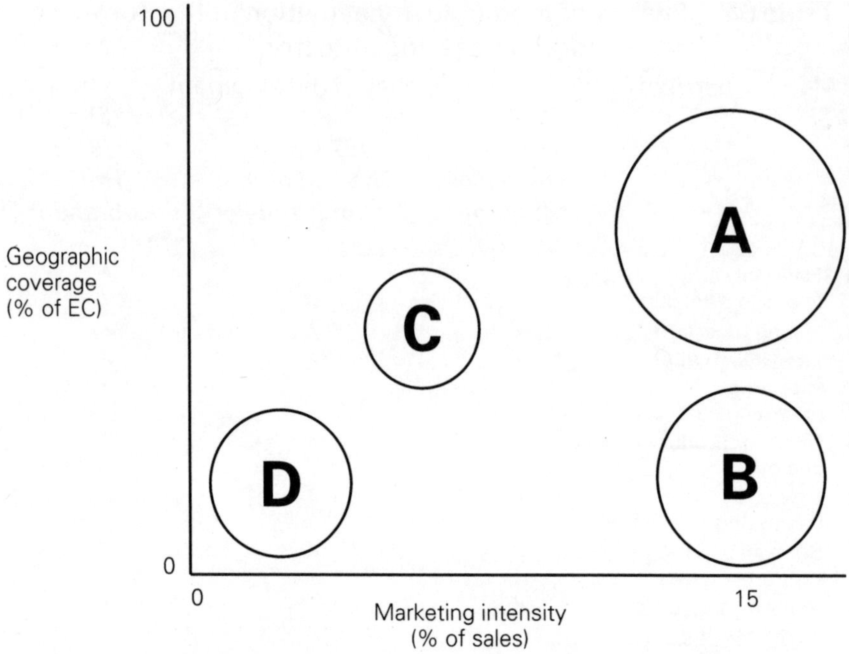


Key: A - Multinational branders

B - National branders

C - Weak national branders with direct (own) branding for retailers outside home territory

D - National direct (own) branders

*Source:* McGee and Segal-Horn[9]

**Figure 6.1** Strategic groups in the European food industry in the 1980s

map of the European food industry in the 1980s. The strength of the brand (product strength) is represented by marketing intensity, which measures marketing costs relative to total costs. It is intended to reflect the importance of the marketing function in this industry in building and supporting brands. This dimension on the map is therefore able to show not only brand strength, but also the centrality of the marketing function and in particular the ability to benefit from scale economies in cross-border marketing and larger segment size. It also, to some degree, reflects new product development capabilities.

The four strategic groups represented in Figure 6.1 were derived from cluster analyses of some markets, data from interviews with industry executives and industry estimates by the researchers. The four groups constitute very different competitive postures.

*Group A*

This consists of the multinational major branders such as Mars, Unilever, Nestle, Kraft, Pepsico. They are all multinational consumer packaged goods companies which operate many related businesses throughout the world. All the businesses offer high product quality supported by robust branding. Reflecting the nationally-determined patterns of demand in this industry, the structure of all these companies has been what Porter[18] labelled 'multidomestic' rather than global, ie structuring all operations separately on a country by country basis.

*Group B*

This contains the national major branders eg Ross Young, Danone, Verkade, St Ivel, Smiths/Walkers/Planters, Cote d'Or, Barilla. These firms are nationally based and nationally focused. Proportionately, they utilise as high a degree of marketing support as the multinationals for branded products which are aimed primarily at the domestic market, in which they occupy strong positions. Their product range is also more restricted than that of the multinational branders.

*Group C*

This is made up of the minor regional branders such as Unigate, Premier Brands, La Familia. These firms occupy lower ranking brand positions and are not normally leaders in any national markets. Their modest market strength leads them to supplement their position and absorb underutilised capacity by acting also as own-label suppliers for large retailers' own brands plus some exporting where possible. Groups B and C are not uniformly represented in all food sectors in all markets.

*Group D*

This consists of national own-labellers (national direct branders) eg Hillsdown Holdings, Hazlewood Foods. Often utilising advanced product and process technology, these private-label suppliers concentrate on highly efficient low-cost production, supplying mainly domestic retail chains. They incur virtually no marketing and branding costs of their own.

Figure 6.2 illustrates the mobility barriers separating these strategic groups. The occupied places on the grid correspond to the four map positions in Figure 6.1. Generally the effectiveness of these mobility barriers has been high, although with some variation from group to group. For group A, the multinationals, the barriers have been highly effective, so that competition is experienced as coming mainly from within that group. Higher levels of cross-border activity such as rationalised production or integrated marketing and heavier advertising can only serve to reinforce these barriers. Some pressures do, however, come from the own-labellers whose lower cost-structure constrains the multinationals' potential margins from premium pricing, and also from innovative national branders.

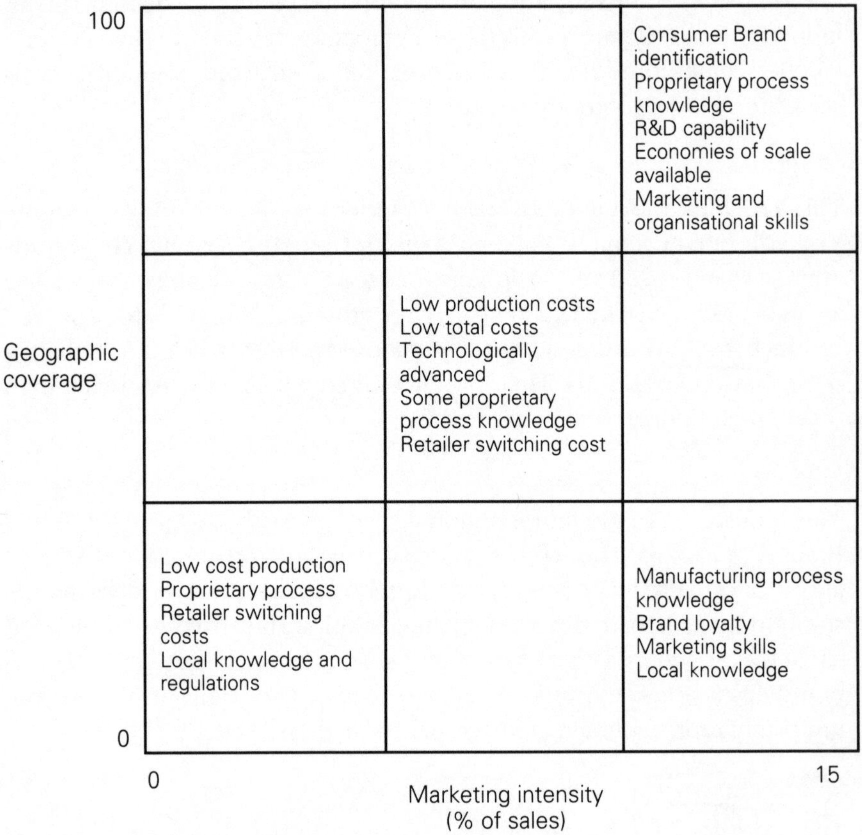


*Source:* McGee and Segal-Horn[9]

**Figure 6.2** Summary of mobility barriers in the 1980s

Figure 6.2 shows the national major branders (group B) in good shape with defensible barriers arising from local market knowledge and conditions. The main competitive pressure on this group is the steadily rising costs attached to the heavy levels of marketing support needed to match that of the multinationals in order to prevent greater inroads in many product sectors. Added to this is the related issue of the cost of new product development and launch, which must be sustained against a smaller potential market size.

The minor regional branders (group C) are revealed by Figure 6.2 as being in a vulnerable position. Their production costs and total costs are low, but do not match those of group D. Their return on investment (ROI) is likely to be poor, making it difficult for them to match the marketing intensity and brand support of groups A and B, with whom they are competing for retailer shelf space. The national own-labellers (group D) are also faced with difficulties. Their barriers are those consistent with a low-cost strategy and they are dependent upon achieving manufacturing economies of scale. These mobility barriers are vulnerable to lower-cost, higher-volume suppliers. The natural arena from which such competitors might appear would be own-label suppliers seeking to enter from other national markets. There are no brands to protect or be protected in this group, so competition is all about volume and the search for scale efficiencies.

## *Strategic space in the European food industry*

Looking again at Figures 6.1 and 6.2, it is possible to identify the pattern of 'empty' space available in the current structure of competing groups in this industry. Cluster analysis by Duckett[19] supports the view that there is enough space available to allow alternative configurations of the strategic groups. Building on the grid used for Figure 6.2, an illustration of how the available strategic space may be occupied is given in Figure 6.3. The existing strategic groups A, B, C and D occupy four of the spaces on this grid. The remaining spaces (V, W, X, Y, Z) offer positions of varying degrees of feasibility under current and (likely) future industry conditions.

External factors have recently been very powerful in shifting the existing mobility barriers. Regulatory change in pursuit of the European Single Market in general, and EC food directives in particular, have increased accessibility to individual country markets, thereby creating the opportunity for potential cost savings to manufacturers from addressing larger scale units. In the longer-term, achievement of such potential efficiencies would require the continuation of trends towards convergence of consumer preferences across the different national markets. Taken together these trends create pressure on firms to move 'north' and 'west' in the available strategic space.

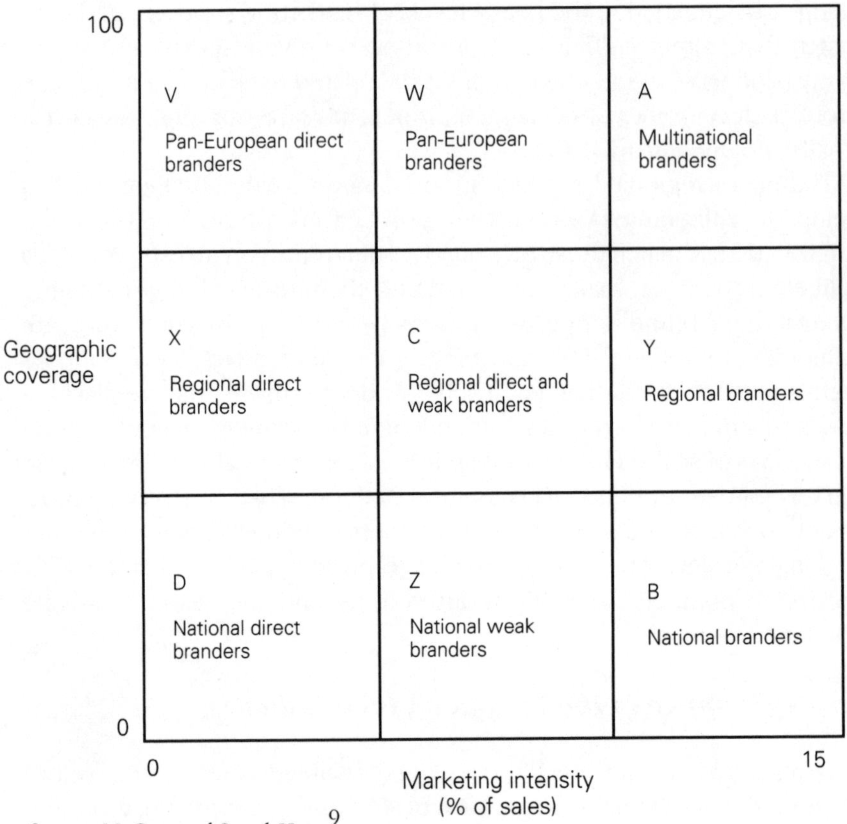


*Source:* McGee and Segal-Horn[9]

**Figure 6.3** Strategic space analysis

*The own-labellers' spaces*

The national own-label suppliers (group D) will be under pressure to respond to the squeeze on costs and volumes by looking for scale. For them the push 'northwards' is inescapably attractive. This means that they must be expected in the short-term to enter space X, ie to extend their customer base to retailers in other national markets, while aiming in the longer-term for space V, ie to supply own-label private brands to retailers across Europe. This would enable them to exploit fully both production and distribution economies, which would only increase yet further with greater congruence in concentration levels amongst retailers in the various European markets.

It is hard to see spaces D and X remaining sustainable in the long-term. That is likely to mean that rivalry within the own-label groups will become intense. The regional strategy (space X) will only be viable if the pan-European strategy (space V) is shown to be non-viable, as a result of continuing high requirements for national differences and large residual structural impediments regardless of EC deregulation. If, however, space V *is* viable, then it must dominate spaces D and X, because of the massive scale effects. Alternative development paths then will be either space X as a stepping-stone to space V ie pan-European coverage, or space X (regional competitors) locked in permanent rivalry, with both bigger (V) and smaller (D) competitors each seeking to address an unconsolidated market. Much of the outcome will depend on the actions of the retail chains in their search to establish regional chains and the buying practices they then follow.

*The branders spaces*

Space W is the home of pan-European branders pursuing an integrated strategy for common branded goods throughout Europe. Economies of scale would be achievable in all functions. Since this would include marketing, it would mean that the marketing intensity would be less than for the multinational branders in space A, as long as the multinationals continue to be organised in a multidomestic mode. Space W would be distanced from the price competition of the own-labellers, whilst in natural competition with spaces A and B, ie the national branders and also the multinational branders who do not adopt either a global, or what Bartlett and Ghoshal[20] call a 'transnational', structure. Although lower logistics costs, regional media availability, reduced regulatory, structural and tariff barriers, together with increasing consumer convergence, all increase the viability of a trans-European multinational group, it would mean significant operational and cultural changes in group A to follow that path. The multinational major branders in space A have the barriers to protect their existing position, or to use as cover while undergoing gradual shifts to strengthen towards a globally integrated position. Any move by them towards space W would undermine their existing investments in national brands and national management structures. The current reorganisation many of this group (such as Unilever, BSN, Kellogg) are now undergoing to rationalise their production plants and logistics across Europe should give them useful insights into how integration in other functions may be managed in due course.

By definition, the competitors in space A, have greater international experience than the occupants of space B. They would undoubtedly be able to exploit this advantage as some competitors from both spaces A and B see benefits from developing a more trans-European integrated structure and both begin moving towards space W. However, many competitors in space B will choose to remain there and protect what will undoubtedly remain some viable national products and segments. Unfortunately it is difficult to predict the eventual size of those national market segments in the longer-term. What can be certainly stated however, is the lack of international experience amongst this group. The mobility barriers for moving towards space W from space B are very high and may involve mergers or collaboration in joint ventures to attempt to surmount them.

*The centre spaces*

Following the discussion of the issues affecting the other spaces, space C at the centre of the grid starts to look very weak. If the own-labellers spread across Europe and strong pan-European regional branders emerge, its' poorly protected position in both brands and own-label becomes even more exposed. As spaces X and V fill up, opportunities for utilisation of spare capacity on private-label supply to other national markets will diminish. Thus the profitability of space C in the long-term looks marginal at best. For the same reasons space Z is not feasible – it is stuck between strong national branders (space B) and national own-labellers (space D), lacking the strengths of either of them even in the short-term.

Space Y (regional branders), although virtually unoccupied at present, could offer a pathway through to space W, or an escape route from space C. However, the rivalry in space Y is likely to be overpowering since the multinationals will be seeking to protect their (national) brand positions, all the more so if these are the ones they wish to develop into 'Eurobrands'. The national branders in space B will oppose any inroads by new regional branders (in addition to existing multinationals) into their national markets and will have strong protective barriers and a stronger resource base behind which to operate.

## *Changes in the strategic group map over time*

The preceding discussion of the strategic space is illustrated in Figure 6.4. It shows the most probable sequence of changes in the configuration of strategic groups in this industry over the next ten years. Clearly the barriers protecting the strategic groups of the 1980s are under threat.

There are two key elements driving the changes illustrated in Figure 6.4. The first is cost and the second demand.

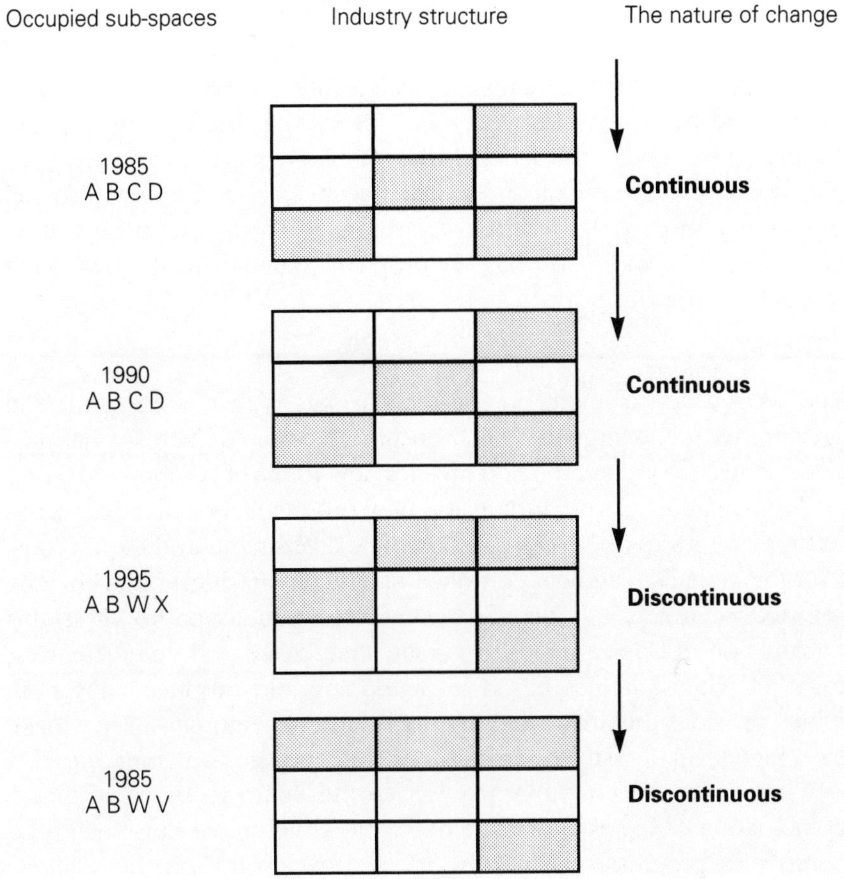


**Figure 6.4** Possible changes in the strategic group map

*Cost*

The potential opportunities for lowering significantly the existing cost base for manufacturers in the food processing industry are extensive. They include increased efficiencies from production, distribution and marketing, which are already encouraging restructuring and consolidation, together with large reductions in the numbers of plants and the numbers of companies (eg Kellogg's breakfast cereal production is now consolidated to just two manufacturing plants for Europe). Successive bouts of acquisitions within the food industry have been directed at acquiring companies with specific assets such as strong brand portfolios or distribution networks. Grover[21] described the food industry as in the midst of major structural change, 'with a handful of mega-scale food conglomerates emerging eg Nestlé, Unilever, BSN'. Acquisition is being used by companies as a route for making strategic moves into 'empty' spaces and constructing the new mobility barriers to protect their new positions. Many small and medium-sized companies may be forced to exit as a more polarised industry emerges. This polarisation will be acompanied by more cost-based European strategies as the own-label strategic groups develop.

*Demand*

The second key element driving the changes is that of demand. The greater the convergence of consumer demand across national boundaries, the greater the potential for new forms of competition based on segmentation, Eurobranding and new product lines. Already this has led to many 'swaps' between companies, ie divestments and acquisitions, to both rationalise segment portfolios, and fill out product lines within the selected segments (eg divest snack foods, add to pasta). It is this conjunction of opportunities to pursue strategies based on efficiencies, together with strategies based on marketing and product innovation, which provides the drivers behind the changes in Figure 6.4. They make for a high level of disturbance of the existing industry structure.

What emerges from this analysis of the strategic space is that a combination of external and internal factors will move European food companies progressively 'northward' and 'westward' on the strategic space map. In order for this analysis to be correct, the existing mobility barriers must be diminishing in strength relative to the mobility 'capacity' of the firms within the existing strategic groups. Fragmentary and inconclusive evidence is usually all that is available when an industry is in the midst of transition. However, the specific kinds of new investments firms are making in technologies, products, and brand portfolios, together with changed approaches to manufacturing, marketing and distribution, suggests that these early indicators are valid.

The two main themes are 'cost-push' and 'demand-pull'. 'Cost-push' is towards scale economies and major changes in unit costs, in an industry historically distinguished by low levels of scale economies determined by national market boundaries. 'Demand-pull' is stretching those market boundaries to encompass emergent European-wide segments, with a corresponding European-wide positioning of firms and brands, and some standardisation of products and marketing. This represents a radical agenda for firms which have traditionally operated close to their national markets, within a fragmented industry structure.

This analysis has suggested that two new strategic groups are likely to emerge in the European food industry: the *pan-European (regional) brander* and the *pan-European own-labeller*. From the strategic space analysis, it has further suggested the likely pathways which these new groups will travel. Finally, it explains the probable nature of the competition to be faced, both en route to the new structure and once the new groups have emerged. It is not, however, able to predict the time the changes will take nor the final winners and losers, although the likely characteristics of the winners and losers are fairly clear.

## CONCLUSIONS AND IMPLICATIONS

This chapter has presented a new methodology for looking at industry dynamics and planning the future strategies of firms. Making sense of industries is difficult because the unit of analysis may itself be unhelpful. In static analysis, 'industry' as the unit of analysis does shed some light on the current situation. For long-term dynamics, however, the strategic group concept is more powerful. Particularly helpful is the pivotal mechanism of 'mobility barriers' (ie barriers to change) beçause these are different for the different members within an industry. This is partly because what we mean by an 'industry' is frequently unclear since many industry boundaries have become fluid and hard to define. It is also because the particular situation is more important than the general industry membership. This does not mean that 'all firms are different': it simply means that the more usable aggregated unit is that of groups of firms serving common customers or having common asset structures.

'Industry' is a portmanteau expression with modest strategic significance. Issues are much more to do with the existence of firms and groups of firms and the investment decisions that particular firms share. Strategic group analysis can offer insights into industry dynamics. Analysis of the strategic space can identify directions of migration and thus an approach to future strategic direction.

Finally, it is important to clarify the issue of performance, either relative to industry structure or within each strategic group. Strategic group membership is only a statement of membership, not of *competence*, therefore, diversity of performance within strategic groups must be expected.

## References


1. Porter, M (1980) *Competitive Strategy*, The Free Press, Macmillan, New York.
2. Lipsey, R (1983) *An Introduction to Positive Economics*, Weidenfield and Nicolson, London 6th edition, p 242
3. McGee, J (1985) 'Strategic Groups: a Bridge Between Industry Structure and Strategic Management?' in Thomas, H and Gardner, D (eds) *Strategic Marketing and Management*, John Wiley, Chichester
4. McGee, J and Thomas, H (1986) 'Strategic Group Analysis and Strategic Management' in McGee, J and Thomas, H (eds) *Strategic Management Research*, John Wiley, Chichester
5. Caves, R and Porter, M (1977) 'From Entry Barriers to Mobility Barriers', *Quarterly Journal of Economics*, vol 91
6. McGee, J and Thomas, H (1989) 'Strategic Groups: a Further Comment' *Strategic Management Journal*, vol 10, no 1, Jan–Feb
7. McGee, J (1985) *op cit*
8. McGee, J and Segal-Horn, S (1988) *Changes in the European Food Processing industry: the Consequences of 1992*, British Academy of Management 2nd Annual Conference, Cardiff
9. McGee, J and Segal-Horn, S (1990) Strategic Space and Industry Dynamics: the Implications for International Marketing Strategy, *Journal of Marketing Management*, vol 61, no 3, pp 175–93
10. McGee, J and Segal-Horn, S (1992) Will There Be a European Food Processing Industry? in Young, S and Hamill, J (eds) *Europe and the Multinationals*, Edward Elgar, London.
11. Kaldor, N (1980) 'The Economic Aspects of Advertising', reprinted in Kaldor, N (ed) *Essays on Value and Distribution*, Duckworth, London.
12. Foy, P (1980) 'The implications for manufacturers of the Retail Revolution', unpublished, McKinsey & Co., London.
13. Segal-Horn, S and McGee, J (1989) 'Strategies to Cope with Retailer Buying Power' in Pellegrini, L and Reddy, S K (eds) *Vertical Relationships and the Distributive Trades*, Routledge, London
14. Cecchini, P (1988) *1992: European Challenge, The Benefits of a Single Market*, Wildwood House, London
15. MAC Group (1988) *The Cost of 'Non-Europe' in the Foodstuffs Industry*, Commission of the European Communities, vol 12B
16. MAC Group, *opcit*
17. Gogel, R and Larreche, J-C (1989) 'The Battlefield for 1992: Product Strength and Geographic Coverage', *European Management Journal*, vol 7 no 2
18. Porter, M (ed) (1986) *Competition in Global Industries*, Harvard Business School Press, Boston

19. Duckett, S (1990) *Competitive Strategy, the European Internal Market Programmes and Van Den Bergh and Jergens*, unpublished paper, Templeton College
20. Bartlett, C and Ghoshal, S (1989) *Managing Across Borders*, Hutchinson, London
21. Grover, J (1989) 'The Changing Structure of the European Food Industry', *Acquisitions Monthly*, October

# 7

# STRATEGIC ALLIANCES: COOPERATION FOR COMPETITION

*David Faulkner*

## INTRODUCTION

Until very recently the reputation of strategic alliances and other cooperative forms of organisation has been mixed at best, and the underlying theory justifying them has been unconvincing and lacking in consensus. In fact many of the most prominent students of the genre have had little good to say about it.

> If firms can do everything equally well and are blessed with infinite cash resources, there is no need for joint ventures . . . . Joint ventures are a transitional form of management, an intermediate step on the way to something else.[1]

> Joint ventures are a trade-off between the drive for unambiguous control, and the quest for additional resources.[2]

The literature is strewn with negative adjectives like, 'impermanent, transitional, second-best, unstable'. Nevertheless, throughout the eighties and into the nineties, cooperative forms of doing business have grown rapidly, and continue to increase as firms of all sizes and nationalities in an increasing number of industries perceive value in them.

Strategic alliances, joint ventures, dynamic networks, constellations, cooperative agreements, collective strategies, all make an appearance and develop significance for the analyst of industry structure as well as for the industrial practitioner. In tune with the growth of cooperative managerial forms, the reputation of cooperation, in the views of the commentators, is enjoying a notable revival, to set against the hitherto unassailable theoretical strength of the competitive model as a paradigm of resource allocation efficiency.

It is probably unhelpful, however, to think of cooperation as the opposite of competition, since firms generally cooperate with each other only in order to harness the resources, skills and power to compete more effectively with others in the market place. The issue, then, is not 'to compete or to cooperate' but rather how best to organise the appropriate set of resources and skills to become a winner in the competitive market place. And since more market places are becoming global, the critical mass of resources needed to succeed is growing faster than many internally developed companies can cope with alone.

This chapter takes the view that competition is not threatened by the growth of strategic alliances and other cooperative variants, as it was by the philosophy underlying the command economies found in the communist world. It is suggested that the questions that really matter are those concerned with the conditions and circumstances that lead to the development of alliances and networks, and the patterns of behaviour that lead to their survival and success.

The growth of interorganisational cooperative forms of business activity calls into question the nature and boundaries of the basic building blocks of economic analysis: the firm, the industry and the national economy. In traditional economic analysis, firms, composed of a set of resources, produce products and services and compete with other firms for the favours of customers in a market place. Firms that produce similar products are collectively gathered together in an industry, and all the firms within a nationally governed geographical area form a national economy. It is assumed that the firm controls its resources and can deploy them at will, and that the success of industries and national economies comes from the interaction of that deployment within constraints set by national governments. However, in a world of globalised tastes and technologies, declining trade barriers, economic turbulence, predictive uncertainty, multinational companies larger than many nation states and fast developing international strategic alliances and cooperative networks, the traditional categories of the economist become less and less useful as basic building blocks for analysis.

The economist Oliver Williamson defines a firm as no more than a cluster of contracts – with suppliers, employees, customers, and distributors.[3] Others talk of the 'hollow corporation'[4] like Clive Sinclair's old Sinclair Research where the entrepreneur and his team perform one key function (product development in this case) and leave all other functions to subcontractors better equipped to carry them out.

In a growing number of areas, a careful consideration of the appropriate make-or-buy options may lead many manufacturers to opt to become mere assemblers, or even purely brand marketing companies. Alternatively, medium sized companies may become global enterprises almost overnight by setting up a wide network of strategic alliances to meet global challenges and opportunities. In this changing structure, the predominance of the traditional firm operating with a complete value chain[5] as the basic unit of strategic analysis becomes somewhat suspect and difficult to define. On the industry front, McGee and Thomas[6] and others find strategic analysis often more usefully carried out at strategic group level (ie the group of strategic entities that recognise each other as competitors) than in industries, the clear existence of which becomes questionable in many areas, and which frequently have major players uncomfortably straddling a number of them. Is it now useful to talk of a computer industry, or is it communications, telecommunications or even microchip that is the most useful descriptor?

At the level of the economy even, the globe-spanning existence of major multinationals has long made national economic management very difficult, and supranationality will soon, no doubt, increase further as Brussels develops its power post-1992. These changes are emphasised by the development of the 'transnational'[7], eg NEC, which may have multiheadquarters in a number of different countries, and which exists to respond sensitively to local needs in a global fashion through the dexterous manipulation of appropriate information flows.

The movement away from simple hierarchy is accentuated by the growth of alliances and other strategic networks, which aid the development of global loyalties and cooperative endeavours, quite distinct from those encouraged by the old national boundaries. Where the old concepts of firm, industry, and national economy begin to lose their usefulness as tools for strategic analysis, the need for an adequate theory of strategic alliances assumes increased importance.

This chapter will, then, address the following key issues:

- What is a strategic alliance?
- What are its fundamental forms?
- What external conditions stimulate the development of strategic alliances?
- What internal conditions lead to their creation?
- What conditions and behavioural patterns make strategic alliances most likely to survive?

The findings are based upon empirical research currently being carried out by the author at Cranfield School of Management.

## WHAT IS A STRATEGIC ALLIANCE?

Organisational forms are conventionally described on a scale of increasing integration, with markets at one end as the absolute of non-integration, to hierarchies or completely integrated companies[8] at the other. There are, however, many forms of organisation between those extremes, as shown in Figure 7.1.

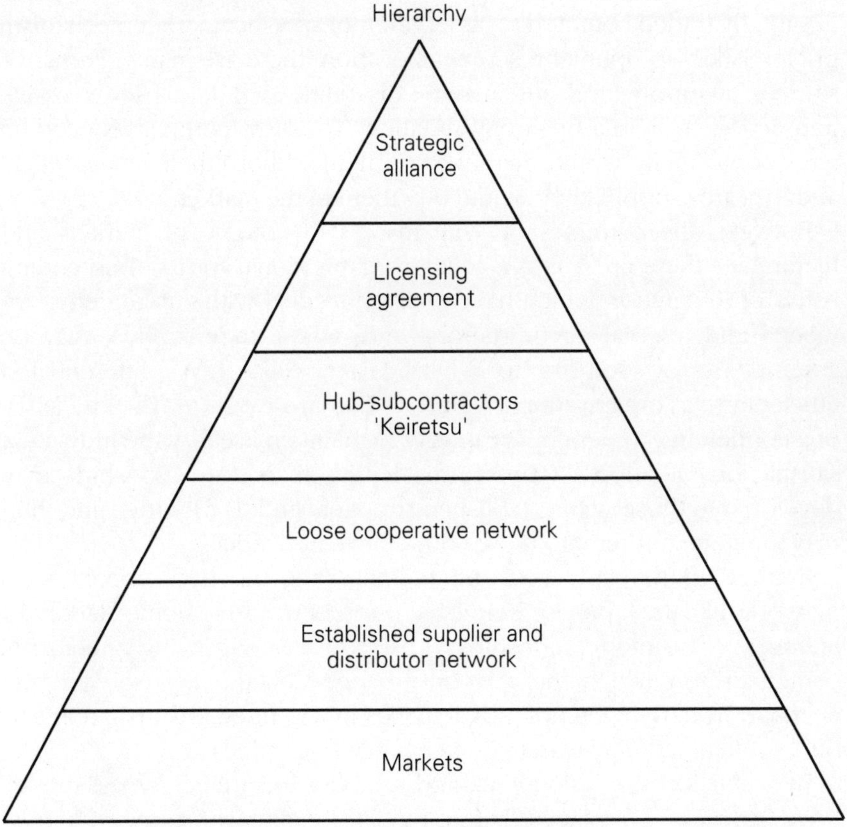


**Figure 7.1** Intermediate organisational forms between markets and hierarchies

It is often assumed that the particular organisational form will be chosen that fits the specific circumstances of the relationship between the set of activities and the environment, and that the pressures of natural selection will cause inappropriate organisational forms to fail. Thus hierarchies[9] will be preferred in situations of high asset specificity, thin markets, conditions of high complexity, uncertainty and infrequency of transaction, when information impactedness and opportunism are likely to be present to an unacceptable degree. Such circumstances would make the transaction costs involved in guarding against the above problems exceedingly high, and make the hierarchical form of organisation the most appropriate one.

At the other extreme, transactions are best performed in markets where no one deal implies commitment to another, and relationships are completely arms length, in the following circumstances: the product is a frequently traded commodity, assets are not specific, market mechanism pricing is key to optimal resource allocation, there are many alternative sources of supply, and bureaucratic disabilities would cause excessive transaction costs in a hierarchy situation. Thus few companies needing nails occasionally would manufacture them without their being critical and in scarce supply: they would buy them in the market.

Between the extremes of Williamson's dichotomy of markets and hierarchies there are a range of interorganisational forms of ascending levels of integration which have evolved to deal with varying environmental and internal circumstances, and, where they survive, may be assumed to do so due to what Masten calls their 'differentiated efficiency'[10] as organisational forms. As Barnard[11] puts it: 'The efficiency of a cooperative system is its capacity to maintain itself by the individual satisfactions it affords'. Thus arms length market relationships may develop into those with established suppliers and distributors, and then may integrate further into loose cooperative networks.

Further up the ladder of integration come the hub-subcontractor networks like the Japanese Keiretsu groups, or nearer to home Marks and Spencers' close interrelationships with its suppliers. Licensing agreements come next, in which the relationship between the licensor and the licensee, from the viewpoint of activities in a defined area, is integrated but both retain their separate ownership and identities.

Between licensing agreements and complete hierarchies, where rule by price (markets) is replaced by rule by fiat (hierarchies), comes the most integrated form of rule by 'adaptive coordination'[12] namely that found in strategic alliances. Alliances may be preferred organisational forms where sensitive market awareness is required, the price mechanism remains important for allocative efficiency, risks of information leakage are not considered unacceptably high, scale economies and finance risks are high, there is resource limitation and flexibility is important.

These diverse forms of cooperative agreements are categorised by

Dephillippi and Reed[13] as either unilateral or bilateral. Unilateral agreements are so called because they typically involve minimal amounts of partner interdependence. Examples would be technical training, supplier contracts, franchising, patent licensing, or marketing consultancy. The agreements have quite specific tasks, and each partner could terminate the agreement without great cost. Strategic alliances are bilateral agreements and involve a larger amount of interdependence. They include non-equity cooperative agreements, equity joint ventures and consortia.

In the literature, strategic alliances are variously defined, and the term is often loosely interchangeable with the term joint ventures. For the purpose of this chapter Johanson and Mattsson's definition will be adopted, namely;

> A particular mode of inter-organisational relationship in which the partners make substantial investments in developing a long-term collaborative effort, and common orientation.[14]

This definition emphasises a number of aspects of the strategic alliance that distinguishes it from other interorganisational forms: namely that the partners make substantial investments, and the effort is intended to be long-term. In addition, the goals of the partners should be orientated in the same direction, although of course their respective goals need not be identical. All of these criteria would clearly be applicable to a bilateral agreement.

The transaction costs approach to the determination of organisational form is that dictated by efficiency criteria. It is not, however, the only dimension that influences form, and may not even be the dominant one for a number of reasons.

1. Transaction costs, especially the qualitative variety, eg information impactedness or asset specificity, are impossible to assess with any numerical accuracy.
2. Organisations develop as a result of human decisions, and human beings have great difficulty in determining the appropriate solution to complex organisational situations. So the actual organisation may, in many cases, not be the optimal one.
3. In the real world, the pressures of natural selection do not operate smoothly or inexorably. There may, therefore, be organisational forms that survive, even though they do not minimise transaction costs. Nonetheless, the transaction cost model provides a useful set of structures against which to assess organisational form.

## THE BASIC FORMS OF STRATEGIC ALLIANCE

Strategic alliances can usefully be classified along three dimensions that define their nature, form and membership:

1. Focused ⟶ Complex
2. Joint venture ⟶ No joint venture
3. Two partners only ⟶ Consortium

### *Focused alliances*

The focused alliance is a collaborative arrangement between two or more companies, set up to meet a clearly defined set of circumstances in a particular way. For each partner, it normally involves only one major activity respectively of its value chain, or at least is clearly defined and limited in its objectives.

Thus, for example, a US company seeking to enter the EC market with a given set of products may form an alliance with a European distribution company as its means of market entry. The US company provides the product, and probably some market and sales literature, and the European company provides the sales force and local know-how. Thus in November 1989 Cincinnati Bell Information Systems of the USA set up an alliance with Kingston Communications of Hull, England to market CBIS's automated telecommunications equipment throughout the European Community. CBIS provides the equipment and Kingston the sales effort. The precise form of arrangement may vary widely, but the nature of the alliance is a focused one with clear remits, and understandings of respective contributions and rewards.

### *Complex alliances*

Complex alliances may involve the complete value chains of the partners. The companies recognise that together, potentially, they form a far more powerful competitive enterprise than they do apart. Yet they wish to retain their separate identities and overall aspirations, whilst being willing to cooperate with each other over a wide range of activities.

Rover/Honda is a good example of a complex alliance. Currently it includes joint R & D, joint manufacturing, joint development and sourcing of parts. It remains separate, however, in the critical marketing and sales areas, and both companies retain clearly distinct images. The alliance involves a 20 per cent share exchange between Rover and the Honda's UK manufacturing company.

## Joint ventures

Joint ventures involve the creation of a legally separate company from that of the partners. The new company will probably start life with the partners as shareholders, and with an agreed set of objectives in a specific area. Thus a US company may set up a joint venture with a UK company to market in the EC. The partners provide finance and other support skills and resources for the joint venture in agreed amounts.

The aim of the joint venture is normally that ultimately the new company should become a self-standing entity with its own employees, and strategic aims quite distinct from those of its parent shareholders. Unilever is a good example of a joint venture set up by a Dutch and an English company in the 1920s, and which has grown into a major multinational enterprise.

## Consortium

The consortium is a distinct form of strategic alliance in that it has a number of partners, and is normally a very large-scale activity set up for a very specific purpose, and managed in a hands-off fashion from the contributing shareholders. Consortia are particularly common for large-scale projects in the defence or aerospace industries where massive funds and a wide range of specialist skills are required for success.

Airbus Industrie is a consortium where a number of European shareholders have set up an aircraft manufacturing company to compete on world markets with Boeing and McDonnell Douglas. The European shareholders, although themselves large, felt the need to create a large enough pool of funds to ensure they reached critical mass in terms of resources for aircraft development, and chose to form an international consortium to do this.

There are, then, eight possible basic configurations of alliance covering the alliance's nature, its form and the number of partners it has. The different categories can be illustrated as in Figure 7.2 overleaf.

1. **Focused collaboration** (Focused/non-joint venture/two partners FN2)
2. **Focused joint venture** (Focused/joint venture/two partners - FJ2)
3. **Focused consortium** (Focused/joint venture/consortium - FJ>2)
4. **Focused multi-partner collaboration** (Focused/non-joint venture/consortium FN>2)
5. **Complex collaboration** (Complex/non-joint venture/two partners CN2)

6. **Complex joint venture** (Complex/joint venture/two partners CJ2)
7. **Complex consortium** (Complex/joint venture/consortium CJ>2)
8. **Complex multi-partner collaboration** (Complex/non-joint venture/consortium CN>2)

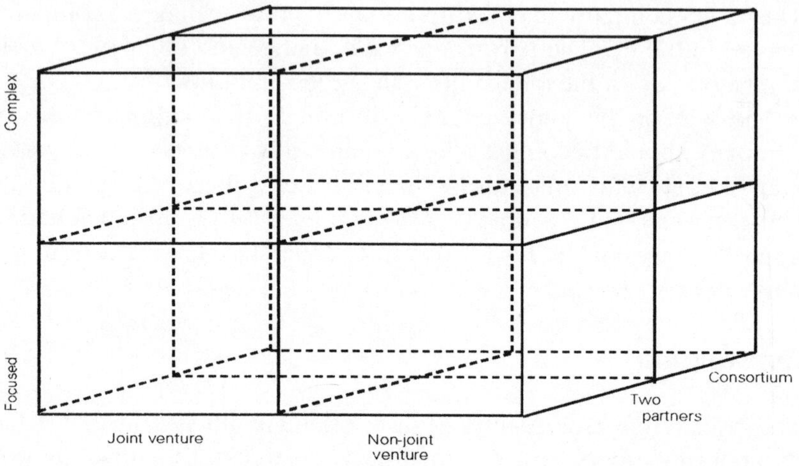


**Figure 7.2** The strategic alliance options

All the categories of alliance are not equally likely to come about, and certain forms are likely to evolve into others. In research conducted at Cranfield into a data-base of 228 international alliances recorded in the British national press and in periodicals, and in which at least one partner was a UK firm, configurations varied as shown in Table 7.1 below.

**Table 7.1** Strategic alliance configurations (%)

| | | |
|---|---|---|
| 1. | Focused joint venture (FJ2) | 25 |
| 2. | Focused consortium (FJ>2) | 20 |
| 3. | Complex joint venture (CJ2) | 20 |
| 4. | Complex collaboration (CN2) | 11 |
| 5. | Focused collaboration (FN2) | 9 |
| 6. | Focused multi-partner collaboration (FN>2) | 9 |
| 7. | Complex consortium (CJ>2) | 3 |
| 8. | Complex multi-partner collaboration (CN>2) | 3 |
| | | 100 |

Although no definitive predictive conclusions can be deduced from the above analysis, since a different sample would no doubt give different percentages, it does demonstrate a number of points:

- The alliance type that involves setting up a joint venture company is currently by far the most popular method, accounting for 68 per cent of the sample total.
- Alliances with focused objectives, rather than more general link-ups between companies, accounted for 63 per cent of the total.
- Although consortia are inevitably difficult to operate, since they involve getting and keeping accord between several partners, at 35 per cent they account for a significant number of alliances.

It should be noted that the configurations analysed above are the 'pure' forms. Situations exists where a joint venture itself becomes a partner in a further alliance – or the partners in a focused alliance subsequently set up a joint venture. There are also well trodden paths by which alliances evolve. For example, focused alliances that are successful frequently develop into complex alliances, as the partners find other areas for mutual cooperation. Two partner alliances often recruit further partners, and develop into consortia, as the scale and complexity of the opportunities becomes apparent. Frequently alliances, initially without joint venture companies, subsequently form them as they experience difficulty in operating in a partially merged fashion, but without clear boundaries between the cooperative and the independent parts.

Other paths of evolution, however, are probably less likely to be followed. Consortia are unlikely to reduce to two partner alliances. Alliances with joint venture companies are unlikely to revert to a non-joint venture situation, but to keep the alliance in being. Also, complex alliances are unlikely to revert to a simple focused relationship between the partners.

A research project at INSEAD [15] has been collecting data since 1976 on cross-border alliances, and has to date recorded nearly 2000. The largest number have been in five industry areas: automobiles, aerospace, telecommunications, computers, and electrical and electronic goods. It is notable that, in general, these industries have similar characteristics. They all require very large investment, have a high threshold of critical mass, are high risk, exhibit large scale economies, and have rapidly changing technologies.

The Cranfield research has revealed similar findings in this area, although the spread of industries seems to be wider, and certain dominant alliance industries are missing from the leaders, notably automobiles, computers and electronics. This may suggest that from an alliance viewpoint these industries have reached maturity, in that most of the key networks have already been established.

**Table 7.2** Industries most frequently cited in the Cranfield research

| | % |
|---|---|
| Defence, aerospace and aviation | 15 |
| Oil, chemicals, and plastics | 15 |
| Telecommunications | 12 |
| Financial services | 8 |
| Food, drink, and hotels | 8 |
| Energy and power generation | 6 |
| Pharmaceuticals | 5 |
| 20 other industries | 31 |
| TOTAL | 100 |

Other notable features are the appearance of financial services as a strong alliance industry, as the financial industry becomes more global; and the spread of alliances over a wide range of industries outside the obvious high-technology, and high critical mass categories.

The stable competitive conditions of the neoclassical economists relate closely to the conditions described in plant and animal life by the biologist Amos Hawley[16]. 'Competition arises whenever individual units with like demands, such as members of the same species, make claims on limited resources'[17] However, in very turbulent, threatening and uncertain conditions, members of the same species (eg ants) do not wait for natural selection, but engage in voluntary collective mobilisation of action and resources to ensure their collective survival.

Hawley identifies other forms of collaboration that are symbiotic and link different species:

> Plants collaborate with animals, as animals live on the fruit and plants have their seed widely scattered . . . Thus the natural environment is increasingly displaced by a social environment that mediates the effect of competition through the construction of a network of cooperative relationships.[18]

The parallel with the economic world is striking.

## EXTERNAL STIMULI FOR STRATEGIC ALLIANCES

There are a number of external conditions that have stimulated the growth of strategic alliances in recent years. Amongst the most important, it is believed, are the following:

- globalisation of tastes and markets;
- the rapid spread and short life cycle of new technology and its products;
- major economies of scale, scope and learning;
- increasing turbulence in international economies;
- a heightened level of uncertainty in all aspects of life;
- declining international trade barriers.

## *Globalisation of tastes*

Theodore Levitt[19] was credited, over 20 years ago, with first having drawn attention to the increasing homogenisation of tastes leading to the development of the 'global village'. Since that time the movement has spread to an increasing number of industries, and it is now possible to travel from New York to London and on to Tokyo, and to see the same articles on display in department stores in all three cities.

As Ohmae emphasises[20], over 600 million consumers in the triad of the USA, EC and Japan are developing very similar tastes in a growing number of areas. One implication is that companies need to be able to serve all three areas simultaneously, and very shortly after a product launch. Alliances are often the only way to achieve this, as few firms have the resources or know-how to undertake this task single-handed.

## *Technology*

Stopford and Turner[21] point out that all of what they describe as the meta-technologies, namely microelectronics, genetic engineering, and advanced material sciences, are subject to truly global competition.

The global technologies inherent in the communications revolution also succeed in 'shrinking' the world, and facilitating the design and manufacture of products with global appeal due to their pricing, reliability and technical qualities. 'Technology is replacing economic and financial considerations as the most common basis for international cooperation.'[22]

But not only is technology becoming global in nature, it is also changing faster, which means a single firm needs correspondingly greater resources to be capable of replacing the old technology with the new on a regular basis, and this is often difficult to achieve.

## Economies of scale and scope

The globalisation of markets and technologies leads to the need to be able to produce at a sufficiently large volume to realise the maximum economies of scale and scope, and thus compete globally on a unit cost basis.

Although one effect of the new technologies is, through flexible manufacturing systems, to be able to produce small lots economically, the importance of scale and scope economies is still critical to global economic competitiveness. Alliances are often the only way to achieve a sufficiently large scale of operation to generate these economies.

However, the movement towards deintegration also stems in large part from some of the same set of circumstances that has led to the growth of alliances. Alliances and deintegrated networks allow greater degrees of specialisation, and consequent cost and quality advantages. Lorenzoni[23] quotes the development of the textile industry in northern Italy where, in 1951, 700 firms deintegrated into 9500 by 1976, with a decrease in the average workforce size from 30 to 5. Total employment more than doubled and the industry is still amongst the most competitive in the world.

The advantages of alliances and networks over integrated firms are in the areas of specialisation, entrepreneurship and flexibility of arrangements. Only major scale economies in terms of capital equipment would push in the other direction, and even this can be achieved by an alliance of two or more major players.

## Growing turbulence

Igor Ansoff drew attention to the growing turbulence of international economic affairs in 1965.[24] The ensuing oil crises of 1973 and 1978, the Middle East wars, and the subsequent aggravated economic cycles of boom and recession, coupled with ever shortening product life cycles has made economic forecasting as hazardous as long-term weather forecasting. Strategic vulnerability due to environmental uncertainty has become a fact of life in most industries. 'Problems arise not merely because organisations are dependent on their environment, but because the environment is not dependable.'[25]

## Declining trade barriers

After the Second World War, trade barriers between nations placed a limit on the development of a world economy. With the dramatic economic recovery of many of the combatant nations, particularly Germany and Japan, the move towards increasing international trade was stimulated by international agreements to reduce trade barriers, and thus increase overall economic welfare by allowing greater specialisation on the basis of comparative costs.

GATT, the EC, EFTA and other trading agreements and common markets enabled national firms to develop opportunities internationally, and to grow into multinationals. More recently the 1992 EC legislation, the reunification of Germany, and the break-up of the Communist bloc have accelerated this movement, and in so doing stimulated the growth of strategic alliances between firms in different nations.

## INTERNAL CONDITIONS FOR ALLIANCE CREATION

A range of external conditions may stimulate the creation of strategic alliances. However, firms will only enter into such arrangements when their internal circumstances make this seem to be the right move. Most commonly, these internal circumstances have included a feeling of resource dependency in that an alliance would afford access to valuable markets, technologies, special skills or raw materials not easily or quickly otherwise available. Other internal circumstances have included the belief that the governance structure involved in an alliance would involve lower transaction costs than those involved with other organisational forms. A third reason has frequently been the belief that an alliance, or a series of alliances, would provide strong protection against takeover predators. Others may be the perceived need to limit risk, or to achieve a desired market position faster than by any other method.

### *Resource dependency*

The theory of resource dependency has been most strongly associated with the ideas of Pfeffer and Salancik.[26] It suggests that the crucial condition determining the survival of a firm is not its competitive advantage but its access to resources. Thus if a highly competitive firm overtrades, ie runs out of resources it fails to survive. On the other hand if a sleepy firm is part of a very large and indulgent conglomerate, it can survive as long as its parent considers it worth supplying the necessary resources.

In conditions of economic turbulence and high uncertainty, resources become at risk, which raises the spectre of potential strategic vulnerability for even the most efficient firm. This leads to the motivation 'to negotiate the environment' to reduce that uncertainty and secure a more reliable access to the necessary resources whether they be supplies, skills or markets. Thus often strategic alliances develop where previously market relationships may have dominated. The level of competitive uncertainty is positively correlated with efforts to manage that uncertainty.[27]

**Access to markets** is a common form of resource dependency. One firm has a successful product in its home market, but lacks the sales force and perhaps the local knowledge to gain access to other markets. The alliance cited above between Cincinnati Bell Information Systems of the USA and Kingson Communications of Hull, England was set up to gain market access into the European community markets from CBIS's viewpoint, with the purpose of selling its automated telecommunications equipment. The market motivator is also a strong one in the current spate of Eastern Europe and former USSR alliances with western firms.

**Access to technology** is another form of resource dependency. Thus in forming Cereal Partners to fight Kellogg's domination of the breakfast cereals market, Nestlé has joined forces with General Mills, principally to gain access to its breakfast cereals technology.

**Access to special skills** is a similar form of resource dependency to the above. The special skills may be of many types, and may include know-how associated with experience in a particular product area.

**Access to raw materials** is a further form of resource dependency. Thus, for example, Monarch Resources has allied with Cyprus Minerals to gain access to Venezuelan gold mines.

### *Transaction costs*

Although accurate calculation of transaction costs is not possible, since it involves adding the quantitative and the qualitative, the transaction cost concept is still valuable in determining whether a particular activity is best carried out by internal means, by purchasing it in the market or by collaboration with a partner. As a general rule, as illustrated in Figure 7.3, for a given external environment the strategic alliance form will be preferred in situations where the dependent resource or activity is of strategic importance but the dependent company is lacking in skills or assets to produce this itself.[28]

It is also likely to be an asset of medium to high specificity, but where the risk of information leakage and consequent creation of a competitor is judged to be acceptably low. The need for speed, resource limitation or potential bureaucratic disabilities due to reduced motivation or adminis-

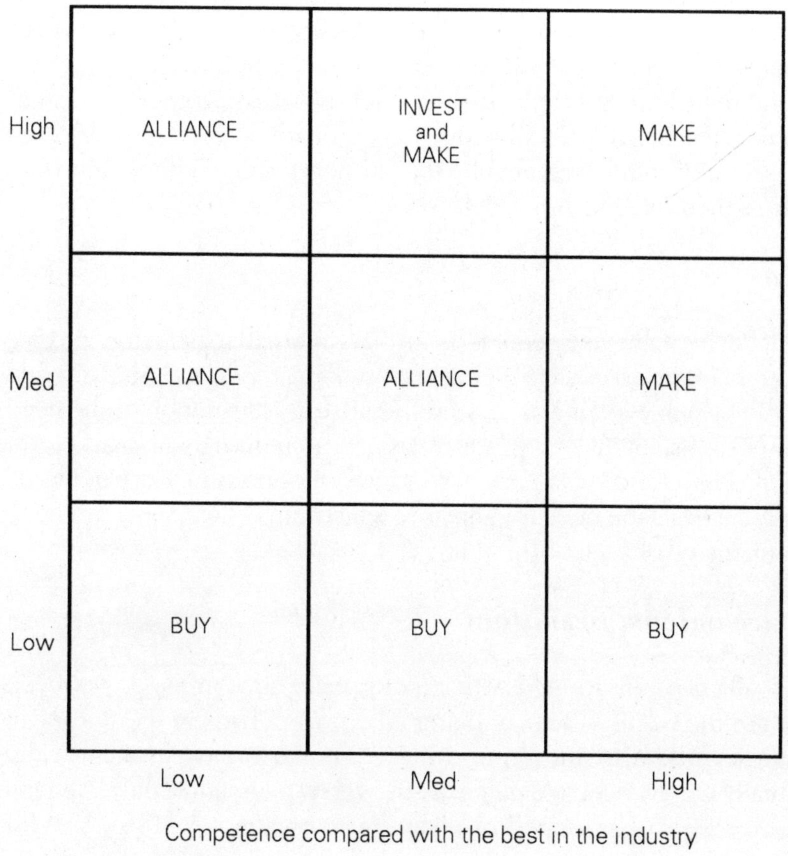


**Figure 7.3** Make, ally or buy decisions

trative inflexibilities are also key in leading to the judgement that the transaction costs would be lower than those of internal development or acquisition.

### *Risk limitation*

Alliances are frequently formed as a result of the need to limit risk. The nature of the risk may be its sheer size in terms of financial resources. Thus a £100 million project shared between three alliance partners is a much lower risk for each partner than the same project shouldered alone. The risk may also be portfolio risk, in which case £100 million invested in alliances in four countries represents a lower risk, *ceteris paribus*, than the same figure invested by one firm in a singe project. The trade-off is between higher control and lower risk. An acquisition represents high control but is expensive, and, however good the due diligence activity, may still reveal unexpected surprises after the conclusion of the deal. A strategic alliance involves shared risk, is probably easier to unravel if it proves disappointing, and enables the partners to get to know each other slowly as their relationship develops.

### *Speed*

The need to achieve speed is a further internal reason for alliance formation. Many an objective in the fast-moving modern business world can only be achieved if action is fast. Ohmae's[29] illustration of the need for almost instantaneous product launches in the retail markets of London, Tokyo and New York if 'windows of opportunity' are not to be missed, suggests the need for alliances which can be activated rapidly to take advantage of such opportunities.

### *Defence against predators*

Not all alliances are formed with expansionary aims in mind, however. Many are the result of fear of being taken over. Thus in the European insurance world AXA and Groupe Midi of France formed an alliance and eventually merged to avoid being taken over by Generali of Italy. General Electric of the UK has formed an alliance with its namesake in the USA for similar defensive reasons.

## CONDITIONS FOR ALLIANCE SURVIVAL

The creation of a strategic alliance does not, of course, guarantee its long-term survival. Research by the consultancy firms McKinsey and Coopers and Lybrand has shown that there is no better than a 50 per cent survival probability for alliances over a five year term. This conclusion is, however, put in perspective when considered against Porter's research[30] into the success of acquisitions, which concluded that this latter route to growth was little better in terms of probable successful outcome. However, one of the aims of such research must be to improve the probability of success by identifying the key qualities required of an alliance for it to endure.

There are three fundamental factors underlying the probability of survival of a strategic alliance:

1. Strategic fit;
2. Cultural fit, including attitude;
3. Appropriate organisational arrangements.

The importance of strategic fit and cultural fit can be illustrated in Figure 7.4.

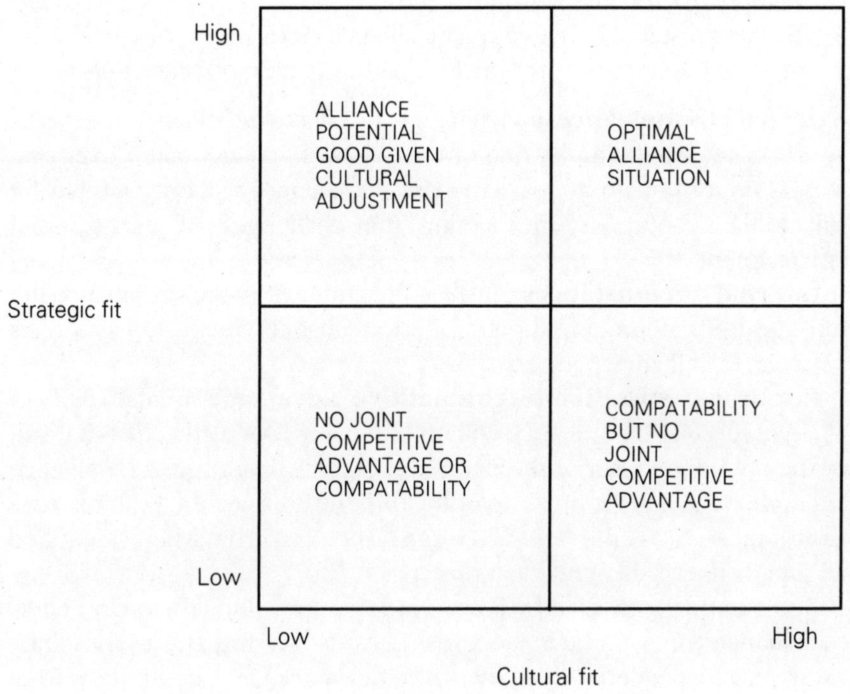


**Figure 7.4** Situations that make alliances appropriate

A high degree of strategic fit is essential to justify the alliance in the first place. However, for it to endure, cultural adaptation must take place leading the most successful alliances to graduate to the top right-hand box.

## *Strategic fit*

Strategic fit, of some form or another, is normally the fundamental reason that the alliance has been set up in the first place. It is important *a)* that it is clearly there at the outset, and *b)* that it continues to exist for the lifetime of the alliance.

Strategic fit implies that:

1. the external and internal circumstances that led to the formation of the alliance are unchanged, or if changed are still such as to make an alliance an appropriate response to them;
2. that the alliance has a clearly identifiable source of sustainable competitive advantage; and
3. that as a result of its activities, the alliance is developing an increasing level of interdependence, including the creation of joint assets.

**External circumstances** may change and make the alliance no longer appropriate. For example, one of the partners may get taken over or a market opportunity may cease to exist. Any alliance will only survive if it still fulfils a purpose in meeting the challenges of the external environment.

**Internal circumstances** must also continue to make the alliance the most appropriate organisational form to realise the perceived synergies between the alliance partners.

**Continued sustainable competitive advantage** is also vital to alliance survival. The alliance will probably have been created as a result of the reconfiguration of the partners' value chains to give the alliance strength in the market place. In doing this, the areas where both partners contribute to each other's resource or skill needs will have been identified and made the focus of negotiations.

If one partner ceases to be able to provide something the other needs, the alliance will soon be in jeopardy. Bertodo[31] of Rover was constantly aware that he needed to be ready with a new package to continue to whet the appetite of his Honda partners. The Shell/BASF alliance broke up because the strategic imperatives of both partners changed, and instead of being symbiotic they threatened to become competitive.

**Growing interdependence** of activity and assets is not a necessary condition for the continued functioning of an alliance; the level of interdependence may remain at the same level as it was at the outset. It is, however, a healthy sign of a thriving relationship, implying strong informal links between the partners and leading to new ideas for joint activities. Royal Bank of Scotland and Banco Santander of Spain set up a complex alliance in 1989, but within a year had developed the relationship further by jointly buying a merchant bank in Germany.

### *Complementary assets*

Whichever partner is sought, it must be one with complementary assets, ie to supply some of the resource or competencies needed to achieve the alliance objectives. In tune with Oliver's[32] view, these complementary needs may come about in a number of circumstances.

- **Legal necessity** – this may be occasioned by the legal requirement, particularly in many developing countries, that international companies take a local partner before being granted permission to trade.
- **Asymmetry** – Alliances are often formed between powerful companies and less powerful ones with specifically needed assets such as technical skills. The aim is to increase power in the market for the more influential company, and to give some resource security to the smaller partner.
- **Reciprocity** – Where the assets of the two partners have a reciprocal strength, ie there are synergies such that a newly configured joint value chain leads to greater power than the two companies could hope to exercise separately.
- **Efficiency** – Where an alliance leads to lower joint costs over an important range of areas; scale, scope, transaction, procurement and so forth, then this provides a powerful stimulus to alliance formation.
- **Reputation** – Alliances are set up to create a more prestigious enterprise with a higher profile in the market place, enhanced image, prestige and reputation.

## *Cultural fit*

The relationship of the partners, as in a marriage, is a key to the success of the arrangement. It may not be a sufficient factor in itself, since the successful alliance needs positive quantifiable results, but it is certainly a necessary condition. An appropriate attitude has two major components, *commitment* and *trust*.

## *Lack of commitment*

This can kill an alliance in a very short time. When the Rover/Honda alliance was set up eleven years ago commentators were concerned lest Rover's commitment to it was not matched by Honda. Rover's economic survival depended upon the alliance however, and its commitment has been high from the outset: this was less important from Honda's viewpoint. However, the Japanese company has shown an equal degree of commitment throughout and the alliance has prospered.

Other alliances have failed because the partners have not allocated their best people to the project, have placed it low on the priority agenda, or have set up too many alliances in the hope that at least a few would succeed. These attitudes have the seeds of failure already sown within them.

### *Trust*

This is the second key factor for survival. Unless trust develops early on in the partnership the alliance soon ceases to be the appropriate organisational arrangement, as transaction costs rise due to monitoring systems installed to overcome lack of trust. Trust does not imply naïve revelation of company secrets outside the alliance agreement, but it implies the belief that the partner will act with integrity, and will carry out its commitments. The appropriate attitude must be set from the start. During the negotiation stage, friendliness should be exhibited, and a deal struck that is clearly 'win-win'; qualities quite different from those that often characterise takeover negotiations. A growing lack of trust may well have been a key factor in the doomed AT&T/Olivetti alliance.

### *Culture*

Culture can be the key to alliance survival, as many an alliance has foundered on the question of incompatible culture alone. The major dissonance between AT&T and Olivetti probably stemmed from a clash between the contrasting cultures of a bureaucratic US giant corporation and an entrepreneurial Italian marketing company. This may lead to difficulties in working together, to mistrust and ultimately to a growing scepticism as to whether the strategic synergy was ever there in the first place. Cultural fit can be analysed under two headings: *basic cultural compatibility* and *goal compatibility.*

*Cultural compatibility*

This can be tested by requiring both partners to draw up a cultural web[33] of their respective organisations in order to identify any potential barriers to working closely together. Cultural difference may not mean incompatibility, however, where there is a strong will to understand differences and bridge the gap. The Rover/Honda cultural differences did not destroy the alliance, because they were evidently visible and the will existed to overcome them.

*Goal compatibility*

This is vital to the long-term success of a partnership. Of course the specific goals of the alliance will evolve over time. However, if there is a fundamental clash between partners at a generic level, the alliance cannot but be a short-term opportunistic affair. Compatibility does not necessarily mean the partners goals must be identitical. Rover's current goals are to be an upmarket niche player in the automobile industry. Honda has more ambitious goals of global success over a wide product range. There is, however, no fundamental incompatibility inherent here.

## *Organisational arrangements*

These may be allowed to evolve to some degree. For best survival chances the most appropriate alliance form for the situational circumstances needs to be adopted. It is not possible to predict definitively which form of cooperative agreement will be adopted in which specific set of circumstances, since certain companies will show policy preferences irrespective of their appropriateness. It is possible, however, to identify certain situational characteristics that make one alliance form more appropriate than another. Important amongst these characteristics are the following:[34]

- Ease of asset separation;
- Level of asset specificity;
- Strength of the need for joint management of the collaborative assets;
- Level of risk of an uncompensated appropriation of some of the assets;
- Degree of certainty of the profit forecast from the collaborative effort.

Unilateral agreements may be preferred when asset separation is easy, assets are not very specific, there is no need for joint management of assets, there is little risk of asset appropriation, and the certainty of the forecasts in relation to the collaborative effort is high.

Strategic alliances or bilateral agreements are best in circumstances where these five circumstances are not found, as shown in Figure 7.4.

Within the strategic alliance category, however, the optimal circumstances for particular forms will also vary. Thus joint ventures and consortia joint ventures (FJ2, FJ>2,CJ2, CJ>2) are generally most appropriate where:

- assets are separable and specific;
- there is a need for joint management of the assets;
- there is a positive appropriation risk (but the joint venture, if the partnership is symmetrical, affords mutual hostages); and
- the profit outcome is uncertain.

**Figure 7.5** Organisation forms: different situational requirements

| SITUATIONAL CHARACTERISTICS → / TYPE OF ORGANISATION FORM ↓ | Asset separability | Asset specificity | Need for joint management | Risk of asset appropriation by partner | Certainty of profit forecast |
|---|---|---|---|---|---|
| UNILATERAL COOPERATIVE AGREEMENT<br>eg Marketing consulting<br>● Training<br>● Subcontracting<br>● Franchising<br>● Licensing | HIGH | LOW/ MODERATE | LOW | LOW | HIGH |
| STRATEGIC ALLIANCE<br>● Non–equity arrangement | LOW | LOW | LOW | ACCEPTABLY MODERATE | MODERATE |
| ● Equity joint venture<br>● Consortium joint venture (inc, equity) | HIGH | HIGH | HIGH | HIGH HENCE NEED FOR "MUTUAL HOSTAGES" | LOW |
| Hierarchy or merged company | LOW | HIGH | HIGH | HIGH | LOW |

The non-equity strategic alliance (FN2, FN>2, CN2, CN>2) may be more appropriate when:

- the assets necessary to the collaboration are difficult to separate from the partners' organisations and of moderate specificity;
- joint asset management is unnecessary;
- there is less appropriation risk than with joint ventures, and more certainty of profit outcome.

Clearly the decision whether to have two or more partners is a trade-off between the need for additional resources and skills, and added complexity of management - and the other variable of whether to cooperate on a specific focused front or more widely in a complex arrangement depends upon circumstances and managerial temperament.

Little definitive research has been carried out to attempt to discover a link between situational characteristics and chosen alliance form, and it is not necessarily the case that companies would be sufficiently aware of the appropriate situational characteristics to choose the best alliance form. However, from a theoretical standpoint the above characteristics provide persuasive arguments for the adoption of particular forms of alliance where the circumstances for them can be identified.

A further factor in the organisational arrangements is the need for clear responsibilities and a good dispute resolution mechanism to be agreed by both parties so that when the first problem emerges it will not sour the atmosphere and lead to a decline in trust. Clearly, responsibility for running the alliance on a day to day basis should be assigned to one chief executive whose performance should be subject to *assessment* by the parties but not to operational *interference*, and the procedure in the event of a wish by either party to end the alliance should be agreed at the outset, since this will increase the feeling of security by both parties that an end to the alliance does not represent a potential catastrophe.

## CONCLUSIONS

Strategic alliances are now widely recognised as appropriate interorganisational forms to meet certain environmental and internal firm conditions. They have certain inherent characteristics like speed of creation, flexibility, opportunities for specialisation, access to additional resources and risk limitation – all of which make them attractive when compared with the alternatives of internal development, acquisition or market purchases.

This is particularly the case in volatile, uncertain environments, where the need to negotiate some resource security and to develop a rapid global presence becomes of paramount importance to the survival of the firm, and the development of competitive advantage in a world increasingly dominated by multinationals. However, alliances can be unstable for a number of factors outlined above, both external and internal. Any one factor from each group may be sufficient to give rise to a strategic alliance. Of the survival factors, however, it is probable that most, if not all of the factors need to be present for the long-term success of the alliance. The problem of maintaining an alliance may, therefore, be far greater than that of creating one in the first place, and it is principally in this that the challenge lies.

## References


1. Harrigan, K R (1984) Joint Ventures and Global Strategies, *Columbia Journal of World Business*, vol 19, issue 2, Summer, pp 7–16
2. Stopford, J M and Wells, L T (1972) *Managing the Multi-national Enterprise*, Longman, London
3. Williamson, O E (1975) *Markets and Hierarchies*, The Free Press, Macmillan, New York
4. Reich, R B and Mankin, E D (1986) 'Joint Ventures with Japan give away our Future' *Harvard Business Review*, vol 64, issue 2, March/April, pp 78–86
5. Porter, M E (1985) *Competitive Advantage*, The Free Press, Macmillan, New York
6. McGee, J and Thomas, H (1986) 'Strategic Groups: theory, research, and taxonomy', *Strategic Management Journal*, vol 7, 2, pp 141–60
7. Bartlett C A and Ghoshal, S (1989) *Managing across Borders*, Hutchinson, London
8. Thorelli, H B (1986) 'Networks: Between Markets and Hierarchies', *Strategic Management Journal*, vol 7
9. Williamson; 1975 *op cit*
10. Masten, S E (1984) 'The organisation of production; evidence from the aerospace industry', *Journal of Law and Economics*, vol 27, issue 2, October, pp 403–417
11. Barnard, C I (1968) *The Functions of the Executive*, Harvard University Press, Cambridge, MA
12. Johanson, J and Mattsson, L G (1987) 'Interorganisational Relations in Industrial Systems', *International Journal of Management and Organisation*, vol 17, issue 1, Spring, pp 34–38
13. Defillippi, R and Reed, R (1991) Three Perspectives on Appropriation Hazard in Cooperative Agreements, SMS Conference Paper Toronto
14. Johanson, J and Mattsson, L G, 1988 *op cit*
15. Morris, D and Hergert, M (1987) Trends in International Collaborative Agreements, Columbia Journal of World Business

16. Hawley, A (1986) *Human Ecology: A Theoretical Essay*, University of Chicago Press, Illinois
17. Astley, W G (1984) 'Towards an appreciation of Collective Strategy', *Academy of Management Review*, vol 9, no 3
18. Hawley, A, 1950 *op cit*
19. Levitt, T (1983) *The Marketing Imagination*, The Free Press, Macmillan, New York
20. Ohmae, K (1985) *Triad Power, The Coming Shape of Global Competition*, The Free Press, Macmillan, New York
21. Stopford, J M and Turner, L (1985), *Britain and the Multinationals*, John Wiley, Chichester
22. Osborn, R V and Baughn, C C (1987) 'New Patterns in the formation of US/Japanese Cooperative Ventures', *Columbia Journal of World Business* vol 22, issue 2, Summer, pp 57–65
23. Lorenzoni, G (1982) From Vertical Integration to Vertical Disintegration, Strategic Management Society Conference Paper Montreal
24. Ansoff, H T (1990) *Implementing Strategic Management*, 2nd ed, Prentice-Hall, Hemel Hempstead
25. Pfeffer, J and Salancik, G (1978) *The External Control of Organisations*, Harper, New York
26. Pfeffer, J and Salancik, G, 1978 *op cit*
27. Pfeffer, J and Salancik, G, 1978 *op cit*
28. Rands, T (1991) A Famework for Managing Software make or buy Decisions, Management Research Paper 91–8, Templeton College, Oxford, June
29. Ohmae, K, 1985 *op cit*
30. Porter, M E (1987) 'From Competitve Advantage to Corporate Strategy', *Harvard Business Review*, May/June
31. Bertodo, R (1990) 'The Collaboration Vortex', *EIU Japanese Motor Business*, June
32. Oliver, C (1990) 'Determinants of Interorganisational Relationships: Integration and Future Directions', *AMR*, vol 15, no 2
33. Johnson, G (1987) *Strategic Change and the Management Process*, Basil Blackwell, Oxford
34. Gupta, A K and Singh, H (1991) The Governance of Synergy: Inter SBU Coordination vs External Strategic Alliances, Conference Paper in Academy of Management Conference, Miami

PART THREE

# MAKING STRATEGIES HAPPEN

8

# HOW STRATEGIES DEVELOP IN ORGANISATIONS

*Andy Bailey and Gerry Johnson*

## INTRODUCTION

This chapter reports on a major research project being undertaken at Cranfield School of Management which explores the nature of strategy formulation. The aim of this research project is both to discover the general patterns of strategy development within organisations and also to explore the managerial implications of strategy formulation. The chapter presents a number of explanations of strategy development: these explanations are illustrated with managerial views of strategy formulation within an organisational context using data collected through the research project. The managerial issues of differing processes and potential conflicts are examined.

The early works of writers such as Ansoff[1] and Andrews[2] and the books of the 1970s, in particular on corporate planning, have both emphasised the importance of strategy and have guided thinking in the area; thinking which has been dominated by the view that strategies are formulated through a particularly analytical and intentional process. The basic framework which this 'rational' planned view offers indicates that through the application of appropriate analytical and systematic techniques and checklists organisations are able to secure their own success. Moreover such an approach allows assumptions to be made about the future, assists in the reduction of uncertainty and facilitates the systematic development of strategy. This view and its associated frameworks have become deeply entrenched within strategic thinking, while the prescriptive and normative modes so generated have substantially influenced the approach to strategy formulation in practice, in education, and in research.

To view strategy development in this logical and rational manner is appealing and as such it is not surprising that this view has enjoyed such prominence. In management education strategic texts have traditionally emphasised the rationality of analysis, planning and implementation as a step by step process. Within organisations this school of thought suggests that formal strategic planning processes and mechanisms can operate in a rational and objective manner to allow the comprehensive analysis of the internal and external environments, the development of alternative strategies, the selection of the best strategy, and the production of objectives, goals, budgets, and targets to guide implementation. In short this rational planning approach is often what is regarded as 'good practice'.

However this view is not without its problems. In particular it fails to account for the social, cultural, political and cognitive aspects of the process of strategy development. Indeed, it's dominance has detracted from the equally valid consideration of less 'objective' aspects of the organisation and their critical influence on strategy development.

## THE EMERGENCE OF STRATEGIES

A natural assumption of this rational planned view of strategy formulation is that strategies are developed and implemented in this linear manner and that an organisation's *intended* strategy will be implemented in its entirety to become realised as *actual* strategy. However this may not always be the case. Unexpected shifts in the environment, unforeseen problems in implementation or limitations in the process can operate to restrict the efficiency of strategy formulation and its realisation. The result of this may mean that an organisation's intended strategy is not realised as actual strategy.[3,4] Indeed even within organisations with effective planning systems intended strategies do not always become realised.

The fact that a planned, intended strategy is not realised does not mean that an organisation has no strategy at all. Indeed the strategies an organisation pursues are not necessarily what is espoused by the organisation or its senior figures and as such they may more accurately be perceived as the direction an organisation is actually pursuing, planned or otherwise. However, the distinction between what is intended and what is realised may not be so defined and the two may interact. A strategy which starts as intended may change and become more emergent as it is implemented, while an emergent strategy may become formalised and more deliberate as it enters the accepted wisdom of the organisation and is encapsulated within its longer-term strategies.

If strategies are defined in terms of future position and consistency of direction or 'the direction an organisation is pursuing', then they may be seen to develop continually in an adaptive or incremental manner. As such, strategies may develop as much from the adaptive processes of the organisation or the actions of management as from deliberate and intended action. In this way strategies emerge gradually as actions are altered to cope with, and adapt to, the environment in a never-ending series of small steps. These small continual changes aggregate,[5] and so reduce the need for large or major change in strategy.

In stable environments strategies may not need to change in a major way. Any change required will, typically, be incremental and enable the organisation to operate in a gradually changing environment. While an organisation is doing well there will be a strong tendency not to change existing successful strategies. As an organisation's strategy develops 'momentum', any changes which occur will generally develop incrementally in a direction consistent with existing strategy and past experience rather than involving large-scale changes in direction.[6] Generally this pattern of strategy development is gradual and continuous, although more dramatic change may occur if the relationship between the environment and organisation alters more substantially. Indeed periods of strategy formulation have been seen to range from those typified by 'continuity', where strategies remain unchanged, to those which are 'continuous' or incremental, to those involving more substantial dramatic frame breaking or 'discontinuous' change, which occur infrequently.[7,8]

In situations where an organisation and its environment are increasingly mismatched, incremental refinements of strategy may not keep pace with environmental changes. As this situation develops and becomes more acute, either through large environmental change or strategic drift (the organisation becoming out of line with the environment), minor or piecemeal change may not easily remedy the situation. Here more global strategic change, incorporating significant and simultaneous reversals in strategy,[9] and involving discontinuous changes, may be required to realign the organisation and its environment.

## THE RESEARCH

This chapter reports on a study of how managers make sense of the different ways in which strategy develops. Given the complexity of this process it is not surprising that various explanations of strategy formulation have been advanced. Through a detailed review of such explanations[10] six perspectives on the process have been defined. While these explanations are not novel or indeed definitive, they do represent meaningful classifications of the process which both make intuitive sense to managers and are understandable.

These alternative explanations or views of strategy formulation were deconstructed to identify characteristics singularly attributable to each of them. Based on these characteristics statements were developed for use in a questionnaire, which was then administered to senior managers, from a cross section of industries, who indicated the degree to which the statements were characteristic of their organisation. Through the analysis of their responses, managerial perceptions of the organisation's process of strategy formulation were revealed. The numerical representation of these perceptions were subsequently plotted to develop strategic decision-making profiles for separate organisations or sub-units. (see Figure 8.1).

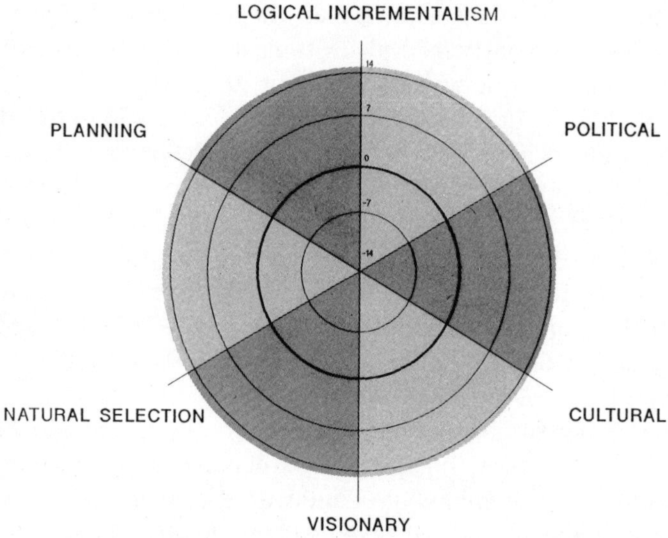


**Figure 8.1** Strategic decision-making profile

Examples of these profiles will be used to illustrate the explanations of strategy development. It is important to note that these profiles represent how managers see the process of strategy formulation within *their* organisations. The interpretation of the strategic decision-making profiles is based on distance from the mid-point ring (highlighted in bold). Points moving away from this ring towards the outside of the map (accompanied by a positive score) represent the degree to which the view and its incumbent procedures are seen to be characteristic of strategy formulation in the organisation. Points moving inwards towards the centre (accompanied by a negative score) represent the degree to which the view is uncharacteristic of the process. Points at zero or low positive or negative scores indicate that the attributes associated with that view are not particularly characteristic or uncharacteristic of the organisation.

## ALTERNATIVE EXPLANATIONS OF STRATEGIC DECISION-MAKING

This section reviews in more detail different explanations as to how strategies develop. However, it is important to stress that it is most unlikely that any one of the explanations given accounts entirely for the processes at work in an organisation; strategy formulation needs to be understood in terms of a *mix* of processes.

### *The planning perspective*

Strategic planning is perhaps the most traditional view of how strategic decisions are made in organisations. The perspective indicates that strategy formulation is a distinctly intentional process involving a logical, rational, planned approach to the organisation and its environment. Further it implies that through the application of appropriate analytical and systematic techniques the 'right' decision can be taken.

The strategies which develop are the outcome of sequential, planned and deliberate procedures and are often the responsibility of specialised departments. Clear and well defined strategic goals and objectives are set by the senior members of an organisation.[11] These goals may be a reflection of shareholder values or reflect potential threats and opportunities which the organisation becomes aware of through its constant monitoring of the business environment. As a goal or strategic issue is defined, the organisation and its environment (both internal and external to the organisation) are systematically analysed in terms of (for example) strategic position, the position of competitors, organisational strengths and weaknesses, and resource availability. The information collected is assessed and strategic options capable of attaining the goal or resolving the strategic issue are generated.

These strategic options, or courses of action, are systematically assessed against the criteria of the strategic goals and objectives to be achieved. This evaluation incorporates an assessment of both the estimated consequences of the alternative courses of action, for example in terms of risk versus return, and the value of these consequences. Similarly the long-term potential of the options are estimated. The option which simultaneously is perceived to maximise the value of outcomes, best fits the selection criterion and presents competitive advantage is chosen. The selected option is subsequently detailed in the form of precise plans and programmes and is passed from the top downwards within the organisation. Throughout this process strategies are determined and guided by those decision-makers in senior management positions and are implemented by those below[12] who act on but are unlikely to decide on strategy.[13]

### *The planning approach – illustrated*

This traditional planned approach to strategy formulation is exemplified in a major regional utilities company (Figure 8.2). Managers in this company saw the process of strategy development as distinctly intentional with strategic decisions being made by powerful senior organisational figures. Definite and precise strategic goals were set within the company, with defined procedures and systems being employed to develop potential strategic options. Options were evaluated against the explicit goals to be achieved; in line with the assumption that the consequences of strategic options are predictable in advance of implementation. The final decision to adopt a particular strategy was taken based on a considered and systematic analysis of the business environment; an analysis supported with quantitative facts, such as, for example, market trends. This intended strategy was subsequently outlined and planned in detail for its implementation.

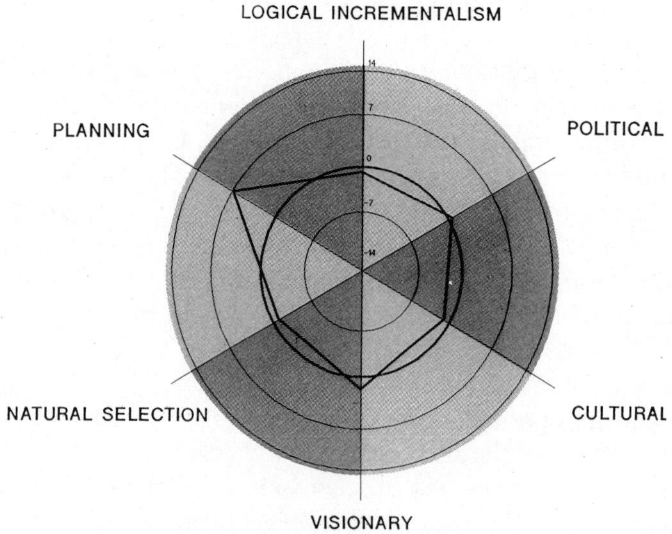


**Figure 8.2** The planning approach

In line with the systematic development of the strategy, the resources required for implementation are determined and appropriately allocated, and similarly the systems for monitoring and controlling the new strategy are determined. It is argued that strategies developed through this planned, sequential routine should be implemented fully and in a 'surprise free' manner.

This formalisation of strategic planning, though appealing, is problematic, and indeed has inherent dangers. In particular it lacks consideration of the less 'objective' aspects of the organisation and their critical influence on strategy development. However, regardless of the problems, the discipline and techniques of planning approaches can be useful because they may provide a framework for strategic thinking; and if managers also address the problems of managing strategy within the social, cultural and political world of organisations, then such thinking can be very helpful.

## *The logical incremental perspective*

In the late 1950s Lindblom[14] suggested that managing strategies through logical, sequential planning mechanisms was unrealistic. He argued that, given the complexity of organisations and the environments in which they operate, managers cannot consider all possible options in terms of all possible futures and evaluate these against preset, unambiguous objectives. This is particularly so in an organisational context in which there are likely to be conflicting views, values and power bases. Rather, strategic choice takes place by comparing options against each other and considering which would give the best outcome and be possible to implement. Lindblom called this strategy building through 'successive limited comparisons', but argued that it took place in the everyday world of managing, not through planning systems.

It is a position in many respects similar to that argued by Quinn.[15] His study of nine major multinational businesses concluded that the management process could best be described as *logical incrementalism.* By this he meant that managers have a view of where they want the organisation to be in years to come but try to move towards this position in an evolutionary way. They do this by attempting to ensure the success and development of a strong, secure but flexible core business, but also by continually experimenting with 'side bet' ventures. This mode of strategy formulation is not seen as the sole responsibility of top management and the corporate centre:those in the lower levels of the organisation and the organisation's 'strategic subsystems' are actively involved. Indeed it is the strategic subsystems, each of which is concerned with different strategic issues (for example acquisitions or major reorganisations), which raise the awareness of potential strategic problems. Here managers accept the uncertainty of their environment because they realise that they cannot do away with this uncertainty by trying to 'know' factually about how the environment will change. Rather they seek to become highly sensitive to environmental signals through constant environmental scanning and by testing and developing strategies in a step by step process of experimentation and limited exposure to the business environment.

The logical incrementalist view does not, then, see strategic management in terms of a neat sequential model:rather the system is seen to be cyclical. It encompasses feedback loops to previous phases where the problem and solution may be redefined or reformulated.[16] Similarly commitment to strategic options may be tentative and subject to review in the early stages of development. There is also a reluctance to specify precise objectives too early as this might stifle ideas and prevent the sort of experimentation which is desired. Objectives are therefore likely to be fairly general in nature.

Through ongoing analysis, assessment and incremental refinement, changes in the environment are matched with changes in procedure.[17] This iterative process ensures the strengths of an organisation are retained as experimentation and learning are undertaken without excessive risk to the organisation. Throughout the process potential options are eliminated or encouraged in accordance with their assessed appropriateness; the process does not operate to identify the best or optimal solution.[18]

Quinn[19] also suggests that different decisions should not be seen as entirely separate. Because the different organisational subsystems are in a continual state of interplay, the managers of each know what the others are doing, and can interpret each other's actions and requirements. They are, in effect, learning from each other about the feasibility of a course of action in terms of resource management and its internal political acceptability. Moreover, this constant readjustment and limited commitment allows the long-term direction of the organisation to be monitored and the organisational mix of resources and skills altered in reaction to environmental changes. The process broadens the information base available, builds organisational awareness and increases the active search for opportunities and threats not previously defined. Further, the formulation of strategy in this way means that the implications of the strategy are continually being tested out. This continual readjustment does, of course, make a lot of sense if the environment is considered to be a continually changing influence on the organisation.

## *Logical incrementalism – illustrated*

This logical incremental form of strategy formulation is seen by managers to explain strategy development within this computer systems organisation (Figure 8.3). The organisation's strategies are seen to emerge in an adaptive manner through a series of continual small scale changes and steps. This adaptive or incremental response to changes enables the organisation to keep in line with its business environment. The strategies it pursues are assessed and development through experimentation and limited exposure in the market place. Commitment to a strategy is initially tentative and builds slowly as knowledge is gained that strategy and environment fit; a knowledge which cannot be gained prior to implementation. This adaptive incremental approach although reactive is not unintentional but is in fact rather deliberate.

Here the systematic planned approach suggested by the traditional planning view is not seen to represent strategy formulation in the organisation. The organisation does not have definite and precise strategic goals, it does not have defined procedures for developing strategies, and the final decision to adopt a strategy is not based on a systematic and considered analysis of the business environment. However the process occurs under some degree of political influence – which will be the next subject discussed in more detail.

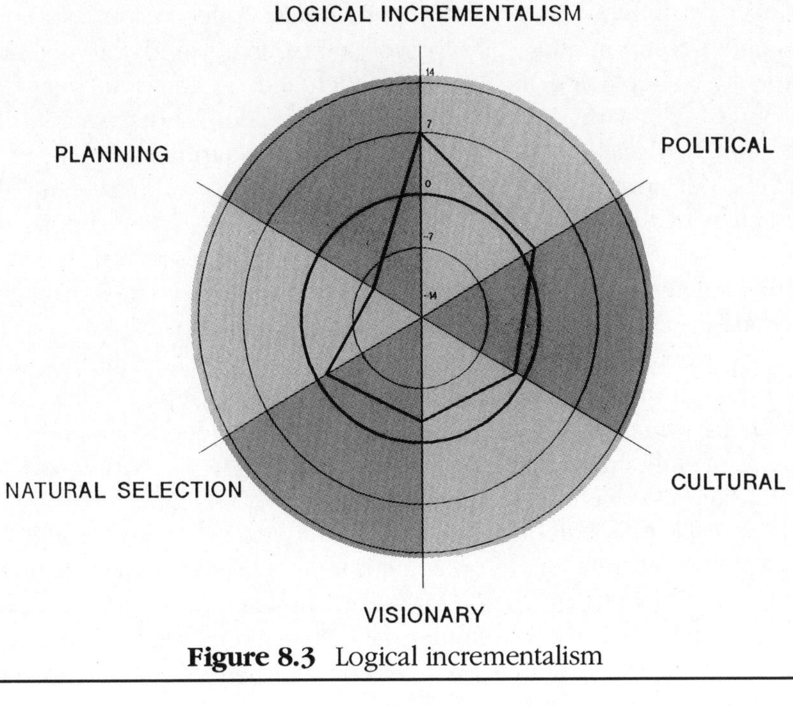


**Figure 8.3** Logical incrementalism

## *The political perspective*

The formulation of strategy can also be explained in political terms. Organisations are political entities and, as such, powerful internal and external interest groups influence the inputs into decisions. These interest groups, each of which have different concerns,[20] may be in conflict; there may be differences between groups of managers, between managers and shareholders, or between powerful individuals. These differences are likely to be resolved through processes of bargaining, negotiation or perhaps edict; with the result that goals and objectives, strategic issues and even strategies are derived from this political process and not from an analytical neutral assessment and choice.

This political process and the strategies followed by an organisation are susceptible to both internal and external influences[21] by stakeholders ('any group or individual who can affect or is affected by the achievement of the organisation's objectives'[22]), which could include customers and clients, banks, trade associations, shareholders, supplier firms, government departments and agencies, competitors, trade unions and organisational members. The level of influence these stakeholders are able to exercise differs[23] and is often conditional upon the organisation's dependency upon these groups for a resource[24] and the potential difficulty in replacing the present stakeholder as the source of that resource.[25] Similarly the influence of a stakeholder is not constant from decision to decision. The decision situation determines the level of stakeholder involvement and both their level of influence and the dynamics of that influence throughout the process. For example, the influence of top level decision-makers decreases as a strategy enters the implementation stage, while the influence of lower level managers increases.

The power and influence of stakeholders can also be used and acquired by other groups. For example, those internal groups or 'boundary spanners' who deal with the external environment tend to attain greater levels of influence and power over strategy[26] by virtue of the organisation's dependency on the external group with which they deal.

Powerful individuals or groups may also influence decision through the provision of information. Information is not politically neutral, but rather a source of power, particularly for those who control that which is seen to be important; so the withholding of information, or the influences of one manager over another because that manager controls sources of information, can be important. Alternatively the organisation's systems may be restricted to reduce information flow and so legitimatise the demands of particular interest groups.[27] Strategic decisions, then, are taken based on information distorted by the preferences of the information providers rather than on information which is politically neutral.

### *A political illustration*

The political process of strategy formulation is seen to typify strategy development in this airline (Figure 8.4). The airline's managers perceived its strategies to be strongly related to the desires of particularly influential interest groups and powerful individuals. The definition of strategic issues and indeed strategies were seen to emerge through negotiation, debate and compromise in an attempt to accommodate conflicting interests. While negotiation and compromise were central to this process it was the powerful individuals or groups who made strategic decisions. However participation in the process was not constant but determined by the issue at hand. Although the same interest groups were not involved in every strategic decision, the influence that these groups could exert over the process and the strategies followed was enhanced by their access to and control of resources critical to the organisation.

Although major influence over strategy came from participation in the process it was not restricted solely to this sphere. The information upon which a decision was based provided a further medium of influence; information which was seen to reflect the desires and interests of certain groups. In line with this political influence the chief executive officer was seen to influence strategy through the power he could exert.

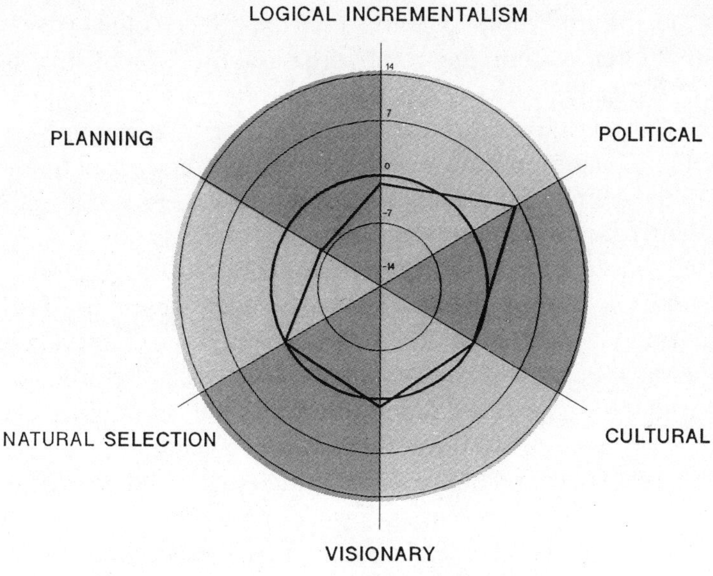


**Figure 8.4** A political illustration

It would be wrong to assume that the identification of key issues and even the strategies eventually selected emerge in a political neutral environment. Differing views will be fought for, not only on the basis of the extent to which they reflect environmental or competitive pressures, for example; but also because they have implications for the status or influence of different stakeholders. Through compromise and mutual adjustment a commonly acceptable strategy will emerge.[28] This strategy will finally be adopted because it is acceptable to both those interest groups influencing the decision-making process and those who must implement the strategy, and not solely because it fulfils any objective criteria.[29]

### *The cultural perspective*

Traditionally strategy has been viewed as the planned response of the organisation to its environment. However, the strategies an organisation follows can also be attributed to cultural factors. Organisations faced with similar environments will respond differently. The strategies they choose to pursue will not result solely from a precise planned approach to the environment, but under influence from the attitudes, values, and perceptions which are common among the members and stakeholders of that organisation. Further, management cannot be conceived of simply in terms of the manipulation of techniques or tools of analysis. Management is also about the application of managerial experience built up over many years; and often within the same organisation or industry. Nor do managers typically work in isolation; they interact with others. Their experience is not only rooted in individual experience, but on group and organisational experience built up over time. It is important therefore to recognise the significance of cultural aspects of management.

By 'organisational culture' is meant the 'deeper level of basic *assumptions and beliefs* that are shared by members of an organisation, that operate unconsciously and define in a basic 'taken for granted' fashion an organisation's view of its self and its environment'.[30] A cultural perspective suggests, then, that managerial experience is likely to be based on 'taken-for-granted' frames of reference which are brought to bear by a manager – or group of managers – and which will affect how a given situation is perceived and how it is responded to. Over time this taken for grantedness is likely to be handed on – or 'inherited' – within a group. That group might be, for example, a managerial function such as marketing or finance; a professional grouping, such as accountants; an organisation as a whole; and more widely an industry sector, or even a national culture. Just as these frames exist at the organisational and subunit level they also exist on an industry wide basis,[31] or indeed at a national level. Managers, then, are influenced by many cultural frames when making a decision. However, especially important for the strategic management of most organisations is the organisational frame of reference, which we call the '*organisational paradigm*'.

The paradigm is likely to contain within it the beliefs which managers talk about in their day to day lives: but it is also likely that it will contain assumptions which are rarely talked about, are not considered problematic, and about which managers are unlikely to be consciously explicit. Examples might include the deep rooted assumption that banks are about *secure* lending; local newspapers about purveying *news* (ie as more their *raison d'etre* than advertising); that universities are about doing research and so on. As such, these deep rooted assumptions can play an important part in strategy development.

An organisation's paradigm is, then, built up from different influences such as history and past experience (both personal and organisational) and may also reflect the desires of particular stakeholders.[32] The strength of these influences will depend on a number of factors. For example an organisation with a relatively stable management and a long-term momentum of strategy is likely to have a more homogeneous paradigm than one in which there has been rapid turnover of management and significant change forced upon it. Organisations with a dominant professional influence, perhaps an accountancy firm, are likely to demonstrate a homogeneous paradigm. Industry influences may be particularly strong if the transfer of staff between firms is limited to that industry, as it often is in engineering or banking for example.

Of course for any organisation to operate efficiently it must, to some extent, have a generally accepted set of beliefs and assumptions. These may not be a static set of beliefs, although it is quite likely that they will evolve gradually rather than change suddenly. What this represents is a collective experience without which managers would have to 'reinvent their world' afresh for all circumstances they face or decisions they need to take; as such it enables new situations to be perceived in a way which is not unique.[33] The paradigm allows the experience gathered over years to be applied to a given situation so that managers can decide upon relevant information by which to assess the need for change, a likely course of action, and the likelihood of success of that course of action.

An organisation's strategies, then, develop in accord and within the confines of its culture and dominant paradigm. The cognitive and perceptual processes operate to orientate the definition and solution of a strategic problem internally ensuring a strategic response is based within the domain of the organisation[34] and the history of its members.[35]

### *The cultural approach – illustrated*

The highly influential nature of organisational culture on strategy formulation is identified by managers from a specialised financial services company (Figure 8.5). This company had until recently been family owned. The company's strategic decision-making process was seen to be directly influenced by the history and past experiences of the organisation and its members. This influence and direction was associated with a 'way of doing things' in the organisation which was based around its particular beliefs and assumptions, which were shared throughout the organisation. They existed in the form of a commonly accepted philosophy which was understood by both those inside and outside the organisation. The cultural factors of the organisation manifested to influence strategic direction through the identification of strategic issues, the definition of appropriate responses, and the development of strategic solutions.

While culture was seen to be particularly influential, some aspects of the planned approach exist. Strategies were assessed against the goals to be achieved and decisions were made based on considered and systematic evaluation of the business environment though inevitably these were guided by culture.

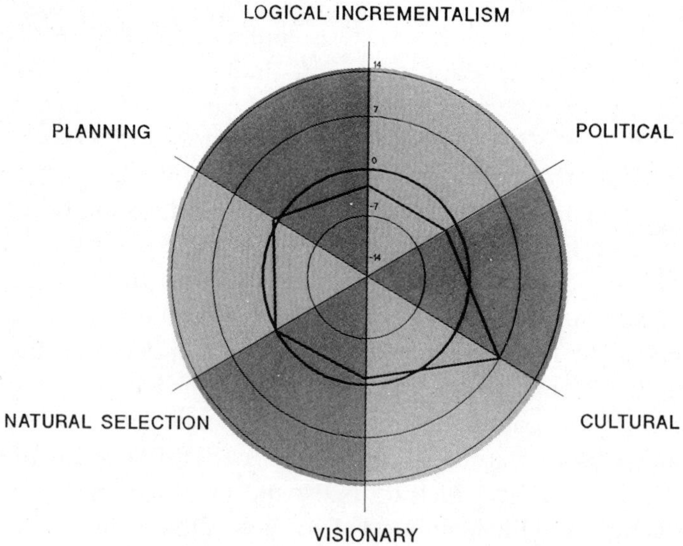


**Figure 8.5** The cultural approach

## *The visionary perspective*

The strategy an organisation follows can also be seen as emerging from a vision which represents the desired future state of the organisation,[36] and which is initially and primarily associated with an individual (for example its leader or a past leader). This might be especially so if the organisation is dominated by a leader: such leaders may exist, particularly in organisations which they have founded, or in situations where an organisation has reached a crisis point. Less commonly, perhaps, a vision could be associated with a small group of individuals, rather than one individual.

One explanation for the source of this vision is that it results from the intuition and innovation of its originator. Here the vision is based both on intuition and a rational understanding of the organisation's strategic problems. This understanding is developed through exposure to, and experience of, the important strategic issues of an organisation and enables innovation to be made through the adding of new to the well understood and certainty of the old. The vision generated is often based on radical ideas and may challenge accepted norms, contradict established principles and paradigm,[37,38] and go beyond familiar experience and knowledge.[39]

However, visionary management might also be seen as the capacity of managers more generally to *envisage*, rather than plan, the future of their organisation. It can be argued that some market environments are so turbulent that trying to forecast, predict or plan what they will be like is futile. On the other hand experienced managers 'have a feel' for what makes sense in these markets (again there are links here with the notion of the paradigm) and can make decisions about the future on this basis. In this case, the notion of visionary capacity is not limited to the leadership role of the organisation, but is seen as a more general aspect of management.

Yet another explanation is more mundane. This is that a new vision in an organisation comes about because a new executive applies his or her existing frame of reference from another context to the new organisation to which they have been appointed. For example some of the new chief executives appointed to newly privatised UK industries in the 1980s came from private sector companies. They brought with them frames of reference from competitive environments in which profit motivation was taken as given. What was normal and obvious to them was often seen as new and visionary in the organisations they moved into. In terms of the emergence of vision and its influence in organisations, this view links into the cultural and political views.

Regardless of how it emerges, for a vision – however appropriate to the organisation – to develop into strategy it must be effectively articulated and communicated. The transformation of a vision into strategy is not unidirectional: a vision must be shared and receive assistance if it is to be realised. The authorisation for a vision's pursuit comes from its acceptance by the organisation's members[40] who 'contract in' to a vision, and

*A visionary illustration*

As with the other views of strategy formulation an illustration of the visionary form can be identified. This small, high-tech organisationoperating in a competitive and new biotechnology market was seen by managers to be very much driven by visionary processes (Figure 8.6). The general direction of the organisation was dictated by a vision of the future which was particularly associated with the chief executive officer (CEO). Indeed the CEO was seen to be particularly powerful, enforcing decisions and typically taking strategic decisions in isolation from the other senior executives, though based on the vision. Further, the CEO was perceived to have led the organisation into the pursuit of high risk, high return strategies. However, these strategies and their driving vision were based on a rational understanding of the organisation and the business environment rather than purely on intuition. While based on the vision the strategies followed by the organisation were seen to emerge in an adaptive manner on a low committal trial basis.

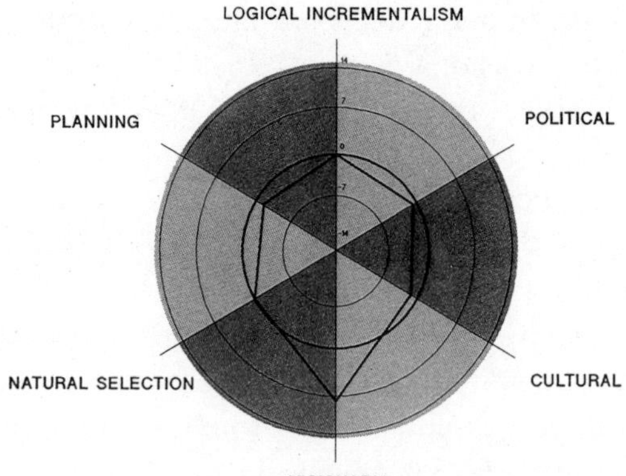


**Figure 8.6** A visionary illustration

so provide the authority for its realisation, concentrating resources to facilitate the vision's enactment.[41] A visionary alone cannot turn a vision into strategy.

While an individual may gain visionary status for himself within the organisation, an organisation's structure and history may be such that it endows an individual with this power, position and authority. Whether the position is achieved through the generation of an idea and vision, the syntheses of existing visions, the communication of a vision, or through the organisation's history, it inevitably places enormous control and power in the hands of the visionary who gains the 'capacity to translate intention into reality and sustain it'.[42]

## *The natural selection perspective*

Some writers on management argue that organisations have little or no control over the choice of strategies they follow. Factors in the environment impinge on the organisation in such a way as to select and encourage the adoption of organisational structures and activities which best fit that environment.[43] These external constraints operate to prescribe strategies and sharply limit the role organisational members play in their selection.[44] Equally the strategies an organisation can follow tend to be common to all organisations within their industrial sector or market; their ability to make strategic decisions outside these are restricted. In short, the success of an organisation is due to a fit between strategy, structure and environment produced via a process bearing more similarities to natural selection rather than any rational and intentional choice.

While intentional strategic choice may be restricted, strategic change *does* occur. Initially changes occur within an organisation through variations in its processes, structures and systems. While the process of organisational innovation and variation may come about as a rational intentional response to the environment, they may occur equally unintentionally, through conflict over control of resources; ambiguity of organisational reality; accident; errors; tactical moves; and luck.[45] It is these variations, however they occur, which produce the potentially advantageous or dangerous innovations for an organisation. Those variations which positively fit the environment and which are appropriate and beneficial to the organisation are selected and retained, while those which do not, fail and die or are altered to match the environment.[46] It is these successful variations, which match changes in the environment, which produce advantage and so contribute to the likelihood of an

*Natural selection – illustrated*

The influence of the external environment was perceived to be a major determinant of strategy by managers in this regional engineering firm operating in a market dominated by a few companies (Figure 8.7). The firm was seen to be strongly influenced in the strategies it pursued by its operating environment. Indeed the external environment was seen to impinge to such a degree that external forces, such as, for example, strong customers and the government, dictated strategic direction. Moreover,the strategies open to the organisation were restricted to those typical of most other organisations within the industry. In line with the influence of external pressures the organisation's position was such that managers perceived it to be less able to influence its operating environment than its competitors.

While the organisation was restricted by its environment managers perceived that strategic decisions were taken. Attempts were made to employ traditional planning approaches and systematically developed strategies, however choice was restricted by barriers and its strategies did tend to be prescribed. Indeed this rational approach may merely represent an attempt to post-rationalise enforced strategies, or alternatively, gain some degree of control over them at the implementation stage.

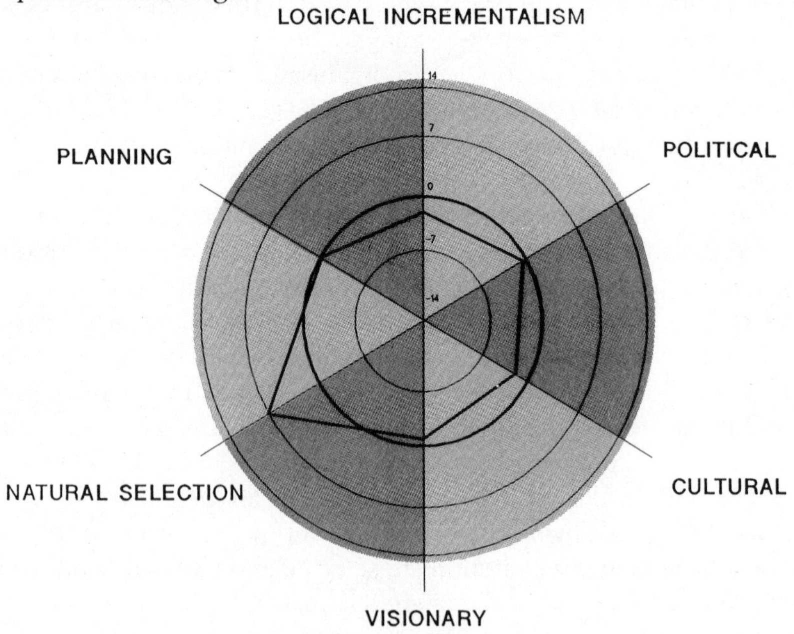


**Figure 8.7** Natural selection

organisation's or subunit's survival.[47] These successful variations are retained and subsequently disseminated throughout the organisation and across its generations through culture, symbols, socialisation, administration and training.

The view taken in this chapter is that for some organisations the impact of the environment is, indeed, very large; and that degrees of managerial latitude are severely reduced: however, this is not so in all environments and even where those pressures are severe, it is the job of managers to develop the skills and strategies to cope with the situation.

## MANAGERIAL IMPLICATIONS

The previous sections demonstrate, to a greater or lesser extent, that each of the perspectives can describe or explain some aspects of the process of strategic decision-making. The very complexity of these decisions makes it unlikely that any one of the perspectives in isolation would adequately capture the complexity of the process operating in all organisations, in every situation, and at any point in time. While the above examples have presented the process in isolation, in many organisations this is not the case: the processes occur in combination. Indeed these different views about how strategies develop are not mutually exclusive and in most organisations managers see strategies developing through a mix of such processes.

In the following cases general patterns which have been identified from the research will be highlighted and the potential advantages and problems these combinations present discussed. In addition examples of differences in the perceived process from within the same organisation will be explored to show the potential conflicts which may be surfaced.

## GENERAL PATTERNS

The following series of four case studies show different sorts of patterns that exist in organisations. The first two cases (A and B) show that where planning is seen to be dominant it is often linked with other views. In these situations the planning process may be seen to operate in a *moderating* role rather than as the sole process of strategy development. Case A shows planning in combination with cultural processes.

## *Case A*

The process of formulating strategy in this major multinational organisation (Figure 8.8) is seen to be characterised by the traditional planning approach, in conjunction with the organisation's history and culture.

The organisation is seen to have definite and precise strategic objectives and to make its strategic decisions based on considered and systematic analysis of the business environment. This analysis is supported by quantitative data and the strategic options generated are evaluated against the explicit strategic option to be achieved. However, the strategies developed are not based solely on this 'objective' approach: the cultural processes of the organisation are seen also to directly influence strategy. The organisation has a 'way of doing things' which has developed over the years and is intrinsically linked to the organisation's history. This way of doing things and the accompanying beliefs and assumptions are seen to be specific to the organisation. The paradigm subsequently operates to ensure that actions are in line with the expectations of the organisation.

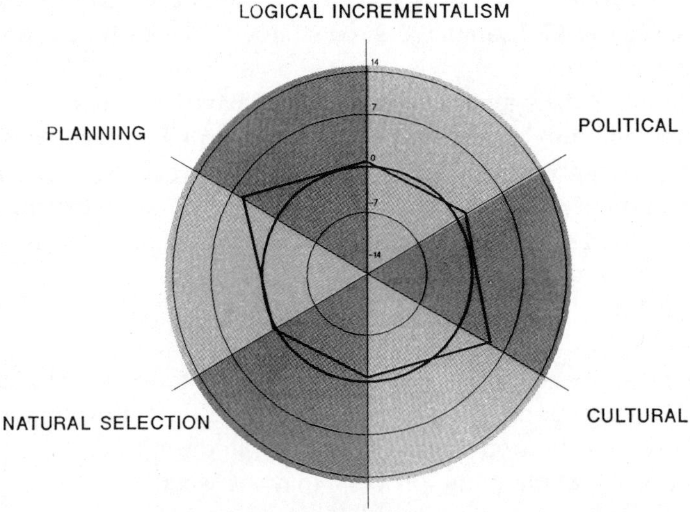


**Figure 8.8** The traditional planning approach

This process of strategy development is seen to be a distinctly intentional process with strategic decisions being made by powerful individuals and in consultation with the whole of the senior management team. These decisions are guided by culture and the planned approach, however: the strategies are not seen to emerge through a process of experimentation and trial within the market place or in response to external pressures. This pattern of a strong cultural process presents inherent dangers due to the internal orientation of strategic issues and their solution. If the definition of a strategic issues and the search for opportunities are confined to traditional area of operation by culture, then the future direction of the organisation will be predetermined by the past regardless of any changes in the operating environment. Because of this the potential for strategic drift is high. In this situation the planning process may operate to either limit or extenuate the potential dangers. However the planners at the corporate centre see the role of planning as acting to challenge the 'taken for granted' and the 'way of doing things' in the organisation. If this were the case, the combination of cultural and planning processes could prove highly beneficial. The question is, does planning actually do this?

Case B shows an organisation in which planning is seen to play a significant role but vision is also seen to be particularly important.

### *Case B*

The strategies of this retail organisation are seen to develop in a manner characterised by visionary and cultural processes (Figure 8.9). Similarly, formulation is associated with the planning process and a logical adaptive response to the environment.

While strategic decisions are made by the same group of powerful figures within the organisation, these decisions appear to be based around a shared vision. This vision, which is highly influential in directing future strategy, is based both on intuition and a rational understanding of the organisation. Although the vision is particularly associated with the chief executive, who consequently secures a high level of influence over the strategy, strategic decisions are not taken in isolation from the rest of the top management team. However if required the chief executive is able to enforce decisions and also to lead the organisation into pursuing high risk, high return strategies. These strategies however are likely to be in line with the organisation's culture and past experience.

Along with the visionary process there is a strong tendency for the history and past experience of the organisation and its members to direct strategy. These factors influence strategy development through the organisation's paradigm, its particular 'way of doing things'. They direct the identification of strategic issues and the development of strategic solutions. They indicate appropriate areas of operation and ensure that strategies are in line with organisational expectations. Indeed these are not restricted by the industry 'recipes' as the organisation is seen to follow strategies which are not common to most organisations in the industry.

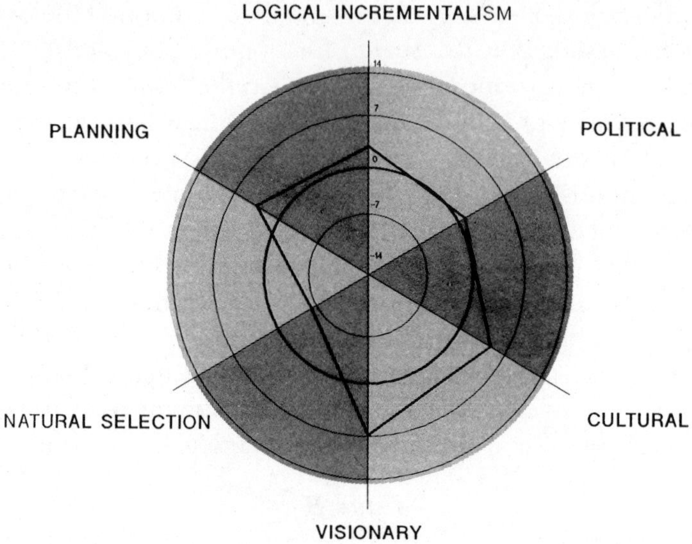


**Figure 8.9** Visionary and cultural processes

This process is not merely reactionary but involves an intentionally analytical, though adaptive, approach. Strategies emerge through a series of continual small scale changes which ensure the organisation keeps in line with its business environment. This adaptive approach involves an active assessment of potential strategic options through experimentation and limited exposure to the market place. Further more traditional approaches are involved. Indeed the organisation has precise and definite strategic objectives, supports its analysis of the environment with quantitative data, and makes strategic decisions based on considered and systematic analysis of it business environment – albeit in a direction determined by the vision. Moreover, strategy development is not restricted or overly directed by the external operating environment.

This combination offers the potential of a powerful benefit if it means that strategic planning and the driving vision of the dominant individual are complementary, acting to check one against another. On the other hand there are signals of potential danger; in particular the extent to which the external environment is not seen to be a dominant influence on strategy, especially in this highly competitive retail environment. The high influence of organisational culture could also present difficulties if the planning role is not exercising the sort of strategic challenge that might be necessary given the powerful influence of individuals.

Case C moves away from the planned approach. It represents a public sector organisation in which the forces of the environment are such that there is relatively little choice, and the natural selection view predominates within a political context.

## *Case C*

In this public sector organisation strategies are developed in response to pressures from the external environment (Figure 8.10). The operating environment is such that strategies are prescribed by external forces such as, for example, local or national government. Further, barriers exist in the industry which restrict strategies and potential choices which can be made. Although limited by these pressures, what choice exists is typically exercised through political aspects of the process. The senior figures in the organisation direct the strategy, though their involvement in the process is determined by the strategic issue at hand and the informal rules of the organisation. While some attempt is made to use quantitative analysis to support decisions, the dominant force in the process is that of compromise between conflicting interests.

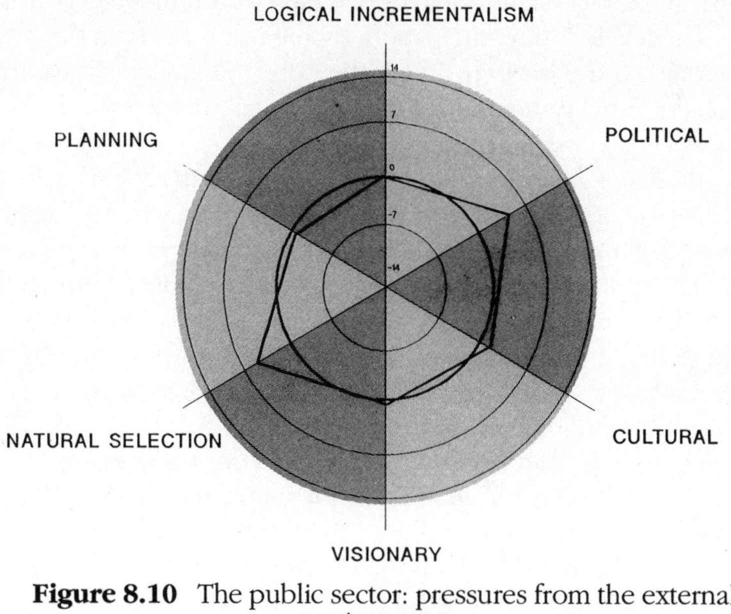


**Figure 8.10** The public sector: pressures from the external environment .

The process of strategy formulation in this organisation presents real problems for change. What strategic change there is, is dictated by forces outside the organisation and through internal power struggles. While this combination may not be too surprising given the industry sector (indeed this combination of processes is typical of the public sector), it does not bode well for future position and success if the operating environment was to change rapidly and perhaps become more competitively oriented.

The final of these four cases illustrates a typical pattern: here the logical incremental, cultural and political views are pronounced. This is a typical linkage in organisations in which adaptive or incremental strategy development predominates.

## *Case D*

Strategy formulation in this large professional services firm (Figure 8.11) is seen to be primarily driven by its political and cultural processes and from an adaptive reactive or logical incremental response to an influential environment. Although the firm operates through subsidiary practices there is a high degree of agreement around strategy formulation.

The firm's strategies, which are strongly related to the desires of certain interest groups, are developed by powerful individuals and groups through negotiation, debate and compromise. In this manner strategic problems are defined and strategies which accommodate conflicting interests are developed. Participation, by interest groups, in the process is determined by the issue involved; the same individuals or groups are not involved in every decision. Equally, though, the firm's history and culture directs the identification of strategic issues and options. These historic influences are such that specific ways of doing things, which are particular to the organisation, exist and as such guide strategic direction.

The strategies pursued emerge in an adaptive manner through a series of continual small scale changes and steps which enable the firm to keep in line with its business environment. Through this iterative process potential strategic options are assessed through experimentation, hence early commitment to strategies is limited, subject to review, and dependent on continuing assessment.

Typically, strategy development is initiated in response to strategic issues and tends to be based on previous strategies, though they are adaptable and easily altered as the environment, culture, history, or internal politics demand. In addition the firm, which does not generally seem to be in a position to influence the environment in which it operates, appears to respond to environmental influences rather than making strategic decisions unprompted by external forces. Indeed strategies are not seen to develop in any systematic planned manner: little in the way of set procedures for the development of strategy exist and the strategies which *do* emerge tend to be common to the industry and not planned in detail.

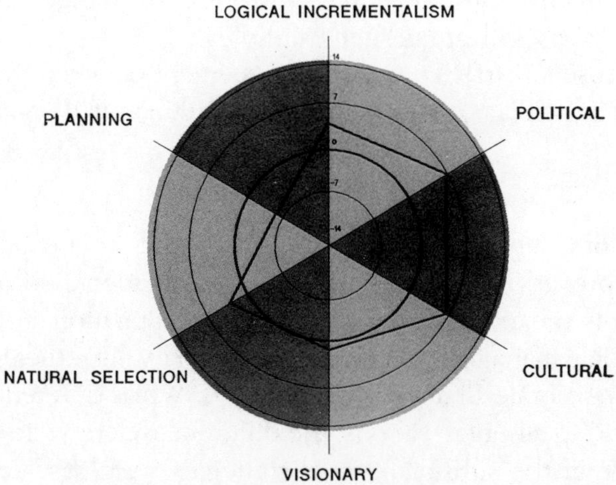


**Figure 8.11** Adaptive or incremental strategy development

This general pattern, which is typically associated with low levels of traditional planning, accords great homogeneity to the process of developing strategy through the incorporation of the organisation's interest groups, its culture and history in the adaptive reactive approach to the environment and strategy. However the lack of planning and the influence of the environment may result in too much reliance on this reactive response and the internally based strategy. Strategic direction may reflect past successes and their power structure and so not entirely fit the requirements for sustained success in the future business environment. The problem of this situation is that there may be little to challenge and question the taken for granted, given that – with the low planning score – planning does not fulfil this role.

In this description of 'logical incrementalism' managers may, in fact, be describing incremental or adaptive change which is the product of political and cultural processes.

## SITUATIONS OF CONFLICT

Of course, very real problems can emerge if different parts of an organisation have markedly different influences on the development of strategy. So while there may be agreement in the process of strategy formulation within some organisations, in others there is not. It is in these situations of conflict where the process or the input of certain groups may become ineffective and potential obstacles to change emerge. The following two cases illustrate such examples.

The first case illustrates a major disagreement between the corporate centre and a subsidiary operating unit of a multinational organisation.

### *Case E*

Disagreement is illustrated in this example from a multinational (Figure 8.12). The process of formulating strategy was identified as distinctly different by two executives from within this multinational organisation, one a divisional manager of an overseas subsidiary, the other his opposite number in corporate finance at head office. While differences may be expected within all organisations, the differences here were particularly acute. While at the subsidiary level strategies were assessed as being developed in the traditional sense of strategic planning involving the setting of goals, the analysis of the environment, and the production of

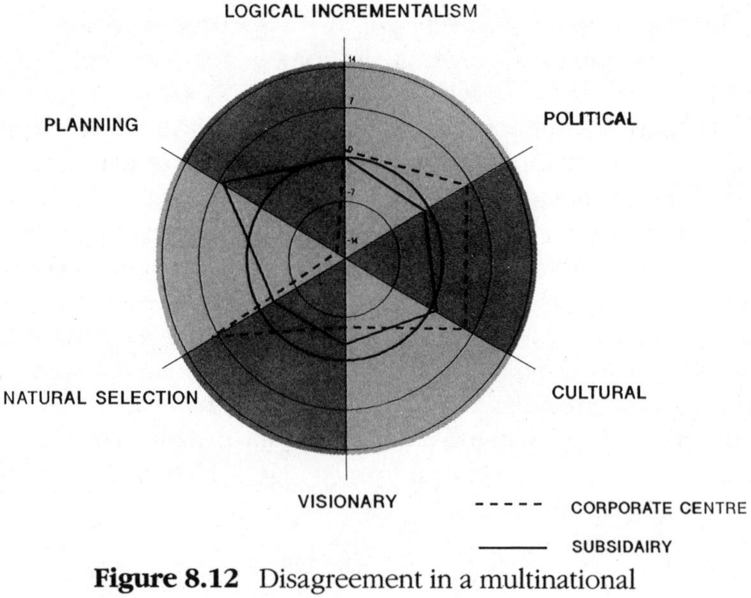


**Figure 8.12** Disagreement in a multinational

detailed procedural plans, this was not the case at the corporate centre. Here the process was evaluated to be distinctly political, to be directed by culture and the way things are done, and under much influence from the external environment: a process most definitely *not* characterised by the traditional planned approach.

Detailed plans outlining the development of a strategy formed the basis for the subsidiary's approach to the corporate centre for approval and allocation of resources. However this approach was not in line with the process at the centre. Here, strategy development and subsequent resource allocation was based on previous requirements and under influence from environmental, political, and cultural pressures – not on the bases of the formalised planning process undertaken in the subsidiary. These differences in the perception of how the organisation develops its strategies have resulted in serious difficulties between the two in relation to defining strategic problems, formulating strategy, and the general discussion of strategic issues, the consequences of which present obvious problems in determining strategies which are acceptable and 'owned' by both the subsidiary and the corporate centre.

### *Case F*

This second case, an example from the aerospace industry (Figure 8.13) identifies differences and disagreements between individuals within senior organisational positions. In such situations problems may emerge due to the differences in how the process is seen by the managers, all of whom must input into the strategic decisions. Here, major differences are seen to exist in the perceptions of the process of strategy formulation by the chief executive and the other members of the top management team (TMT). Particularly large differences can be seen in relation to the extent to which the planning, the political and the visionary processes characterise the organisation.

The CEO who is relatively new to the organisation sees strategies developing through the cultural process of the organisation. Here he sees strategies as being directed and developed in line with the beliefs and assumptions of the organisation and its widely shared philosophy. Further, there is some level of planning seen in the process, although the political view is seen to be uncharacteristic.

This view is not one shared by the other members of the senior management team. Their view of strategy development is characterised by the political view, the influence of vision, and to some extent the external environment. Strategies are seen to be made by powerful individuals with informal rules guiding their involvement. Influence over the process is enhanced by control of critical resources and the diagnosis of a strategic problem emerges through negotiation rather than from quantitative analysis. While the political process is seen to influence strategy development the dominant force is seen to be visionary. The strategies the organisation follows are seen to be directed by a vision of the future which is particularly associated with the CEO – indeed the influence of the CEO is seen further in his readiness to enforce decisions and his tendency to impose strategies rather than consulting the rest of the TMT.

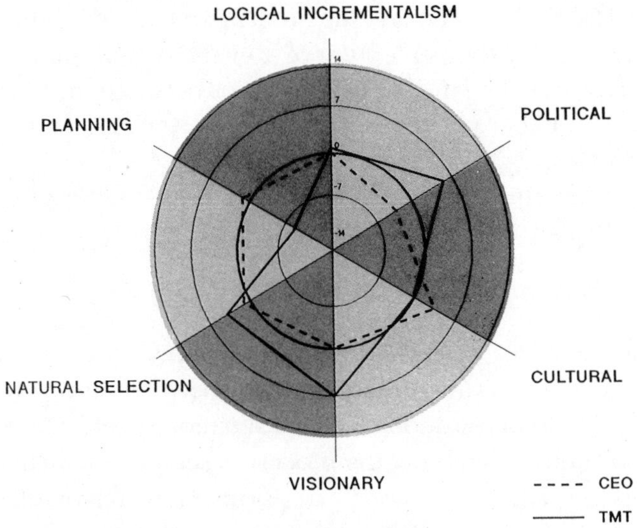


**Figure 8.13** Disagreement in an aerospace industry

This driving vision is not seen by the TMT to be based on any rational understanding of the organisation but rather on intuition. Correspondingly the TMT perceive a distinct lack of planning in the organisation: a view not endorsed by the CEO. Indeed, where the CEO sees the organisation to have definite and precise strategic goals, to support its analysis of the environment with quantitative facts, and to develop strategies based on considered and systematic analysis, the other members of the TMT do not. In addition, this group does not perceive the organisation as making intentional strategic decisions; rather they see strategies developing in response to environmental influences; again a view not share by the CEO.

The influence of the external environment is seen to be greater by the

TMT, although both see strategic choice to be restricted by the external business environment and barriers in the environment which limit the strategies they can follow. However the influence of external interestgroups over strategy, such as strong customers, is seen to exist by the TMT but not by the CEO.

This situation of conflicting perceptions does not suggest a process easily accessed by all the organisation's senior figures. Consequently the input into strategy of diverse but relevant sources may be reduced while the influence of any one individual may not be effectively challenged. This situation taken to an extreme may result in the CEO being marginalised in the pursuit of what he considers to be the organisation's strategy particularly as he appears to be out of touch with the views of his senior executives. Similarly the other members of the TMT may pursue actions which are consistent with their view of the process though inappropriate in terms of the CEO's view. The overall result of this situation is likely to be a lack of continuity in strategy formulation and the emergence of a potential crisis as an undirected strategy emerges through the conflict.

## CONCLUSIONS

This chapter has dealt with the processes of strategic management as they are to be found in organisations: it is therefore *descriptive* not *prescriptive*. There is no suggestion here that, because such processes exist, this is how strategy *should* be managed. However, it is important to understand the reality of strategy making in organisations, not least because those who seek to influence the strategy of organisations must do so within that reality. There is little point in formulating strategies which may be elegant analytically without having an understanding of the processes which are actually at work.

The strength of this approach to understanding strategy formulation comes from its combined use of the six explanations of the process. Indeed, as has been demonstrated, this approach can differentiate between organisations – all of which do not develop strategies in identical manners. This approach, then, provides a clearer understanding of the process of strategy formulation and its complexity.

There are practical benefits to managers in this work. By establishing and documenting the underlying processes of strategy development, managers are provided with a better understanding of strategy formulation in their organisations: an understanding which can act to stimulate discussion and exploration by senior executives of the strategic decision-making processes operating within their organisations. The information enables organisations or business units to address any deficiencies they perceive in their decision-making processes and reduce their reliance on the 'taken for granted' way of dealing with strategic issues. Further, this allows managers to identify any conflicts or disagreements in the perception of the process which in turn may affect how individuals operate within the system of strategy formulation.

Future research can build on these findings in a number of areas and our research programme is doing so. These areas include:

- The identification of differences and similarities in the process operating within organisations – that is, for example, whether managers within the same organisation agree or disagree on the patterns of processes at work within their organisation and whether this perception differs systematically across managerial groups; between organisations; across industrial sectors; or indeed across national cultures.
- Similarly, differences in process may emerge between situations and organisations due to the affects of time; context; or the strategic issues.
- The influence of the process of strategy formulation on the organisations generally and particularly the relationship with organisational performance requires further attention.

In conclusion, it is apparent that the process of strategy formulation is seen by managers to occur in a number of different ways. To attain the best from the process within an organisation managers should both understand the process as seen by their colleagues and understand the range of possible alternative aspects of formulating strategy. This understanding should enable the various aspects of the process to be addressed and consequently increase efficiency and reduce conflict in formulating strategy.

## References

1. Ansoff, H I (1965) *Corporate Strategy,* McGraw Hill, London
2. Andrews, K R (1980) *The Concept of Corporate Strategy* Revised edition, R D Irwin, Georgetown, Ontario
3. Mintzberg, H (1978) 'Patterns of strategy formation', *Management Science,* 24, 9, pp 934–48
4. Mintzberg, H and Waters, J A (1985) 'Of strategies, deliberate and emergent', *Strategic Management Journal* 6, pp 257–72

5. Lindblom, C E (1959) 'The science of "muddling through"', *Public Administration Review*, 19, pp 79–88, Spring
6. Miller, D and Friesen, P H *Organisations: A Quantum View*, Prentice-Hall, Englewood Cliffs, NJ
7. Mintzberg, H and Waters, J A, (1985) *op cit*
8. Nadler, D A and Tushman, M L (1989) 'Organisational framebending: Principles for managing re-organisation,' *Academy of Management Executive* 3, pp 194–202
9. Miller, D and Friesen, P H, (1984) *op cit*
10. Bailey, A and Johnson, G (1991) 'Perspectives on the process of strategic decision-making', Cranfield School of Management Working Papers Series, SWP 66/91
11. Chaffee, E E (1985) 'Three models of strategy', *Academy of Management Review* 10, 1, pp 89–98
12. Mintzberg, H, (1978) *op cit*
13. Mintzberg, H and Waters, J A, (1985) *op cit*
14. Lindblom, C E, (1959) *op cit*
15. Quinn, J B (1980) *Strategies for Change – Logical Incrementalism*, R D Irwin, Georgetown, Ontario
16. Lyles, M A (1981) 'Formulating strategic problems: Empirical analysis and model development', *Strategic Management Journal* 2, pp 61–75
17. Schwenk, C R (1988) *The Essence of Strategic Decision-Making*, D C Heath & Co
18. Mintzberg, H, Raisinghani, D and Theoret, A (1976) 'The structure of "unstructured" decision processes' *Administrative Science Quarterly* 21, pp 246–75
19. Quinn, J B, (1980) *op cit*
20. Pfeffer, J and Salancik, G R (1978) *The External Control of Organisations*, Harper & Row, New York
21. Hickson, D J, Butler, R J, Gray, D, Mallory, G R and Wilson, D C (1986) *Top Decisions – Strategic Decision-Making in Organisations*, Basil Blackwell, Oxford
22. Freeman, R (1984) *Strategic Management: A Stakeholder Approach*, Pitman, Boston
23. Heller, F, Drenth, P, Koopman, P, and Rus, V (1988) *Decisions in Organisations: A Three Country Comparative Study*, Sage Publications, London
24. Pfeffer, J and Salancik, G R (1978) *op cit*
25. Hickson, D J et al (1986) *op cit*
26. Jemison, D B (1981) 'Organisational versus environmental sources of

influence in strategic decision-making', *Strategic Management Journal* 2, pp 77–89

27. Pfeffer, J and Salancik, G R (1978) *op cit*
28. Mintzberg, H and Waters, J A (1985) *op cit*
29. Johnson, G (1987) *Strategic Change and the Management Process*, Basil Blackwell, Oxford
30. Schein, E H (1985) *Organisational Culture and Leadership*, Jossey-Bass, San Francisco
31. Spender, J-C (1989) *Industry Recipes: The Nature and Source of Managerial Judgement*, Blackwell Ltd, Oxford
32. Mason, R O and Mitroff, I I (1981) *Challenging Strategic Planning Assumptions*, Wiley, New York
33. Schon, D A (1983) *The Reflective Practitioner: How Professionals Think in Action*, Temple Smith, London
34. Schwenk, C R (1988) *op cit*
35. Nutt, P (1984) 'Types of organisational decisions processes', *Administrative Science Quarterly* 29, pp 414—50
36. Rowe, A J, Dickel, K E, Mason, R O, and Snyder, N H (1989) *Strategic Management: A Methodological Approach*, 3rd edition, Addison-Wesley, New York
37. Trice, H M and Beyer, J M (1986) 'The concept of charisma', in *Research in Organisational Behavior*, vol 8, JAI Press, pp 118–64
38. Conger, J A and Kanungo, R N (1987) 'Towards a behavioural theory of charismatic leadership in organisational settings', *Academy of Management Review* 12, 4, pp 637–47
39. Trice, H M and Beyer, J M (1986) *op cit*
40. Rowe, A J et al (1989) *op cit*
41. Conger, J A and Kanungo, R N (1987) *op cit*
42. Bennis, W and Nanus, B (1985) *Leaders: The Strategies for Taking Charge*, Harper & Row, New York
43. Hannan, M T and Freeman, J H (1974) 'Environment and the structure of organisations: A population ecology perspective', paper presented at the American Sociology Association, Montreal, Canada, August
44. Aldrich, H E (1979) *Organisations and Environments*, Prentice-Hall, Englewood Cliffs, NJ
45. Aldrich, H E and Mueller, S (1982) 'The evolution of organisational form: Technology coordination and control' in Staw, B M & Cummings, L L (eds) *Research in Organisational Behavior*, vol 4, pp 33–89
46. Aldrich, H E (1979) *op cit*
47. Aldrich, H E and Mueller, S (1982) *op cit*

9

# SURFACING COMPETITIVE STRATEGIES

*Cliff Bowman and Gerry Johnson*

## OVERVIEW

Recent developments in the management of strategy have advocated greater attention to managerial debate and involvement; and the surfacing of managerial assumptions about strategy. This chapter illustrates an approach to surfacing and mapping managerial assumptions about competitive strategy, explaining the process by which this is done; then giving a number of case examples of managerial workshops in which the approach has been applied. The chapter shows the benefits of surfacing managerial assumptions about competitive strategy so as to galvanise strategic debate, trace managerial differences, challenge the 'taken for granted' of strategy and enhance the ownership of strategy debate and directions.

## INTRODUCTION

In the last decade there have been a number of important developments in the literature on, and the practice of, strategic management. One development has been the realisation that strategies cannot be accounted for, and may not best be developed, through the types of planning systems of which so many writers were fond in the 1960s and 70s. Rather there has developed more concern with managerial involvement in the strategy making process, so the emphasis has moved to managerial debate and a search for commitment around strategic direction. Hand in hand with this has gone a concern by researchers to examine how strategies emerge in organisations rather than to show that any one best way of strategic decision-making is most appropriate.

However, a highly influential set of ideas about competitive strategy has also entered the language of management. The work of Michael Porter[1] has been more influential in setting the agenda for debate around competitive strategy than any other writer for years. It is not unusual to find managers using terms such as 'differentiation', 'cost-leadership' and 'focus' in their discussions about strategy – and certainly in the business schools such concepts have become central to many syllabuses.

This chapter reports on a project which has developed ways of assisting managerial debate about strategies around the concepts of competitive strategy based upon Porter's generic strategy concepts. It is derived from work that has been undertaken with senior teams of managers, usually as part of 'live' debate about the strategy of their organisations, and shows how the surfacing of managerial views and assumptions about bases of competitive strategy can be a powerful tool in strategic decision-making, and sometimes a trigger for change in the strategic direction of the organisation.

## DEVELOPING VIEWS OF STRATEGIC MANAGEMENT

This section reviews briefly four linked concepts that underpin the reasons for the research on which this study is based, and the way in which our work with managers has developed.

### *Espoused and realised strategies*

The idea that strategy formulation is the preserve of the board, or of some corporate planning process has increasingly been questioned; and a good deal of evidence has emerged which shows that this is not so in many organisations. Moreover, many of the assumptions implicit in traditional planning models are not borne out in an examination of managerial action. Planning systems, even when they exist, may not be central to the formulation of strategy; strategic options often are not systematically analysed, and objectives may be ill defined, diverse, post-rationalised, unstated or very generalised.[2] Even when organisations have highly formalised systems of strategic planning these may give rise to what Mintzberg *et al*[3] have called intended, or *espoused* strategies. However, as they point out, very often these become 'unrealised'. 'Realised' strategies may emerge out of opportunistic action, or emergent processes in the organisation. An important question to be dealt with then, in the examination of organisational strategies and managerial debate around them, is whether or not there is a difference between the espoused strategy as stated, and the realised strategy being pursued.

## *Realised strategies and the taken for grantedness of management*

None of this is to say that managers behave in irrational ways. The formulation of strategy is strongly influenced by what might loosely and positively be called managerial experience (or less positively, the received wisdom of management). Managers also tend to take decisions in a context of action, and through active experimentation, rather than analysis: they do not tend to consider in abstract responses to problems, but rather enter active stages of problem resolution and implementation.[4] Donald Schon suggests that it is a mistake to conceive of managerial thought and managerial action as separable: he suggests that management is characterised by 'reflection in action'.[5] In effect, managers develop over time and through experience an understanding and interpretation of the context in which they operate, which they apply to the situations they face. In this sense there is a 'taken for grantedness' or 'presumed logic'[6] brought to bear.

However, such 'taken for grantedness' does not operate merely at an individual level. No organisation could function if, in all respects, each manager had a different view of his or her organisational world. There exists in organisations a 'relatively coherent sets of beliefs that bind some people together and that explains their worlds in terms of cause and effect relations'.[7] It is an organisational view of the world which helps interpret the changes facing the organisation and the individual within it. These sets of core beliefs and assumptions are referred to, for example, as 'dominant logic',[8] and 'paradigms'.[9] However the extent of their homogeneity within an organisation is a matter of debate. It may be that, whilst differences occur within an organisation, perhaps associated with managerial level or function, career background, or length of tenure in the organisation, managers within an organisation subscribe to a more common set of assumptions than a group of managers taken from different organisations; and managers in different organisations within an industry subscribe to a more common set of assumptions – the industry 'recipe'[10] – than those outside that industry.

Implicit in the planning literature on strategic management is the notion that agreement on strategy across a firm is required and that planning systems can help build such agreement. An alternative view is, of course, that there may be consensus within a firm around the realised strategy but that this is rooted in that which is taken for granted at the organisational level, the functional level, or whatever. There are those, then, who would argue that the realised strategy of organisations is better explained as the product of the taken for grantedness of management arising from organisational paradigms, or individual cognition. Indeed a common complaint about planning systems is that they do not give rise to innovation or new thinking. It can be argued that the reason for this is that the analysis and evaluation of strategies through such systems tend to be within the context of, rather than a challenge to, the cognitive limits within which managers work. If such a view of strategy formulation is taken then an implication which arises is the importance of surfacing that which is taken for granted in the processes of strategy formulation[11]: and that by surfacing the taken for granted, managers will be better able to critique the assumptions and examine the extent of agreement or disagreement on (realised) strategy. The research instrument described below has been used in this way, and the chapter reports on the benefits and outcomes of such interventions. The particular issues surfaced also arise from a sociocognitive perspective on strategy formulation, and are identified in the following points.

## *Competitive strategies: prescribed, intended and realised*

The arguments that Michael Porter puts forward about competitive strategy are now well known. Competitive advantage, he argues, is achieved in one of three ways; through cost-leadership, through differentiation or through focus based strategies. He argues that it is important that the organisation is not 'stuck in the middle' – that it is clearly following one of these strategies. Elsewhere he goes further[12] to argue that, whatever other components of strategy may exist, for example, at the corporate or operational levels, clarity of thinking and action around a competitive strategy are vital for the high performing firm. He also argues that clarity must be carried through to operational levels, linked through the different activities of the firm, and that the strategy should be clearly understood by all managers.

Even where such clear prescription is reflected in the statements of strategy made by firms – their intended strategies – this does of course beg the question as to what extent they are being carried out in practice, or managers perceive them as being carried out in practice. The question of intended and realised strategies is therefore raised, again, but at the competitive strategy level. Even if we accept the wisdom of Porter's prescriptions, the strategies of firms need to be examined in terms of what is happening rather than that which is espoused: and this is the perspective adopted by this project.

Bringing together these three different perspectives, this chapter describes a project which provides a means whereby managers can examine the extent of agreement or disagreement within their managerial teams about realised competitive strategies. What follows is a brief explanation of the research instrument used in the project and the workshop events with managers; this is followed by case examples of the way in which strategy debate has been enhanced within a number of firms using the approach.

## THE RESEARCH PROJECT

The case studies which follow arise from a programme of workshops typically carried out with boards of firms or groups of senior executives. These workshops were characteristically of two or three day duration and were designed to discuss and develop the strategies of the organisations concerned. In each of the workshops the researchers acted as facilitators. One part of the workshop activity was concerned with discussing and developing competitive strategy. The discussion on this topic was enhanced by means of a research instrument which resulted in the surfacing of managerial views about the realised competitive strategy of their firm. This research instrument used was a 21 statement questionnaire requiring managers to rate their perceptions of the current competitive strategic posture of their business.

The questionnaire consisted of strategic priority statements derived from Porter's generic strategy concepts. Other established strategic management texts[13] were also consulted, and discussions held with academic colleagues to refine and develop the statements. (In addition other statements about the extent of change in organisations were included but are not relevant to the discussion in this chapter). It is recognised that the link between statements so derived and the 'actual' way a manager sees the strategy of the SBU is problematic since managers may define categories differently from researchers. However there are precedents for such an approach[14] and it must be remembered that, in the context of this paper, the results are used primarily as a means of surfacing issues for debate and discussion by the managers. Moreover considerable attention was paid to ensuring that the statements made sense in managerial terms and were meaningful to managers.

To avoid presenting managers with an overly dichotomised choice between 'cost-leadership' and 'differentiation', each of the generic strategies was dissembled into a set of statements about strategic priorities which related to one or other of the strategies. In so doing a risk was introduced insofar as the selected statements, taken as a set, may not accurately reflect Porter's intended description of each generic strategy. However, statements were required to which managers could easily relate. For example, the term 'differentiation' was never used in any of the statements; instead strategic orientations and priorities that were related to Porter's 'differentiation' strategy were converted into broad statements about current business practice, and discussed with managers in the pilot testing of the questionnaire. In this pilot stage, it was found that 'cost-leadership' was variously interpreted. For some, it meant being lowest cost *to the customer* (ie lowest *price*); others interpreted it as Porter intended but felt that it would be difficult to pursue such a strategy. However, in spite of these problems one statement was retained which reflected the 'pure' cost leadership strategy ('We aim to be the lowest cost producer in our industry'). Other statements were constructed in managerial language to reflect cost-control activities, which taken together, would be required for a firm to achieve cost-leadership. Also as a result of feedback from discussions with managers in the pilot testing and development phase, when interpreting results from the final version of the questionnaire 'cost-leadership' was referred to as a 'cost-efficiency' orientation. The questionnaire was then further tested to ensure that practising managers were able to complete the questionnaire without difficulty, saw the statements as meaningful and were capable of relating them to their own firm.

The outcome was the 21 statement questionnaire shown in Appendix 1. It requires managers to rate their business unit on a five-point scale from 1 ('This statement does not apply to our firm') to 5 ('This statement accurately describes the situation in our firm'). Numbers 2 to 4 enabled them to indicate intermediate positions between these two extremes. The introductory rubric also makes clear that the statements refer to what the firm is doing *now*, not what respondents think it might do in the future.

Two further tests of validity of the questionnaire were conducted. The first involved the use of the questionnaire in a business that, a priori, we would suppose would display high consensus about its strategic priorities, namely the partners of a small strategic management consultancy.[15] This did, indeed, reveal a very high degree of consensus around the strategy of differentiation. The second test involved the selection of a business that, a priori, we would expect to display low consensus. A business within a large multinational corporation was selected, and newly recruited graduates were asked to complete the questionnaire. The combination of relative newness to the business, a spread of functional experiences, and being located at low levels of the hierarchy would suggest that these trainee managers would not share the same perceptions of strategic priorities. Indeed, the tests did produce low consensus.

The questionnaire was then administered to a total of 309 managers in 35 different businesses, and the resulting data factor analysed specifying a three factor solution. This analysis produced three factors that corresponded with the intended structure of the questionnaire ie a 'cost-leadership' factor, a 'differentiation' factor, and a 'change' factor. The tests therefore showed that the statements not only made sense to managers, but made sense in Porter's terms. To date we have collected questionnaire responses from over 1600 managers from a wide variety of businesses; the three factors have remained stable.

For the purposes of presenting the information to managers the factor score coefficients were then applied to the responses for each manager to yield a factor score for each manager. The factor scores were then adjusted (by means of a standard algorithm) to percentiles for the purpose of conveying the results to the managers. (It was found that managers could not easily interpret the factor score plot where the axes were presented in terms of standard deviations.) These adjusted factor scores were then used to construct two-dimensional plots for each business unit as shown in Figure 9.1. Managers located in the 'efficiency' quadrant scored statements to do with cost-control high, and other statements low. Managers located in the 'differentiation' quadrant scored statements about being unique, innovative and offering distinctive products/services high, and cost-related statements low. The 'hybrid' quadrant included managers who scored both efficiency and differentiation statements high. In the 'impoverished' quadrant, managers who did not rate their business high on either group of statements were located. We did, however, recognise that because the two dimensional plots use aggregated data, it was possible that an overall lack of consensus could disguise quite high levels of agreement about individual statements. Accordingly, descriptive statistics (means and standard deviations) were also calculated for each individual statement. Where appropriate, these statistics were also used to feedback the results to managers.

## SURFACING MANAGERIAL PATTERNS OF COMPETITIVE STRATEGY

The use of the results of the questionnaires in management workshops

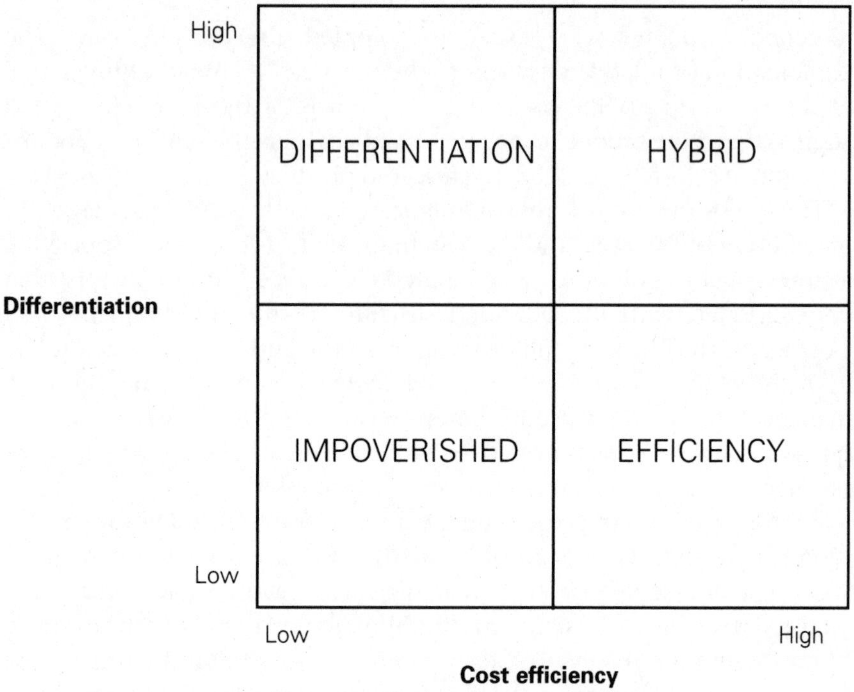


**Figure 9.1** The four realised strategies

has been to promote and facilitate debate on competitive strategy by focusing managers' attention on the competitive strategy of the organisation as they perceive it. The purpose of this section is to provide a number of case examples of the benefits of this approach by showing how managerial debate and management learning on a variety of complex issues of strategy formulation has been stimulated.

### *Mapping levels of managerial agreement*

Figure 9.2 represents the main board team of a major retail organisation which had suffered some years of deteriorating performance. The board had been debating the need for strategic change for some months, a debate which had proceeded as though members of the board had a common understanding of what the current strategy was and the broad direction in which it should be moving. Indeed, to the outside observer, the intended strategy seemed clear enough: the company had been acquired by a group, the chairman of which was wedded to the notion of 'design excellence'; as such the stated strategy of the firm was to gain

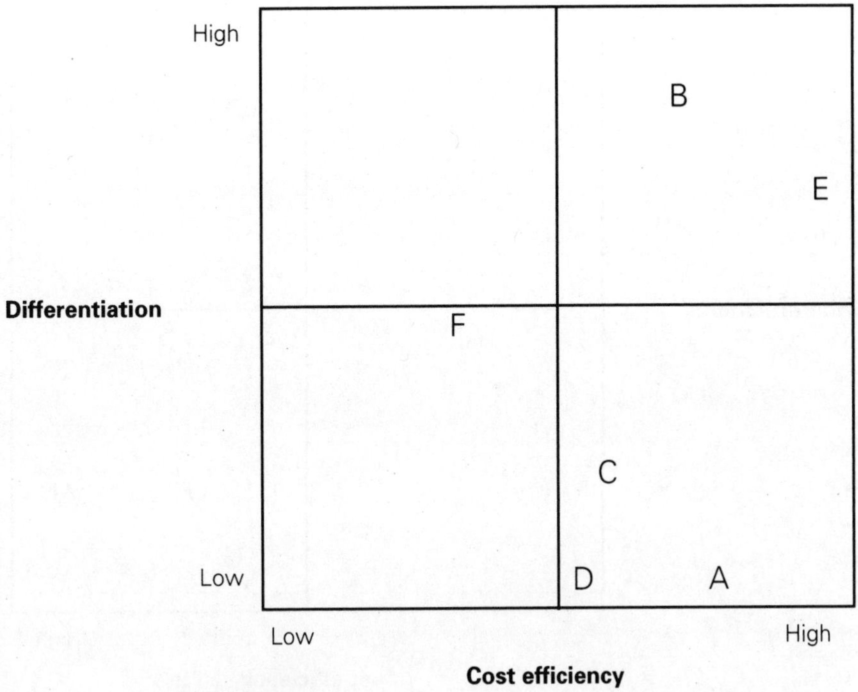


**Figure 9.2** Major retailer: the board

competitive advantage through differentiation by means of a merchandising and marketing policy which stressed the importance of customer oriented design. However the questionnaire uncovered considerable differences.

In Figure 9.2 the chief executive is A; he sees a push towards efficiency and low cost as the current strategy: however, whilst the personnel director (D) and finance director (C) have a similar understanding; the merchandise director (F) is less clear, the property director (E) and particularly the development director (B) also believe the current strategy to be one of differentiation – a hybrid strategy. Not only is there a clear difference between the views of the board and the espoused strategy, but the differences within the board are considerable, and were startling to them.

It was even more of a shock for them to find that, when they looked at their senior management team by function (Figure 9.3) the spread of views was even wider. Although most of the senior managers in store operations (V W X Y Z) and finance (S T U) functions coalesced around an efficiency strategy, the spread of managers in the merchandising

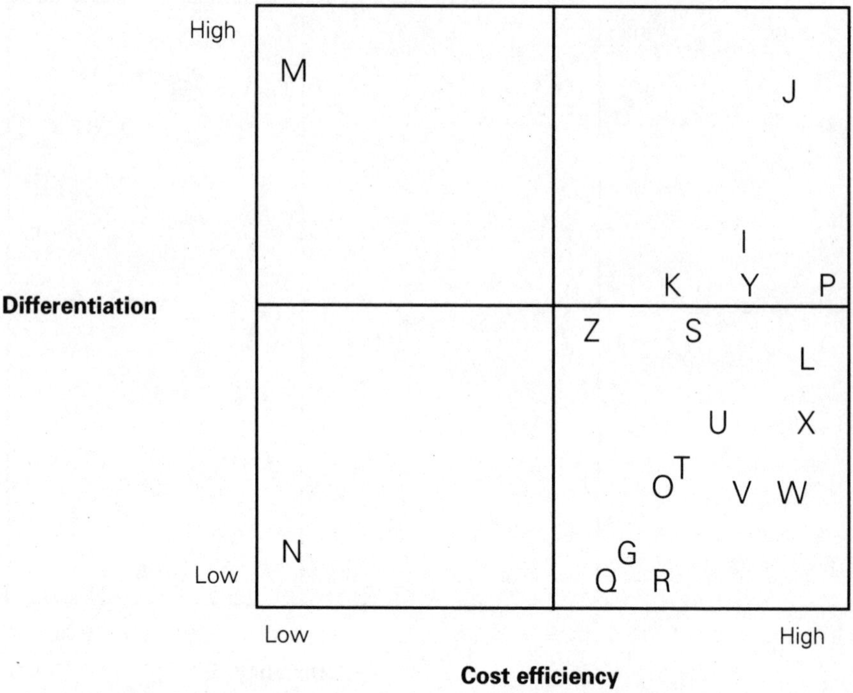


**Figure 9.3** Major retailers: functional managers

function (I to R) was initially seen as remarkable. However it emerged that it might be understood as a reflection of the historic role of the product group for which they were responsible. N, a senior buyer for a product range which had never been successful in the company, had a view of the company's strategy as 'impoverished': M, the senior buyer for a fashion range, had a view of strategy as differentiation and nothing to do with cost or efficiency: and J, who was responsible for the range with the greatest historic profit contribution, saw the company strategy as both differentiation and efficiency based. In short, perceptions of competitive strategy were better explained by functional and historical roles than by reference to the intended strategy, even though there was active and current debate on this.

Differences were, then, surfaced between members of the board, between functions and, in the crucial merchandising area, within function. Surfacing these differences changed the nature of the strategy debate. Hitherto this had assumed common understanding about the agenda for debate and the assumptions about strategic issues facing the company: it shifted towards unearthing and changing fundamental strategic assumptions about competitive positioning.

## *Uncovering the specifics of difference*

A second example shows how such investigation of managerial differences uncovered problems in the processes of managing the business. Figure 9.4 represents the management team of an engineering business which had suffered years of performance decline. In 1989 three executive directors were faced with the company being sold off by the major shareholder, or the opportunity of a management buyout. They decided that, despite an intensely competitive environment they faced, there was sufficient market opportunity, and customer goodwill to merit going ahead with the buyout. As part of the preparation for this they undertook a strategy mapping exercise for themselves and their management team. The three board members had expected that, at least, there would be agreement amongst themselves, yet the managing director (A) clearly saw the firm following an efficiency driven strategy, whilst the sales director (C) emphasised differentiation as well as efficiency, and the finance director (B) really saw the firm as following neither. They were able, however, to look back into the data to find what they agreed on, and what they did not and why. They agreed that the firm had been trying to control costs, though even within this there was some disagreement. The managing director and sales director thought that the firm had gone just about as far as it could in cutting overheads: the finance director disagreed. On the other hand, the managing director and finance director agreed that the company had been following a strategy to become the lowest cost producer in the industry: the sales director disagreed. On the product development side the sales director believed that the company was developing new products and was able to offer unique offerings to customers. The managing director disagreed. Surprisingly, perhaps, what they *did* agree about was that the company was trying to follow a different course from that which it had followed over the past decade: what the investigations showed was that at board level there really was no agreement about what this direction was.

Indeed, a comparison with findings in the other firms in the sample showed that managers here had a lower level of overall agreement than any other firm in the sample. There was little the executive team did agree about, except that there was constant pressure on overheads, and since there was very little emphasis on product line changes, or innovation, managers believed the company had to maintain competitive prices.

Executives could only see a basis of competition on low cost and low price, since there was no attempt at anything else.

Other problems were unearthed at the operational level. There were disagreements on what the firm had been trying to achieve between the contract manager (D) who received orders, and the production manager (E) who processed them. Within the marketing team, the sales director (C) was generally more bullish about the innovatory capabilities of the firm, whilst his sales manager (F) could see the firm doing very little more than attempting to cut costs. Worse, the production manager (E) saw the firm's strategy quite differently from members of the executive; and yet he was responsible for the team briefings in the factory. As the managing director said, 'God knows what the workforce think we're doing if we don't know and Bill doesn't agree with us'.

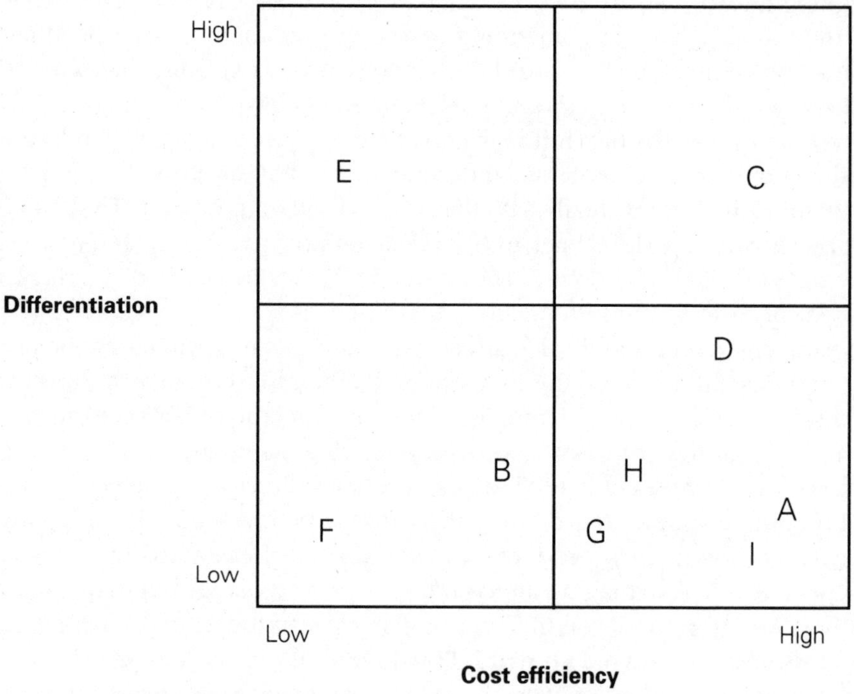


**Figure 9.4** Engineering firm: top management team

## *Challenging managerial perceptions of strategy*

The business described in the next case produces insulation material for industrial and domestic applications. It is part of a large multinational corporation. The industry is highly competitive, there is excess capacity and fierce price competition. It became clear that the managers saw themselves in a true 'commodity' industry, with no real scope to differentiate their products.

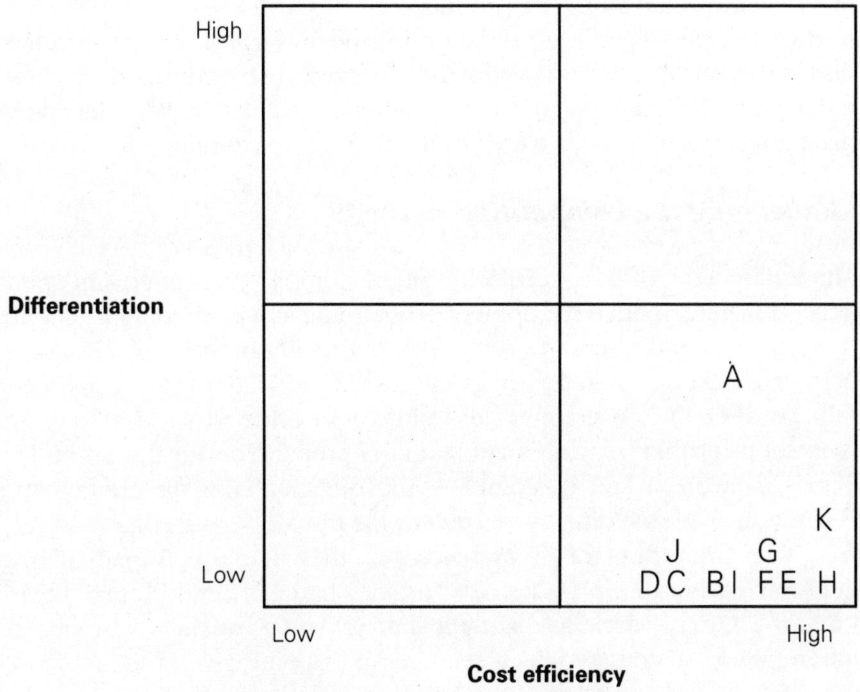


**Figure 9.5** Insulation materials supplier

This 'realised strategy' was presented to a small group of managers, excluding the CEO, who were taking part in a corporate-wide executive development programme. The plot (Figure 9.5) surprised managers from other businesses in the corporation who were able to compare it with plots from their businesses. These had generally displayed a greater dispersion than the insulation business plot. However, the plot did not surprise the representatives from the insulation business who said that it merely confirmed the view that they were in a commodity industry. The 'outlier' (A) on the plot, was correctly identified by these managers as the managing director. He was known to believe that the assumption that they were in a commodity business should be challenged, and that, through product and service development, the business might find ways to avoid competing solely on price and consequent cost-cutting. The representatives on the programme were not at all persuaded of such views but began to debate if they were tenable. Managers from other businesses then began to put forward views that challenged the assumptions revealed through the plot, and argued that whilst the core product might be a commodity, there could be ways of differentiating the service surrounding the core product.

The managers from the insulation business began to concede in the discussions that it was possible for the accepted 'rules of the game' in their industry to be challenged to good effect, and that maybe the new managing director's ideas were worth rather more attention.

## *Challenging the competitive strategy*

Three directors of a specialist nutrition company attended an open general management development programme in which Porter's generic strategy concepts were presented, and the importance of choosing between generic strategies was discussed and advocated. Eighteen months after the programme, the directors decided to run a strategy workshop for their management team. As preparation for the event the managers were asked to complete the questionnaire. In preliminary discussions with the directors to determine the scope and content of the workshop, the directors remarked that they had been particularly impressed with the Porter framework, and had explored Porter's ideas further. They had decided that their strategy had to be that of a focused differentiator, a strategy which seemed appropriate given the nature of their products – specialist nutritional supplements for people with in-born, or disease-related intolerance to different foods.

Prior to the workshop, the firm was taken over by a Scandinavian company, and three executives of this company became members of the board. The plot on perceptions of competitive strategy is shown as Figure 9.6. All the managers perceived the strategy to be about offering superior products, and developing new products. Cost-efficiency and price competition were not seen to be part of the strategy. The only managers who appeared to be slightly different from this strong consensus were two of the three Scandinavians (O and P). They, too, perceived priorities to do with product superiority and innovation, but they also emphasised cost-control.

On this evidence it appeared that the efforts of the directors to implant a strategy of focused differentiation had been remarkably successful. However, the business was not especially profitable and the question was raised as to why this was so if there was so much agreement about competitive strategy. An interesting issue about strategic choice emerged.

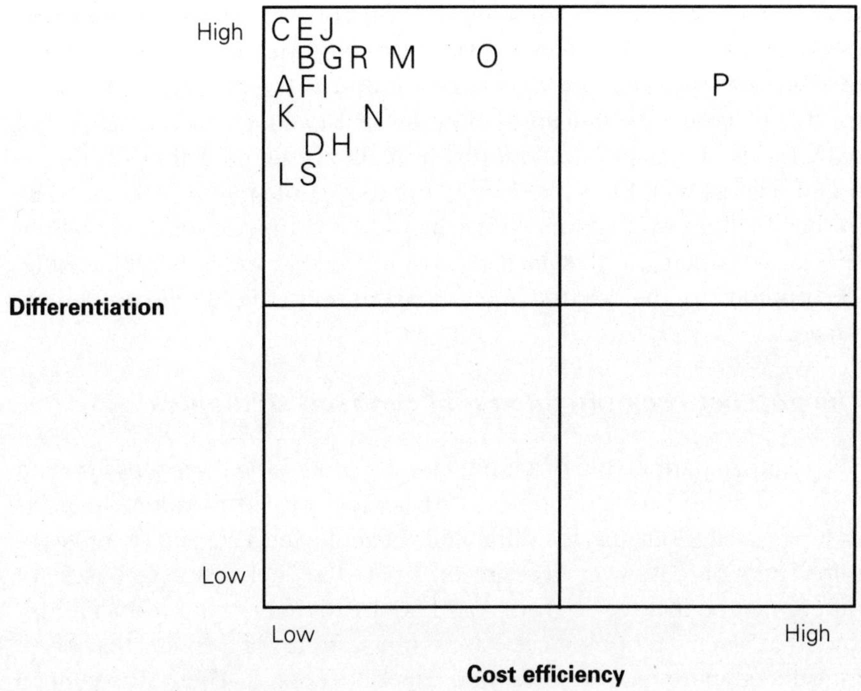


**Figure 9.6** Specialist nutrition company

Given the nature of this firm's products, and the markets it sells into, to what extent were the perceived priorities determined by the products and markets the firm was competing in, rather than being determined by the management? Discussion followed on the extent to which any 'competitive thrust' should be combined with cost-control; and the extent to which their view of 'focused differentiation' clearly explained how the firm was to outperform other firms perceived by customers to be offering substitutes.

One manager remarked that he had a feeling that the focused differentiation strategy was rather too glib and simplistic. One of the Scandinavians said he was surprised at the lack of concern for cost-control in the firm, which was confirmed by the realised strategy plot. The finance director, who was one of the original proponents of the focused differentiator strategy, indicated that he was beginning to understand why they were not making the kind of profits that their 'niche' strategy should be delivering.

The discussion then moved on to whether they could raise the concern for cost-control from its present low level, without jeopardising their sources of uniqueness and innovation. The issue of 'cost-leadership' was raised in this context. The group felt that they could not, and should not, try to be the lowest cost producer in the industry. But their reference point for this view was an industry definition that included manufacturers of baby foods. It was pointed out that it might not be relevant to compare their business with firms like Nestlé; but they could become cost-leaders in the small group of firms with which they competed directly in their specialist markets, ie that *focused* cost-leadership might be achievable. The outcome of the discussion was a major revision of their competitive strategy.

## *The gap between intended and realised strategies*

The regional partnership of a multinational professional services firm had recognised the problems both of achieving any cost-leadership in its industry sector, but also the difficulties of achieving a sustainable basis of differentiation. It was recognised that the delivery of bases of differentiation in a service firm could not be thought of in product terms, and that such technological based innovations of service that were introduced were readily, and often speedily, copied. There was general acceptance in the firm that bases of differentiation had to be sought, and much greater focus on different market segments, even specific corporations, was necessary. The problem was how to deliver such a strategy in a firm with a long established professional culture and a structure wedded to the provision of historically rooted professional services.

The debate proceeded for some two years and had reached the point of a recognition that products and technology were not necessarily the way forward. All the competitors espoused differentiation based around service quality; and service quality was essentially to do with the ability of partners to ensure the delivery of such service. As the managing partner put it:

> I don't think there is a difference between the strategies of competing firms: competitive advantage will only be gained for those firms that do more than state what the strategy is; that deliver against it. Differentiation is about delivery.

A number of strategy workshops were set up to explore how a strategy of greater focus and greater differentiation could be delivered. At the beginning of the strategy workshops the results of the questionnaires (Figure 9.7) were shown to participants – all senior partners in the firm.

These results came as a shock. More so than any other firm, or any other group of managers, the partners' view, common across all the workshops, was that the firm had no competitive strategy at all – that it was 'impoverished'. The partners' views were that the firm was not only unable to compete on cost, but was making no attempt to differentiate.

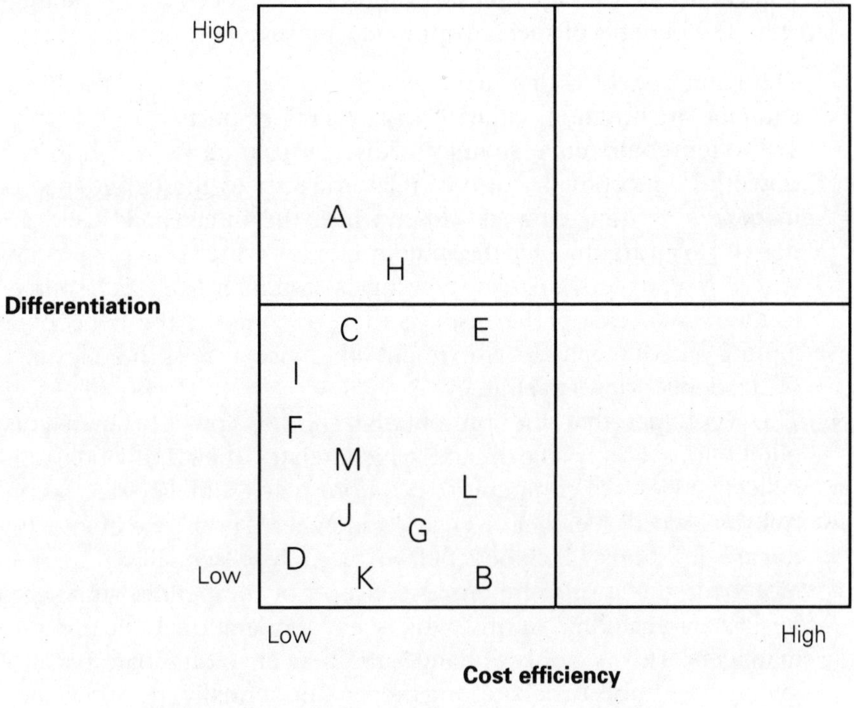


**Figure 9.7** Professional services firm: partners

The debate moved to the reasons for this set of perceptions. Was it that they did not accept the logic of a strategy of focused differentiation; or was it that they believed they were not capable of delivering against it; or perhaps it reflected a deep-seated reliance on old ways of operating; or a cynical view about notions of strategy? The view which emerged was one which formed the context for the rest of the workshop: it was not that those present did not accept the logic of the need for a differentiation strategy, it was that they had not realised the extent of movement required from old ways of operating to the demands of such a strategy. The rest of the workshop concentrated on identifying specifically what needed to be done to deliver against such a strategy.

## THE BENEFITS OF SURFACING REALISED COMPETITIVE STRATEGIES

This chapter has shown how research to uncover the realised competitive strategies in organisations and the levels of managerial consensus around these strategies has been employed as a basis of intervention in strategy debates. The benefits of such an approach are several:

- The main benefit is that managers are provided with the facility to examine organisational strategy from *their* perspective.
- Too often competitive strategy is discussed in terms which, whilst powerful conceptually, do not relate directly to the experience of managers or their context. Here, whilst the dimensions used are derived from argument in the strategy literature, they provide a means whereby managers can relate typologies of strategy from such sources to their own reality. The result is the avoidance of the conceptual 'opting out' of managers who might otherwise dismiss the relevance of 'academic' views of strategy.
- The very fact that the presentation of the 'plot' of managers' perceptions is a visual image which relates their individual and collective views to competitor's positions helps stimulate discussion. 'Why are we all seeing it this way?' and 'where should we be moving to?' are questions which benefit from visual representation.
- Moreover, the approach permits concepts of competitive strategy to be disaggregated in terms which have operational meaning to managers. This not only enhances the relevance of debate because managers are able to debate tangible, organisationally specific aspects of strategy; but also allows agreements and disagreements to be traced to specific operational or functional sources.
- In the experience of the authors, the consequent benefit is a higher likelihood of the internalisation and ownership of the process and outcome of the debate, resulting in a greater managerial commitment to the strategy which is being developed.
- There does, indeed, seem to be a momentum of strategy in organisations. In many of the workshops, managers found difficulty initially in conceiving of strategic options different from those pursued in the past; or if there was discontent with the existing strategy, in identifying specific causes for such discontent. The surfacing of managerial perceptions of competitive strategy, and their mapping in ways described here often provided a stimulus – in some cases a shock – which was needed to galvanise debate outside the traditional ways of thinking. The stimulus was the greater because the

basis of it – the maps and their significance – were self-generated, rather than commentaries by outsiders on their strategic posture.

It is also worth noting that the exercise has proved to be of value to the process of learning for the researchers too: it became clear that the managerial logic uncovered by taking this approach in itself provided a critique of the academic literature. Whilst not the subject of this paper, such a critique allows us to raise the interesting prospect of the emergence of a profitable dialectic between traditional academic analysis and managerial logic surfaced in relatively structured ways through the sort of research reported in this paper.[16]

# APPENDIX 1

## The perceptions of strategy questionnaire

Company:

Division/Business unit:
(if appropriate)

Name:

Function/department

Position in organisation:

Indicate your position in relation to the managing director of firm – eg

managing director

marketing director

sales manager
(me)

### INTRODUCTION

This brief questionnaire is designed to help discover your perceptions of your firm's strategy. In answering the questionnaire assume each statement applies to the most logical 'unit' in the firm. For example, in a diversified organisation, these statements would apply to a single business unit or division. If the statement does not apply at all to your firm/division/unit then circle (1). If the statement accurately describes the situation in the firm, circle (5). The numbers (2) to (4) enable you to indicate intermediate positions in between these two extremes.

Please note that we are interested in your firm's *CURRENT STRATEGY*; the statements refer to what your firm is doing *NOW*, not what you think it might be doing some time in the future.

Thank you for your help.

Cliff Bowman

| | | This statement does not apply to our firm | | | | This statement accurately describes the situation in our firm |
|---|---|---|---|---|---|---|
| 1. | We place considerable emphasis on the control of operating costs | 1 | 2 | 3 | 4 | 5 |
| 2. | The strategic direction we are now pursuing represents a significant change from that pursued in the past | 1 | 2 | 3 | 4 | 5 |
| 3. | We emphasise our distinctive products or image in our marketing communications | 1 | 2 | 3 | 4 | 5 |
| 4. | Our organisation, and the way things get done within it, have changed little in recent times | 1 | 2 | 3 | 4 | 5 |
| 5. | There is constant pressure here to cut overhead costs | 1 | 2 | 3 | 4 | 5 |
| 6. | We make extensive efforts to secure the lowest cost sources of supply | 1 | 2 | 3 | 4 | 5 |
| 7. | We regularly develop new products/services, or significantly change the line of products/services we offer | 1 | 2 | 3 | 4 | 5 |
| 8. | We try hard to maintain the maximum feasible utilisation of our capacity/resources | 1 | 2 | 3 | 4 | 5 |

| | This statement does not apply to our firm | | | | This statement accurately describes the situation in our firm |
|---|---|---|---|---|---|
| 9. We try to offer unique products/services enabling us to charge premium prices | 1 | 2 | 3 | 4 | 5 |
| 10. We give new product/service development top priority | 1 | 2 | 3 | 4 | 5 |
| 11. We emphasise competitive prices in our marketing communications | 1 | 2 | 3 | 4 | 5 |
| 12. Our line of products/services seldom change in a substantive manner | 1 | 2 | 3 | 4 | 5 |
| 13. We carefully monitor operations to help us keep costs under control | 1 | 2 | 3 | 4 | 5 |
| 14. Currently, we are trying to operate this business in significantly different ways to those we have in the past | 1 | 2 | 3 | 4 | 5 |
| 15. As our customers are very price sensitive, we devote considerable time and effort to improving efficiency | 1 | 2 | 3 | 4 | 5 |
| 16. The organisational structure and/or processes we are now using represent a noticeable change from our recent past | 1 | 2 | 3 | 4 | 5 |
| 17. Information about sales performance is considered to be more important than cost control information | 1 | 2 | 3 | 4 | 5 |
| 18. We aim to offer superior products/services to those of our competitors | 1 | 2 | 3 | 4 | 5 |

| | | This statement does not apply to our firm | | | | This statement accurately describes the situation in our firm |
|---|---|---|---|---|---|---|
| 19. | We aim to be the lowest cost producer in our industry | 1 | 2 | 3 | 4 | 5 |
| 20. | We try to operate this business in much the same way today as we have in the past | 1 | 2 | 3 | 4 | 5 |
| 21. | Because we offer very similar products/services to the competition, we try to maintain competitive prices | 1 | 2 | 3 | 4 | 5 |

## References


1. Porter M E (1980) *Competitive Strategy*, The Free Press, Macmillan, and New York Porter; M E (1985) *Competitive Advantage*, The Free Press, Macmillan, New York
2. Fahey L (1981) On Strategic Management Decision Processes, *Strategic Management Journal* vol 2, pp 43–60; Johnson, G (1987) *Strategic Change and the Management Process*, Basil Blackwell, Oxford; Lyles M A (1981) 'Formulating Strategy Problems – Empirical Analysis and Model Development', *Strategic Management Journal*, vol 2, pp 61–75; Mintzberg, H, Raisinghani, O and Theoret, A (1976) 'The Structure of Unstructured Decision Processes', *Administrative Science Quarterly*, vol 21, pp 246–75; Pettigrew, A M (1985) *The Awakening Giant*, Oxford Basil Blackwell, and Quinn, J B (1980) *Strategies for Change: Logical Incrementalism*, Irwin, Homewood, Illinois
3. Mintzberg, H (1978) 'Patterns in Strategy Formation', *Management Science*, pp 934–48 May; and Mintzberg, H and Waters, J A (1983) The Mind of the Strategist(s) in Srivastva, S (ed) *The Executive Mind*, Jossey Bass, San Francisco
4. Kolb, D A (1974) 'On Management and Learning Process' in Kolb, D A, Rubin, I M, McIntyre, J M (eds), *Organisational Psychology*, Prentice Hall, New Jersey, USA
5. Schon, D (1983) *The Reflective Practitioner*, Temple Smith. London

6. Weick, K E (1983) 'Managerial Thought in the Context of Action', in Srivastva, S (ed), *The Executive Mind*, Jossey Bass, San Francisco
7. Beyer, J M (1981) 'Ideologies, Values and Decision Making in Organisations' in Nystrom, P C and Starbuck, W H (eds) *Handbook of Organisational Design*, vol 2, Oxford University Press
8. Prahalad, C K and Bettis, R A (1986) 'The Dominant Logic: A new linkage between diversity and performance', *Strategic Management Journal*, vol 7, pp 485–502
9. Sheldon, A (1980) 'Organisation Paradigms: A Theory of Organisational Change', *Organisational Dynamics*, vol 8, no 3, pp 61–71
10. Spender, J-C (1989) *Industry Recipes: The Nature and Sources of Managerial Judgement*, Basil Blackwell, Oxford
11. Cosier, R A and Schwenk, C R (1990) 'Agreement and thinking alike: Ingredients for poor decisions', *Academy of Management Executive*, vol 1, pp 69–74; and Mason, R O and Mitroff, II *Challenging Strategic Planning Assumptions*, Wiley, New York
12. Porter, M E (1987) 'From Competitive Advantage to Corporate Strategy', *Harvard Business Review*, May/June
13. Johnson, G N and Scholes, K (1989) *Exploring Corporate Strategy*, Prentice Hall Hemel Hempstead; and Thompson, A A and Strickland, A J (1987) *Strategic Management: Concepts and Cases*, 4th edition, Business Publication, Plano, Texas
14. Dess, G G and Davis, P S (1984) 'Porter's (1980) Generic Strategies as Determinants of Strategic Group Membership and Organisational Performance', *Academy of Management Journal*, vol 27, pp 467–88; Hambrick, D C (1981) 'Strategic Awareness Within Top Management Teams', *Strategic Management Journal*, vol 2, pp 263–79; Hambrick, D C (1980) 'Operationalising the concept of business-level strategy in research', *Academy of Management Review*, vol 5, pp 567–75; and Miller, D (1988) 'Relating Porter's Business Strategies to environment and structure: Analysis and performance implications'. *Academy of Management Journal*, vol 31, pp 280–308
15. Wilkins, A L and Ouchi, W G (1983) 'Efficient cultures: exploring the relationship between culture and organisational performance', *Administrative Science Quarterly*, vol 28, pp 468–81
16. Bowman, C (1991) *Perceptions of Competitive Strategy: Realised Strategy, Consensus and Performance*, PhD Thesis, Cranfield School of Management; Bowman, C A Managerial Critique of Porter's Generic Strategies, Cranfield Working Paper Series, SWP 53/91.

10

# MANAGING STRATEGIC CHANGE : STRATEGY, CULTURE AND ACTION*

*Gerry Johnson*

## OVERVIEW

One of the major problems facing senior executives is that of effecting significant strategic change in their organisations. This paper develops a number of explanatory frameworks which address the links between the development of strategy in organisations, dimensions of corporate culture and managerial action. In considering such linkages, and by illustrating them with examples from work undertaken in companies, the paper also seeks to advance our understanding of the problems and means of managing strategic change.

A good deal has been written in the last decade about the links between organisational strategy and culture, the problems of strategic inertia in firms, and the need for managers to manage the cultural context of the organisation so as to achieve strategic change and an adaptive organisation to sustain the change for long-term success. However much of what has been written, whilst striking chords of reality for managers, is frustrating because it lacks precision in explaining links between organisational culture, strategy and managerial behaviour. This chapter seeks to help remedy this situation. It does so by clarifying the links between the development of strategy in organisations and organisational culture, so as to provide quite precise frameworks and explanations by which managers can discern reasons for strategic inertia and barriers to

* This chapter first appeared in *Long Range Planning*. vol 25, no 1. February 1992.

strategic change. It goes on to consider the implications for managerial action in the process of managing strategic change. In so doing the chapter builds on developing concepts and research, and also the application of tools of analysis and intervention that have been employed within companies.

## EXPLAINING STRATEGY DEVELOPMENT IN ORGANISATIONS

### *An incremental perspective*

There are discernible patterns of strategic development in organisations. Organisations go through long periods when strategies develop incrementally; that is, decisions build one upon another, so that past decisions mould future strategy. More fundamental shifts in strategy may occur as major readjustment of the strategic direction of the firm takes place, but this is an infrequent occurrence. Some writers have argued that such incremental development in organisations is consciously and logically managed by executives as a means of coping with the complexity and uncertainty of strategy development. Managers are aware that it is not possible to 'know' about all the influences that could conceivably affect the future of the organisation. They are also aware that the organisation is a political entity in which trade-offs between the interests of different groups are inevitable: it is therefore not possible to arrive at an optimal goal or an optimal strategy; strategies must be compromises which allow the organisation to go forward. To cope with this uncertainty and such compromise, strategies must be developed gradually so that new ideas and experiments can be tested and commitment within the organisation can be achieved whilst maintaining continual, if low scale change. This is what has become known as 'logical incrementalism'.[1] It is a view of the management of strategy which is often espoused by managers themselves, although of course they may not use the same terminology.

However, we need to be careful about building too much upon what managers espouse: because they espouse the idea of logical incrementalism does not necessarily mean they behave in such ways. Still less does it mean that we can confidently build guidelines about strategic management upon such views. There is no denial here that an incremental development of strategy takes place in many organisations, but there are other explantions as to how such patterns come about. Indeed, the whole idea of 'logical incrementalism' can be seen as a rationalisation of processes which can be accounted for in quite different ways; and which shows the important links between strategy and organisational culture.

There is a good deal of difference between the rational handling of a messy organisational situation in an uncertain environmental context and the building of a strategy. The notion of strategy is to do with the long-term direction of the organisation and not just the response to difficulties. If some discernible patterns of strategic direction emerge in an organisation then it must be because there is some guidance to that strategy. This guidance may not, of course, be explicit and conscious as is assumed in much strategic planning literature. However, strategies do not arise by pure chance. The evidence from research which has looked at the decision processes which give rise to strategic decisions and the development of strategy in organisations,[2] show that the decisions arise through the application of managerial experience as a filter of external and internal stimuli, within a politicised social setting. The 'guidance' that gives rise to strategy is, then, most likely to be related to the 'taken for granted' assumptions, beliefs and values that are encapsulated within the idea of managerial experience and organisational culture. The observed patterns of incremental change that occur can be understood in this way just as readily.

## *A cultural perspective*

Strategy has long been associated with logical systems of analysis and planning. However, such frameworks have been based rather more on what writers say managers *should* do rather than observations about how strategies actually come about. If managerial processes which give rise to the development of strategy are examined and understood in cultural, political and cognitive terms then it becomes clear that the strategic complexity that managers face cannot readily be analysed objectively and continually within the managerial task. Managers have a set of core beliefs and assumptions which are specific and relevant to the organisation in which they work and which are learned over time. Whilst individual managers may hold quite varying sets of beliefs about many different aspects of that organisational world, there is likely to exist at some level a core set of beliefs and assumptions held relatively commonly by the managers. This has variously been called ideational culture, a mind-set, an interpretative scheme, a recipe, or the term used here, a *paradigm*. This paradigm is essentially cultural in nature in so far as it is the

> 'deeper level of basic *assumptions and beliefs* that are shared by members

of an organisation, that operate unconsciously and define in a basic "taken for granted" fashion an organisation's view of itself and its environment'.[3]

It is likely to evolve over time; might embrace assumptions about the nature of the organisational environment, the managerial style in the organisation, the nature of its leaders, managerial style and the operational routines seen as important to ensure the success of the organisation. It may also be perceived more easily by outsiders than those inside the organisation, to whom its constructs are likely to be self-evident. The paradigm is, then, a cognitive structure likely to be found to a greater or lesser extent in all firms.

*It is this paradigm which, in many organisations, creates a relatively homogeneous approach to the interpretation of the complexity that the organisation faces.* The various and often confusing signals that the organisation faces are made sense of, and are filtered, in terms of this paradigm. Moreover, since it evolves over time and is reinforced through the history and perhaps the success of the organisation, it also provides a repertoire of actions and responses to the interpretations of signals which are experienced by managers and seen by them as demonstrably relevant. It is, at one and the same time, a device for interpretation and a formula for action. At its most beneficial, it encapsulates the unique or special competences and skills of that organisation and therefore the bases by which the firm might expect to achieve real competitive advantage. However, it can also lead to significant strategic problems.

## *The paradigm as a filter*

Environmental forces and organisational capabilities undoubtedly affect the performance of an organisation but do not in themselves create organisational strategy: people create strategy, and one mechanism by which this occurs at the cognitive, cultural level is the paradigm. Figure 10.1 is a representation of this process. The strategies that managers advocate and those that emerge through the social and political processes previously described are typically configured within the bounds of this paradigm. Changes going on within or without the organisation will affect organisational performance; however even if managers, as individuals, perceive such changes they may not necessarily acknowledge them as impinging on the strategy or performance of their organisation. The examples of this are common. Executive teams who discount competitor activity or changes in buyer behaviour as aberrations; who persist with outmoded practices or dying products, successful in the past, but now facing declining markets or competitor substitution; management teams that choose to ignore or minimise the evidence of market research, the implications of which question tried and tested ways of doing things. Any manager who has found it frustrating to use apparently objective evidence to persuade a management team of the need to change their way of thinking or their behaviour will be familiar with the problem.

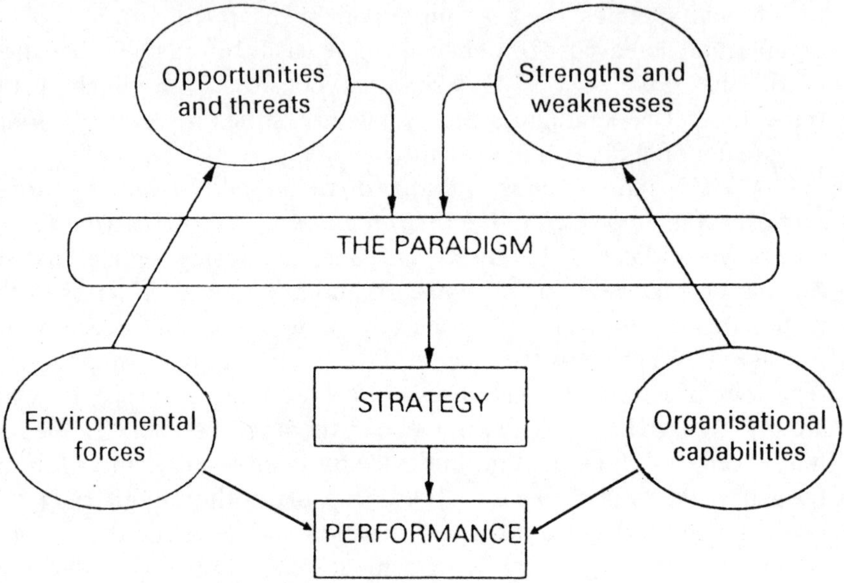


*Note:* A paradigm is a core set of beliefs and assumptions which fashion an organisation's view of itself and its environment

**Figure 10.1** Strategy development – a cultural perspective

The likelihood of the paradigm dominating the development of strategy and causing resistance to significant change becomes clearer when the wider cultural context in which it is embedded is considered. The paradigm is a cognitive structure or mechanism: however, this set of taken for granted assumptions and beliefs, which is more or less collectively owned, is likely to be hedged about and protected by a web of cultural artefacts. The routinised ways that members of the organisation behave towards each other, and between parts of the organisation; the rituals of organisational life which provide a programme for the way members respond to given situations and prescribe 'the way we do things around here'. The more formalised control systems and rewards which delineate the important areas of activity focus. The stories told which embed the present in organisational history; the type of language and expressions commonly used and the organisational symbols such as logos, offices, cars and titles which become a shorthand representation of the nature of the organisation. Moreover it is likely that the most powerful managerial groupings in the organisation are those most closely associated with the key constructs of the paradigm. It would therefore be a mistake to conceive of the paradigm as merely a set of beliefs removed from organisational action. It lies within a cultural web which bonds it to the action of organisational life. It is therefore continually, if gradually, evolving. This notion of the paradigm and the cultural web is shown in Figure 10.2 and the company cases shown in Table 10.1.

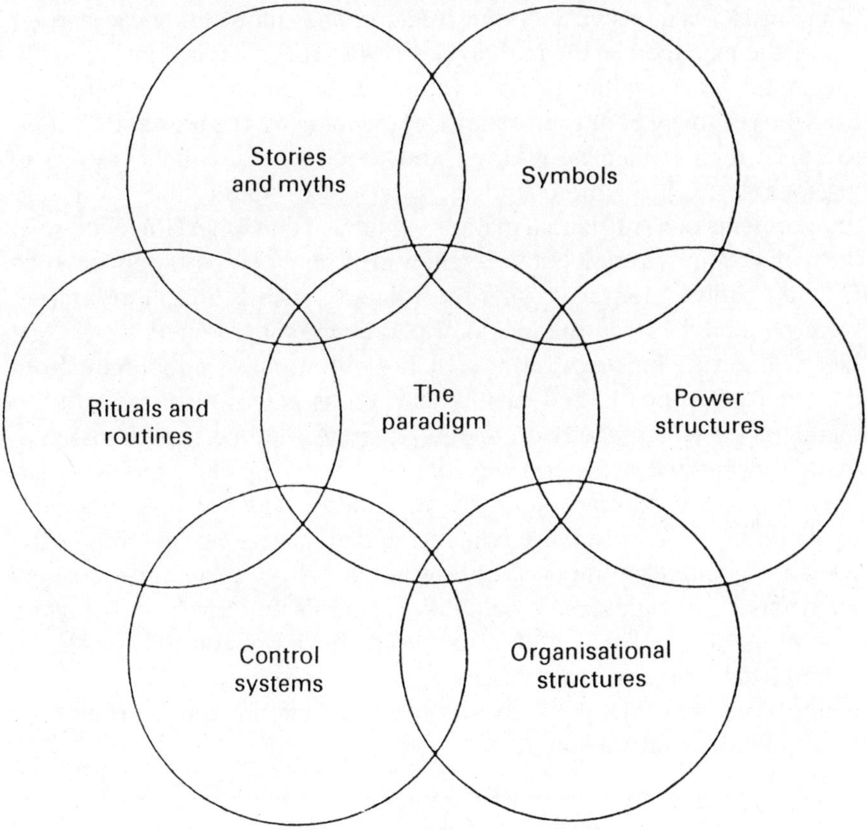


**Figure 10.2** The 'cultural web' of an organisation

## *Culture audits by managers*

The cultural web itself can be used as a convenient device for a culture audit. The company cases shown in Table 10.1 are drawn up on the basis of work undertaken by managers themselves on the culture of their organisations. It is an exercise which is used frequently by the author to allow managers to 'discover' the nature of their organisation in cultural terms, the way it impacts on the strategy they are following, and the difficulties of changing it.

---

### *Case A: A menswear retailer*

Company A is a menswear clothing retailer. The culture audit was carried out by the managers in the mid- to late 1980s. This company had a highly successful decade in the 1970s. As a menswear outfitter it had benefited from the relatively poor performance of the menswear tailors as they tried to adjust their strategies: its tried and tested downmarket, low price, 'reasonable value' merchandise offer also fitted the customer requirements of a substantial market segment at that time. However, with the revitalisation of competitive retailers in the early 1980s its performance suffered badly. Attempts to shift the strategy towards a fashion offering were painfully slow in the face of a paradigm that assumed a low cost, high volume buying driven approach, heavily emphasising sourcing from the Far East. Shops had always been seen as places to dispose of the merchandise which had been bought: there was little comprehension of marketing and the wider concepts of merchandising. Outsiders who had been brought in to effect such changes did not last for very long, and market research reports were reinterpreted to make sense in terms of the taken for granted assumptions of how to trade. Even when the managers intellectually recognised the cultural constraints under which they were labouring, the political and ritualised behaviour, controls on costs, hierarchical organisation, managerial inbreeding and symbolic connections with hierarchy and the past, militated against questioning behaviour or significant changes.

---

### *Case B: A consultancy partnership*

Company B is a consultancy partnership linked to an accountancy firm. Here the emphasis had always been on providing a broad general service to meet client needs in a professional manner, under the close scrutiny of partners. The result was a service to customers which was reliable but avoided risk, and a belief within the firm that it could turn its hand to anything. Since the 'product' was seen by many as the report at the end of the assignment, close supervision of the assignment, and especially report writing, was seen as essential and was mirrored by close attention to monitoring consultancy activities as a way of ensuring professional service, the utilisation of consultants' time and the control of costs. This was supported by a superstructure of partners, many of whom were chartered accountants whose role was not always very clear but who jealously guarded a fragmented and informal organisation structure and cultural trappings, preserving of their influence, autonomy and power. By the late 1980s, new senior partners believed that the consultancy lacked focus in the face of more targeted competitors, but it was an organisation with any number of ways to frustrate the change agent.

---

### *Case C: A regional newspaper*

Company C is a regional newspaper business operating in a market in which it had enjoyed long-standing dominance with its local evening newspaper. It now faced increasing competitor pressure from free newspapers and entry by competitors historically based elsewhere. Moreover a changing local population meant less traditional loyalty to the newspaper – and longer-term developments of media alternatives for the public raised both strategic opportunities and possible threats. The need was for a substantial short-term rethink of competitive strategy and longer term rethink of the direction of the business. Yet the culture audit undertaken by the managers revealed a taken for granted view that their paid-for daily newspaper 'would always be around', and that the local community somehow needed them. Moreover the technology, structure and routines of the business did little to promote strategic thinking: the business was necessarily run on short-term deadlines – hours, not days – the 'macho' self-image of those running the business, and the vertical, hierarchical ways of doing business, prevented a free flow of ideas across management boundaries. Suggestions by some younger managers that the prime purpose of the business was to create an effective advertising medium (the main source of revenue) were set aside given the dominant belief that 'we are a *news*paper': a view reinforced by the symbolic significance of the presses, the associated technical jargon, street distribution system and the stories linked to news gathering and coverage.

---

**Table10.1** How managers define the cultural web – three cases

| A<br>A menswear clothing retailer | B<br>A consultancy partnership | C<br>A regional newspaper |
|---|---|---|
| *Paradigm*<br>We sell to 'the working lad's market'<br>Retailing skills (as they define them) centrally important<br>Retailing is about buying: 'we sell what we buy'<br>Volume is vital<br>Staff experience and loyalty important<br>Low cost operations (eg distribution channels) important<br>A 'big-man' view of management<br>(Note what is *not* here: retailing is not about shop ambience, service etc) | *Paradigm*<br>We are the biggest, the best, certainly the safest<br>Client satisfaction at all costs<br>Any job is worth doing – and we can do it<br>Professionalism is important<br>Avoid risks<br>(The implication is that this consultancy is concerned to provide a very wide range of services, but it is unlikely to provide services which are contentious or risky) | *Paradigm*<br>We are in the newspaper business<br>Our paid-for daily will always be there<br>Readers will pay for news<br>Advertisers need newspapers |
| *Power*<br>The chairman regarded as all-powerful – 'but nicely'<br>Divisions of power significant: the major menswear business, vs ('peripheral') businesses; head office operations vs field retail operations<br>Insiders with experience traditionally powerful: outsiders without company experience not powerful and do not last long | *Power*<br>Diffuse and unclear power base in a partnership structure<br>However an external power base clearly important in the parent audit firm | *Power*<br>The parent company – a newspaper group<br>The autocratic CEO<br>Department rivalry between production, commercial and editorial departments |
| *Organisation*<br>Highly compartmentalised operations with vertical reporting relationships (eg buying distinct from store operations)<br>Every department with a director leading to a heavy superstructure<br>Top down decision-making with board 'fingers in every pie'<br>Paternalistic | *Organisation*<br>The regional partnership structure of the organisation giving a flat if complex matrix<br>Decision-making through a networking system loose and flexible but based on 'who you know' | *Organisation*<br>Vertical, hierarchical system with little lateral communication and much vertical referral.<br>Autocratic management style |

| | | |
|---|---|---|
| *Control systems*<br>Margin control<br>Long established 'proven' rigid and complex systems<br>Paper-based control systems | *Control systems*<br>Emphasis on time control and utilisation of consultants | *Control systems*<br>Emphasis on targeting and budgeting<br>To achieve a low cost operation |
| *Rituals and routines*<br>Long established merchandise sourcing in the Far East<br>Introduction to the company way of doing things through attrition and training: 'outsiders serve an apprenticeship until they conform'<br>Emphasis on pragmatic rather than analytic decisions<br>Lack of questioning or forcing: 'you can challenge provided I feel comfortable'<br>Heavy emphasis on grading systems<br>Promotions only within functions | Rituals and routines<br>Writing and re-writing of reports – 'the product of the firm'<br>Partners signatures on anything that goes to clients<br>Gentlemanly behaviour – particularly with clients and partners | *Rituals and routines*<br>'Slaves to time' to meet deadlines for publication<br>'Product' developed in hours and minutes, not days and months<br>Long working hours common<br>Ritualised executive meetings at senior level |
| *Stories*<br>Big buying deals of the past<br>Paternalistic leaders (usually chairman) of the past<br>More recent 'villainous' leaders who helped cause problems<br>'The Mafia' who excluded outsiders and achieved their exit | *Stories*<br>Big fee assignments<br>Big disasters and failures<br>Stories of the dominance of the audit practice<br>Mavericks who would not follow the systems | *Stories*<br>Macho personalities and behaviour<br>Scoops and coverage of major events<br>Stories of the past<br>Major errors in print<br>The defeat of the unions |
| *Symbols*<br>The separate executive directors' corridor<br>Use of initials to designate senior executives and 'Sir' for the chairman<br>The dining room for directors and selected senior executives – but against what criteria?<br>Named and numbered car parking spaces rigidly adhered to | *Symbols*<br>The partnership structure itself<br>The symbols of partnership – the tea service, the office size, partners' secretaries, partners' dining rooms<br>One regional partnership that had always refused to integrate with other partnerships | *Symbols*<br>Symbols of hierarchy: the MD's Jaguar, portable phones, car parking spaces etc<br>The 'press'<br>Technical production jargon<br>The street vendors |

## PROBLEMS OF STRATEGIC CHANGE

If we view the process of strategic management in such ways, the phenomenon of incremental strategic development in organisations is also explained rather differently. Rather than being a logical testing out of strategies in action, strategic management can be seen as an *organisational response over time* to a business environment which is essentially *internally constructed* rather than objectively understood. The idea that external events have a self-evident reality is clearly not so for us as individuals: two spectators from opposing sides watching a sports event will interpret reasons for success and failure quite differently and quite partially. We should not expect it to be very different for groups of managers.

### *Resistance to change*

This explanation of resistance to change also helps us understand how strategies come about in organisations. Faced with pressures for change, managers are likely to deal with the situation in ways which are in line with the paradigm and the cultural, social and political norms of organisational life. This raises difficulties when managing strategic change, for it may be that the action required is outside the scope of the paradigm and the constraints of the cultural web – that members of the organisation would be required to change substantially their core beliefs or 'the way we do things around here'. Desirable as this may be, the evidence is that this does not occur easily. Managers are much more likely to attempt to deal with the situation by searching for what they can understand and cope with in terms of the existing paradigm. In other words, they will attempt to minimise the extent to which they are faced with ambiguity and uncertainty by looking for that which is familiar. Faced with a stimulus for action, for example declining performance, managers first seek for means of improving the implementation of existing strategy, perhaps through the tightening of controls. In effect, they will tighten up their accepted way of operating. If this is not effective, then a change of strategy may occur, but a change which is in line with the existing paradigm.

For instance in the menswear clothing example (case A), the early attempts to the company to be 'more fashionable' took the form of trying to copy fashionable merchandise from UK boutiques, have it cheapened in the Far East and distributed through their low cost distribution channels in order to sell it below competitive prices. It was a merchandise and buying driven response, rather than anything to do with the expectations of customers; nor did it address the ambience of stores, the service of the staff, the behaviour of managers in head office, or indeed the fundamental quality of the product range. The evidence is that strategic management is, in the main, the predominant application of the familiar and that a fundamental change to the paradigm is unlikely until the attempt to reconstruct strategy in the image of the existing paradigm is demonstrably unsuccessful.

It is difficult to change aspects of the paradigm unless such changes are evolutionary. Challenges to the legitimacy of constructs within that paradigm are not only likely to be disturbing because they attack those beliefs which are central to managerial life, they will also be interpreted as threatening by political elites in the organisation whose roles are likely to be closely associated with the constructs of the paradigm. Those who believe that an objective, analytical assessment of, for example, a changing environment can yield knowledge which managers should interpret intellectually and objectively, and assimilate in such a way as to change strategy, neglect the understanding that such analysis may well achieve a political rather than intellectual response and might well lead to heavy resistance. For example the change agent who attempted to introduce a revised strategy in the consultancy firm (case B) was faced with resistance from some of the most senior and powerful partners trying to preserve the potential threats to partnership structure and the professional nature of the consultancy.

### *Strategic drift*

In these circumstances it is likely that, over time, the phenomenon of 'strategic drift'[4] will occur: that is, gradually, perhaps imperceptibly, the strategy of the organisation will become less and less in line with the environment in which the organisation operates. This may be a process which takes very many years and may not be discerned by the managers until the drift becomes so marked that performance decline results. It is then that more fundamental changes in strategy are likely to occur. The reasons for this drift arise out of the explanations given above. Managers are likely to discount evidence contrary to the paradigm but readily absorb that which is in line with the paradigm. Change which is within the paradigm is therefore likely to be more comfortable. Moreover, radical challenges to the paradigm are likely to give rise to political resistance and reaction which further embeds the organisation in its existing strategy: and since the organisation is likely to be making changes of an incremental nature anyway, managers can point to the extent that change is occurring.

The outcome of processes of decision-making of this kind is not likely to be the careful, logical, adaptive strategy making which keeps in line with environmental change. Rather it is likely to be an adaptation in line with the perceived management wisdom as enshrined in the paradigm. Nonetheless the forces in the environment will have an effect on performance. Over time this may well give rise to the sort of drift shown in Figure 10.3 (Mode 1) in which the organisation's strategy gradually, if imperceptively, moves away from the environmental forces at work. This pattern of drift is made more difficult to detect and reverse because not only are changes being made in strategy – albeit within the parameters of the paradigm – but, since such changes are the application of the familiar, they may achieve some short-term improvement in performance, thus tending to legitimise the action taken. As this drift becomes recognised the strategy of the organisation is likely to enter a period of flux (Figure 10.3, Mode 2) in which there is no clear direction and a good deal of disquiet and counterargument about the strategic direction of the

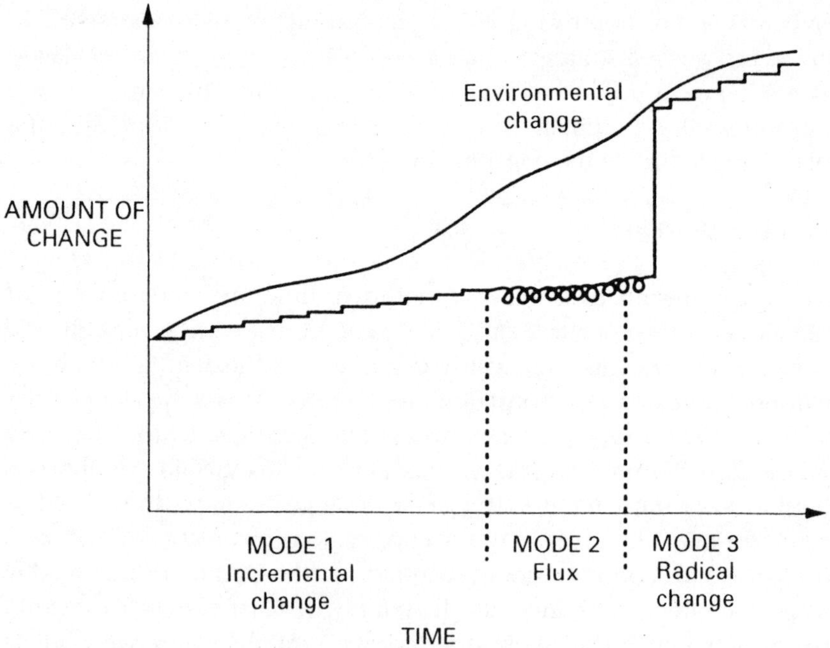


**Figure 10.3** Patterns of strategic development – drift, flux and radical change

organisation. This will be likely to affect performance negatively and, perhaps, be followed by a more radical change in strategy (Figure 10.3, Mode 3).[5]

## IMPLICATIONS FOR MANAGING STRATEGIC CHANGE

The main aim of discussing these links between the development of strategy, organisational culture and the social, political and symbolic behaviour of managers has been to provide explanations of the reasons for the pattern of strategic development observed in organisations, and in particular the strategic inertia and problems of managing strategic change experienced by managers. However, the explanations do help in providing some guidelines in the management of strategic change.

### *Traditional planning approaches*

Views on strategic management espoused by managers tend to be rooted in traditional planning models of strategy. Strategic change may be seen as equivalent to the planning of strategy implementation. Managing strategic change becomes a matter of planning how the systems and structures of the organisation can be employed to achieve behaviour in line with the logic of the strategy.

The rationale for this view is clear enough, if dubious. If managers are clear about the aims and objectives of the business in the long term, and they have carried out an analysis of the factors affecting the strategy of the business, then they can make logical choices from strategic options. If the resulting decision on strategy is logical, then it is capable of being planned in detail and systematised in terms of implementation – and because it is logical and planned, it will work. The problem with this notion of planned change is that it neglects many of the processes that we have seen to be central in actual processes of strategy formulation and change: namely the sociocultural and symbolic processes which preserve current ways of doing things; the cognitive bounds of those who take and influence decisions; and the importance of political processes, including the potential of analysis to be politically threatening. There is nothing wrong with analytic, planning approaches as *thinking* devices for strategic management: they do not, however, address the *process* of managing strategic choice or strategic change. Issues relating to the planning of strategic change need to take account of the sociopolitical and cultural realities of management described in this chapter. They also need to recognise that, certainly when it comes to major strategic change, paradigm shifts are likely to be important, and they are obviously the most difficult of all to achieve.

For such planning systems to be useful, there already needs to exist a climate capable of embracing and promoting strategic change: and the developments of this by managers needs to be understood and managed in ways which address the cultural constraints on strategy discussed earlier.

## Managing strategic change

This chapter has not set out to deal primarily with mechanisms of strategic change. However, there are some guidelines on such mechanisms that are informed by the frameworks which have been discussed.

If strategy development in organisations is driven by the taken for granted assumptions that have been called the paradigm and the aspects of organisational culture that surround and protect it, the first implication is the importance of surfacing that which is taken for granted. One way in which this might be facilitated is to undertake the sort of culture audit described above, which helps to make explicit that which is taken for granted, and to generate managerial debate about the cultural barriers to change that exist. These might be political in nature, to do with the organisational or control systems within the organisation; or they may be more symbolic in nature, manifested in the stories or symbols of tradition and history that exist, or in the everyday routines that people take for granted. The important point is that such aspects of culture cannot be challenged or changed unless they are explicit and they will not necessarily become explicit through the debates on strategy that may take place within the planning agenda.

## Creating a climate for change

Even where a clear direction of strategy has been established, the likelihood of achieving fundamental strategic change is low unless the climate for change exists. The acceptance of such change is likely to depend either on a widely accepted perceived need for it, or a significant trigger for change such as crisis or major threat. Such threat may typically result from a major downturn in performance, perhaps resulting from the sort of strategic drift discussed in this chapter, or from major competitive moves in the market place. There is however, evidence that some chief executives 'fabricate' or 'enhance' organisational stimuli to create a climate suited to more fundamental questioning of that which is taken for granted. This may include inflating internal negative performance indicators or external threats; setting up internal devices for challenging the status quo; or visibly signalling the need for change by political manoeuvres. Such activity may take on both political and symbolic significance, for example by the removal of the 'old guard', or the visible passing over of ideas from traditional power elites; and the encouragement of 'young turks' in the organisation, or the adoption of recommendations of those advocating more substantial change.

Such political activity is common but, in isolation, can be counterproductive unless members of the organisation see it as an opportunity to contribute to organisational revitalisation. Yet in many organisations hierarchical structures, autocratic leadership or unwritten rules about deference and delicacy in questioning may militate against such opportunities. Although there has been a good deal of advocacy of the need for more open 'organic management systems' to replace traditional hierarchies where change is required, senior management may still not understand the responsibility they hold as role models and builders of structures which encourage challenge and questioning.

### *Interventions by outsiders*

Fundamental strategic change may also be associated with the intervention of 'outsiders'. By outsiders is meant those who either literally come from outside the organisation, for example as a new chief executive, or those who are not, by origin or inclination, part of the mainstream culture. Such individuals bring different perspectives to the organisations, perhaps rooted in the paradigm of their previous organisational experience; they see the context of the organisation afresh, and are less linked to the political systems and traditions of the organisation. Yet the value of outsiders as agents of questioning and change is often overlooked in firms: non-executive directors are too infrequently encouraged to question the taken for granted; consultants may feel their recommendations have to be within the current paradigm in order to stand any chance of being implemented; and boards, whilst ready to condone, even encourage, strategic management development for middle or senior executives, often argue that they personally are too busy to step outside the task of running the business.

### *Providing signals and symbols*

Managing change is often conceived by executives as control systems and structural changes; however these are typically thought of as means of monitoring, rather than signalling, change. In fact they should be seen as both. A change in emphasis, for example from control of costs to an emphasis on monitoring effective customer service is not simply a means of monitoring the progress of a changed strategy, it is also a major signal of a change in corporate culture. The example can be taken further. Too few executives conceive of strategic change in terms of the symbols and routines which underpin organisational life. The executive who is planning change needs to ensure that the routines of the organisation are changed in ways which affect the everyday behaviour of those in the organisation. For example in the menswear retailer described earlier, it was neither written plans nor the words of managers that had the most significant affect on staff; it was when staff were, for example, required to wear clothes sold in the shops in which they worked that the changes became meaningful to them. As one executive put it, it was then 'they began to wear the new strategy' that had been developed.

Symbols of change are important for they signal change at the level of mundane reality for those operating in the organisation. There are countless examples, from changes in company logos, the expensive withdrawal from the market of old stocks, the closure of privileged dining facilities for executives, or factories associated with the traditions of a business, to changes in language and terminology employed in a firm; changes to informal forms of address or clothing styles by senior executives, to dramatic signalling of change such as the smashing of old equipment associated with the past of a business in front of the workforce.

## CONCLUSIONS

This article provides a framework for the consideration of strategic management in terms of the social and cultural processes in organisations: it has proposed explanations for the strategic inertia that exists in organisations and the consequent strategic drift that can occur, and has also proposed ways to consider the sorts of managerial change processes in cultural terms that can help achieve strategic change in organisations.

The core of the argument is that it is the social, political, cultural and cognitive dimensions of managerial activities which both give rise to the sort of incremental strategic change typical in organisation – but which can also be employed to galvanise more fundamental strategic change. These aspects of management are employed by managers in their everyday working lives. Managers behave in ways which are political and symbolic: such approaches provide familiar, if not explicit, tools of management. Managers also recognise the powerful influence of cultural and political systems. What they lack is an explicit framework to make sense of the links between strategy, culture and managerial processes of strategic change. This paper has set out to provide this framework and thus of better considering problems and means of strategic change in such terms.

## References

1. Quinn, J B (1980) *Strategies for Change: Logical Incrementalism.* Irwin.
2. Grinyer, P H and Spender, J C (1989) '*Turnaround: Managerial Recipes for Strategic Success: The Fall and Rise of the Newton Chambers Group*' Associated Business Press; Pettigrew, A M (1985) *The Awakening Giant*, Basil Blackwell; Johnson, G (1987) *Strategic Change and the Management Process*, Basil Blackwell.
3. Schein, E H (1986) *Organizational Culture and Leadership*, Jossey Bass, p 6
4. Johnson, G (1988) 'Re-thinking incrementalism', *Strategic Management Journal* 9, pp 75–91
5. Mintzberg, H (1978) 'Patterns in strategy formation', *Management Science*, May, pp 934–48

## Further Reading

For readers who wish to follow-up the links between the processual issues raised in this paper and other concepts and techniques of strategic management, see *Exploring Corporate Strategy* by Gerry Johnson and Kevan Scholes (Prentice Hall 2nd edition 1988; 3rd edition 1993).

11

# INFORMATION MANAGEMENT AND ORGANISATIONAL STRATEGY

*John Ward*

## INTRODUCTION

Over the last 30 years the cost of information technology (IT) has been decreasing dramatically. In general terms hardware costs have been reducing at 20 per cent or more per annum. In the last ten years the capabilities of the technology have increased equally dramatically. As a result it is now feasible to provide powerful technology, effectively 'on the desk', to enable managers, professionals and clerical staff to carry out information based tasks more productively and exploit the information resources of the organisation in new ways.

Over the same period companies have had to achieve success in increasingly demanding competitive environments. Organisations have been forced to seek major improvements in product quality, or provide new services to create sustainable advantages or obtain significant reductions in the costs of business or all of these. Achieving these step changes in business performance has usually involved radical changes in what the organisation does and/or how business is conducted and managed. Many enterprises have achieved some of these changes by investment in new information systems (IS) and the supporting technology. Others have found that their ability to change has been inhibited by the poor quality of their information resources and their inability to obtain the benefits expected from IS/IT investments.

The traditional view of IS/IT was that it provided a means of improving what was already being done 'manually' – to reduce the cost of clerical activities by improving productivity or to enhance managements' effectiveness by the provision of better information, thus improving the control and planning of the business. In the early 1980s a number of examples of businesses who had invested in IS/IT to gain direct competitive advantages were being quoted by consultants and academics to argue a more strategic role for information management. Some of the examples such as American Airlines, American Hospital Supplies and Thomsons Holidays acquired almost legendary status! Behind the hype was the reality that in most of the examples the organisations had used new IS investments to change the conduct of business in some significant way. They had either transformed aspects of how the industry worked; created new valued services for customers or changed the cost-structure of the industry, ie used IS/IT to change the competitive environment in their favour. Many organisations now understand that information systems investments which lead to greater exploitation of information resources are an essential ingredient of any business strategy. As yet however, it would appear that fewer organisations understand either how to identify which investments are likely to create advantages or how to manage the delivery of the new information systems to ensure that the advantages are realised. These are key challenges for management in determining and implementing appropriate business strategies in the 1990s.

## THE ROLE OF IS/IT: A TRADITIONAL VIEW

Whilst the purpose of this chapter is to consider the strategic challenges of the 1990s, it is worth a brief recap on how the use of IS/IT has evolved for two reasons:

1. An organisation's existing suite of information systems is a product of the past. Hence the organisation's ability to move forward successfully will be affected by the quality, variety and extent of the existing base of information, systems and technology. That base may be an asset – a firm foundation on which to build – or a liability that is unsuitable as a basis for future development. The capability of the associated IT people and skills may also significantly influence the chances of future success and they will be closely related to the existing systems base.
2. The management attitude to IS/IT investments will also be heavily influenced by that past, both in terms of understanding the potential benefits available and in having the confidence that further investments will deliver the expected benefits. There is sometimes a huge gulf of credibility in management's view of IS/IT between the vision presented by the IT industry and academics, and the disappointing reality of previous benefits obtained.

Both of these factors will influence an organisation's ability to manage IS investments successfully in a more complex, challenging environment. Hence the past and what it has taught us needs to be assessed in the context of the future demands.

Until the 1980s the evolution of information management could be considered as having been through three eras:

### *Pre-1960*

Prior to 1960 before information technologies (initially 'computers') were available, all information was dealt with manually or with basic electro-mechanical devices. Information was barely understood as a business resource. It was something that was embedded in the majority of business processes, some parts of which – normally accounting information – were extracted to provide business control. A simplified view perhaps, but essentially true.

### *1960s to 1970s*

From 1960 onwards the concept of Data Processing (DP) developed with the arrival of large computers whose capabilities slowly evolved to provide batch and on-line automated processing of business transactions. Given the early high costs of computers and the complexity of systems development, investments could only be justified by significant cost displacements, mainly people savings. Hence only high volume, repetitive, relatively structured processes could justifiably be automated. This led to two major problems that still exist today:

- The limited view some managers have of the benefits available from IS/IT – cost reduction, essentially through people savings – and the consequent view that all IS/IT investments must be financially justified. The latter view has been very prevalent during the late 1980s recession when the term 'Value for money from IT' was on many managing directors lips – and was interpreted as the need to show a clear financial payback from all IT investments.
- In order to produce the most cost-effective system it was better to use information in the system in the simplest and most efficient way for the particular process being computerised. Little regard was paid either to the interfaces with other processes and systems or to other uses of the same information. Since only some functions were automated a mixed manual and computer based information resource

was produced and even the latter was not designed as a coherent whole.

## 1970s onwards

During the 1970s the demands from management to get more value from the information stored on computers to improve the effectiveness of decision-making, exposed the problems which had been developing during the DP 'era'. The partial and fragmented information resource was a severe limitation when required to provide comprehensive, coherent management information systems (MIS) and the new systems were difficult to justify by cost reduction – how many people would better information save? The latter problem was overcome by using per cent reductions in working capital, increased sales or profits and avoided costs to provide figures for financial evaluation – ie the issue was essentially fudged.

There was a technical solution available to resolve the information resource issue. Database software was the solution, albeit a costly, slow and painful one given the need to capture new, and restructure existing, data in a way which met all systems needs effectively plus the need to reengineer most existing systems to use the new databases. Many organisations pursued the database dream in the late 1970s only for it to turn into a nightmare of high cost and little apparent benefit by 1980. At least a partial solution arrived with the personal computer (PC) which enabled managers to produce some management information, initially locally but eventually on a wider scale once the PCs could be networked together. But the result, whilst undoubtedly providing localised improvements in management effectiveness, did not resolve the problems of poorly integrated systems and a fragmented information resource, and often made the situation worse. In the late 1980s many organisations were readdressing the need to provide coherent databases to support effective use of information in the operations and control of the business.

In summary, many organisations face the challenges of the future with an inheritance from the last 30 years which consists of fragmented information resources and systems whose integration was achieved by fitting them together retrospectively, not by forethought and design. Two of the conclusions of the 'Management in the 1990s' (Scott Morton 1990)[1] research programme by MIT are particularly pertinent:

1. that integration (internal and external) provides the main opportunities for improving business effectiveness through information systems;

2. Information Resource Management will remain a major problem and limit the rate at which business changes can be made.

Or, in the words of the oft-quoted Irish farmer when asked to provide a traveller with directions – 'If I was going there sir, I wouldn't start from here'. Another way of putting it, as an IT manager in a major manufacturing company said to me recently, is 'the most logical thing to do would be to scrap everything we've got and start all over again!'

## THE STRATEGIC ROLE OF INFORMATION SYSTEMS

Whether or not an organisation developed good DP and MIS systems was very much under its own control and the quality of those systems probably only had a marginal effect on corporate performance overall. Evidence from those who have studied the use of IS/IT in depth over the period 1960–1985 such as Paul Strassman (1985)[2], is that on average DP type investments have produced efficiency gains but only sufficient to give a 10 per cent return on the investment overall, not the much larger savings often claimed. Whether or not MIS investments have made managers more effective is far less clear – how well the systems are used is the key and that depends very much on the calibre of the management themselves. There is some evidence that giving poor managers new systems merely speeds up the mess!

The key differences between the traditional and strategic roles of IS/IT are:

- the external impact of the investments;
- the degree of associated business change;
- the resulting need to change job roles and organisation structures.

These are quite obvious points given that the purpose of the investments is to gain some business advantage through change of conduct of business, but the implications of these key differences for executives and managers considering IS/IT investments are significant.

In recent years, many writers have attempted to describe these implications to management. Some, such as Davis and Davidson (1991)[3] have argued that many future products will be heavily information based and companies need to 'informationalise' their products to increase their value to consumers. They, along with many others, also emphasise the need to consider systems in terms of business processes, not organisational structures. This is not new. Systems theory has suggested for a long time that information systems should be implemented to improve business activities, *not* to match the organisation structure in which those activities are performed. Others have taken the arguments further, in two directions, proposing that organisations should be designed around their information resources, *and* that business processes should be redesigned around the information flows associated with those processes.

In considering the first of these, Drucker (1988)[4] made the following observation.

> We are entering a period of change – a *shift* from the command and control organisation, *to the information based organisation* – the organisation of knowledge specialists . . ., it is the management challenge of the future.

Zuboff (1988)[5] talks about 'informating' the workforce, whereby job scope is extended due to the information available to the clerical and professional staff, 'empowering' them to make more decisions without the need for functional separation and control of activities. This leads to team based organisation structures rather than hierarchical ones – also proposed by Drucker. Handy (1991)[6] opens up the whole subject of what future organisations will look like and speculates on how they will be structured, if at all. Like others he suggests that 'intellectual capital' will become the critical strategic resource from which organisations achieve advantage. That is almost certainly already true – the problem is how to unlock that capital and exploit it through the people in the organisation without losing control of the business. All of these writers propose novel structures which revolve around the organisation's information resources and are made possible by new uses of information technology. However, how many chief executives today ask either of the following questions when deciding on a new organisation structure?

- What effect will our proposed reorganisation have on the use of our information resources or systems?
- Could we reorganise to exploit our information resources or systems to greater advantage?

It seems that such questions will only get asked when some imperative exists other than solely as internal recognition that there is a need to improve how things are done. That pressure for change will – almost inevitably – come from outside, due to general economic conditions, major changes in the industry or the specific actions of other companies with whom the firm competes or trades, ie by forces which cause business processes to be reassessed first, and then drive a subsequent review of the organisation. That is not to suggest it should happen that way, merely that it is the more likely sequence of events. Hence, we need to understand how information systems have the potential to change business relationships and processes.

## INFORMATION SYSTEMS AND TECHNOLOGY AS CAUSES OF BUSINESS CHANGE

Whilst it was the power of the computer that enabled information based tasks to be carried out more productively, it is the more recent development of communications technologies which have enabled business processes to be rethought. Networks which link organisations together and improve internal linkages within organisations, combined with well organised information mean that business processes can be rationalised, reconfigured and even eliminated. The MIT Report – Management in the 1990s – explains this rationale at length. One paper in the report by Venkatraman (1991)[7] entitled 'IT Induced Business Reconfiguration' discusses a five level model which relates the potential benefits available from IS/IT investments, to the degree of business and organisational change needed to obtain them. The lowest level 'localised exploitation' (low benefit, low change) relates to the traditional approach to investment described earlier in this chapter. The four other levels are of particular relevance to the arguments here. They are defined as:

- **Internal integration** – which involves some internal reorganisation and the creation of new job roles and relationships to obtain the benefits of systems which integrate major business activities. Whilst change is needed, it is entirely within the organisation's ability to define the changes and implement them.
- **Business process redesign** – involves the realignment of business activities to improve relationships with customers and suppliers and hence the overall performance of the businesses. This may well create direct external systems links and require internal processes to be redefined to fit better the overall set of processes in the industry, ie it will require change in the way the business is conducted.
- **Business relationship redesign** – involves the reconsideration of *how* information is shared and used by the organisation and its business partners. This is more than merely linking the processes together and may require the development of new relationships based on mutually designed information systems, and probably further organisational changes. Some activities may be done by different parties, to avoid duplicated effort or to enable subcontracting of non-core activities. This will normally require new management

control systems to monitor the performance of these new business relationships.

- **Business scope redefinition** – involves the realisation that based on points one to three above the organisation may be able to extend its market or rationalise its activities to grow or become more profitable as part of a restructuring of the industry. This will obviously depend not only on the extent and quality of its information systems but also on the vision of the management to see how new opportunities can be derived from its information resources. In this case the organisation may change what it does as well as how it does it and this may well require more external industry information being available to the executive team to decide on future directions. Figure 11.1 summarises the relationships.

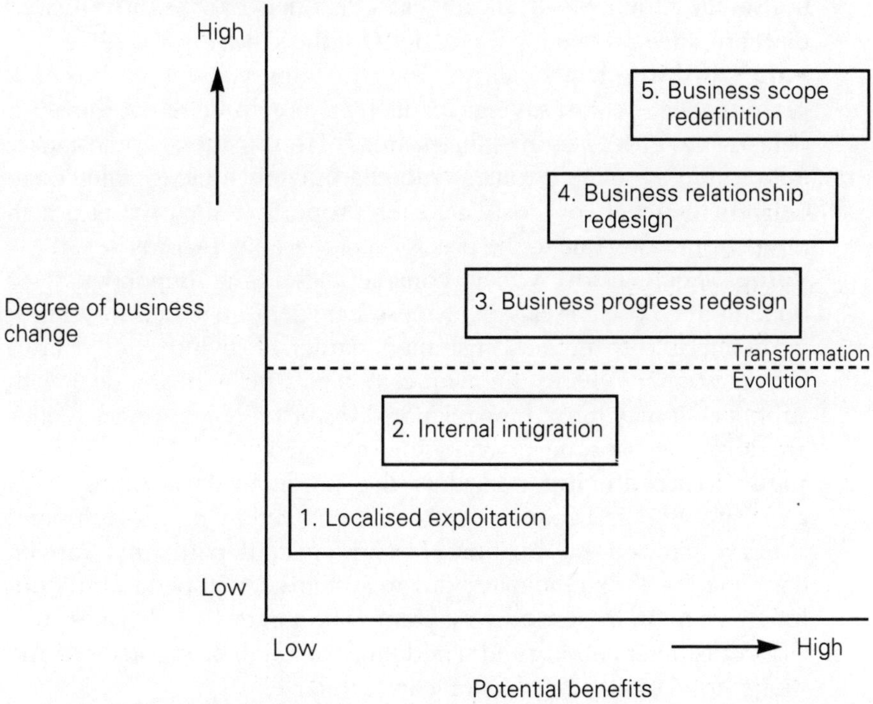


**Figure 11.1** The relationship between the benefits of IS investments and the degree of business change needed to realise them

Whilst this may seem rather theoretical, many companies are moving through these various stages of evolution and transformation, often at a pace that is controlled by others in the industry. The choice is either to react to change as and when it arises – effectively deal with threats to the business – or attempt to understand the implications and identify the potential opportunities for the business. The key message of the MIT study is that benefits from IS/IT investments are inextricably linked over the long term with business and organisational change.

In the book *Information Economics*, Parker et al (1988)[8] look in more detail at the potential benefits that improved information systems can provide in terms of how they affect the value adding processes of an industry and a particular business. They describe four types of benefits which are interrelated in much the same way as described by Venkatraman, ie that the higher order benefits are dependent on achieving benefits of the earlier types. The suggested sequence is as follows.

1. **Cost displacement** through automation of business tasks to improve efficiency. For example, preparing invoices by computer and transmitting them electronically via a data network is more efficient than printing and posting them, both for the sender and receiver.
2. **Value linking** which allows for the improvement to business performance, not just savings made, by a more precise coordination of tasks and processes in different areas of the business. For instance, being able to bill customers more accurately due to immediate delivery feedback, or satisfy a greater proportion of customer orders direct from stock due to the precision of the stock records.
3. **Value acceleration** which considers the time dependency of benefits and costs in related business activities due to better systems, eg being able to invoice customers earlier or giving sales data to buyers sooner, giving them time to negotiate a better deal with suppliers. It may mean new relationships between existing activities are developed or some activities are bypassed.
4. **Value restructuring** considers the productivity resulting from reorganisation and change of job roles enabled by new systems and better organised information. For instance, departments can be combined or even eliminated due to systems developed to carry out functions in an integrated way. Information intensive activities such as forecasting, planning and scheduling can often be rationalised and reorganised to be more accurate and effective.

By bringing these various views together a picture can be drawn of the overall information management environment which organisations face in the 1990s – Table 11.1 attempts to summarise this by considering the purpose in IS investments and their focus.

Stages 1 and 2 in Table 11.1 are those described earlier as 'traditional' DP and MIS eras, although the latter has recently been revitalised by the concept of executive information systems (EIS) whereby top management have direct access to a range of internal and external information for use in strategic decision-making. How many of these systems actually deliver the pertinent strategic information to the 'board' and how many are just glossier presentations of existing management information is not yet clear, but the latter are probably more prevalent than the former.

**Table 11.1** The information management environment

| Focus / Purpose | Operational efficiency | Management effectiveness | Business advantage through change |
|---|---|---|---|
| Internal | 1. Data Processing – automation of business tasks and processes | 2. Management Information Systems [and 'Executive Information Systems'] | 3. Internal Business Integration by process, job and organisation redesign |
| External | 4. Electronic links between organisations automating data exchanges | 5. Sharing information by direct access from one company to another's information resources | 6. External Business Integration, changing the roles of the firms in the industry |

Whether an organisation then moves towards stage three or stage four depends on a number of factors, but above all whether or not management has a vision of the long-term implications of the role of information in their industry. Stage four can be approached at a tactical level to merely improve the efficiency of data exchanges and hence reduce cost, or as the basis for future strategic change – just as internal automation can lead to further possibilities for improved business performance. Stages one, two or four do not, in themselves, demand the redesign of business processes or organisation structures, but often the full benefits are only realised by restructuring after the new systems are in place and have produced cost and time savings. In essence, therefore, top management can adopt a *reactive* but not a *passive* position, ie they need to react appropriately to the new opportunities as they occur, but a proactive approach is likely to lead to earlier benefits and hence an ability to identify and plan further stages of development.

However, in order to gain business advantages through change top management cannot be purely reactive. In stage three many of the business's information systems need to be integrated to enable the business as a whole to respond more effectively to its environment. This requires top management to understand and then drive the need for change. To achieve success requires an appropriate theme as the basis for integration, since the restructuring might well be different if the theme were dramatic cost reduction rather than improvements to customer service or shorter lead times for getting new products to the market. The particular information resources and flows around which the restructuring would take place, the objectives for change would be different and different parts of the organisation would be affected. Therefore the agenda for change must be set at the top, otherwise disintegration is just as likely as integration.

Stage five in Figure 11.1 also requires a degree of management vision to understand the implications of organisations sharing information about, for instance, stock levels, costs, forecasts and capacity availability. If used properly both parties can benefit enormously through accelerated response to change and more accurate matching of demand and supply. But there is always the risk that the trust involved is abused to the disadvantage of one of the parties. Once new information relationships have been established within an industry then scope exists for stage six to develop, whereby who does what in the industry begins to change. This often produces major improvements in the efficiency of the industry overall, potentially to the benefit of all, but unless an organisation has by now integrated its own internal systems effectively (stage three) it may find it cannot fit efficiently into the new industry structure. This restructuring of the industry is very likely to lead to further internal restructuring of each of the organisations involved.

A recent Butler Cox Foundation report (1991)[9] quotes a number of examples of companies from a variety of industries who have made radical changes to core business processes, either internally or in cooperation with trading partners. Many have achieved considerable cost reductions in the processes and/or dramatically improved service levels to customers. In every case the new information systems were integral to the process redesign and in all cases organisational and role changes were essential to achieve the business change. In order to uncover such business options the report suggests that there are five key stages which need to be coordinated by a changed management task force. The stages in summary are:

1. developing a business vision of potential new ways of working and setting objectives for change;
2. analysing the business processes and redesigning them;
3. establishing the new organisation structure required;
4. gaining commitment of the staff involved;

5. developing and implementing the new information systems.

It is important to note that whilst it is the capabilities of IT which enable new ways of doing business, the actual development of the new systems is the last stage of the process. The report argues that unless the earlier stages are achieved successfully, then the systems themselves will fail to deliver the range of business benefits available. The starting point is senior management establishing a vision for how the business could be different in the future. Historically senior management have played a relatively reactive role in approving the IS/IT investment plan devised by others. In the future they must instigate the themes which will drive the IS strategy and create the organisational culture and climate within which IS/IT investment is one of the routes to achieving step-changes in business performance.

## MANAGING INFORMATION SYSTEMS TO SUCCESS

Whilst it is vital that top management have the vision to initiate appropriate change in their business's process and structure based on what IS/IT can enable, it is also important that they understand some key aspects of how to bring the IS developments to success. It is not enough to have the vision, if the organisation cannot achieve it in practice. The earlier part of the chapter described how IS/IT is being used to bring about change in general terms, but any organisation at any one time is faced with a specific set of business and IS/IT challenges and is living with the legacy of its previous developments. The existing systems have to be managed as well as the new developments and over time the *portfolio* of information systems the organisation has, is developing or needs, will change. It will even be necessary to get rid of old systems, although this often proves just as difficult as removing 'dog' products from the product portfolio.

Management need a framework for understanding how to manage the IS portfolio in a coherent way over an extended period in order to ensure that overall they are 'getting real value for money' from IS/IT – or, as it might be better expressed, 'maximising the business contribution of information system and technology investments'. A portfolio analysis technique which is very similar in concept to a product portfolio approach can be used to help management maximise that contribution. It has proved very valuable to many organisations in achieving a consensus view amongst senior managers, users and IT specialists of how to manage the different systems. That understanding and agreement on what is to be done and how is essential if developments are to succeed, benefits are to be realised and resources used effectively, in both the short and long term.

The detailed rationale for the approach is explained elsewhere by the author (Ward et al 1990).[10] The purpose here is to explain its use as a way of ensuring IS/IT investments are appropriately managed. The portfolio is described in terms of a 2 × 2 matrix as shown in Figure 11.2, the axes of which allow assessment of the current and future importance of any existing or new system, ie how it contributes to current business performance and/or enables future strategies to be achieved. The matrix classifies systems and their associated information into one of four types.

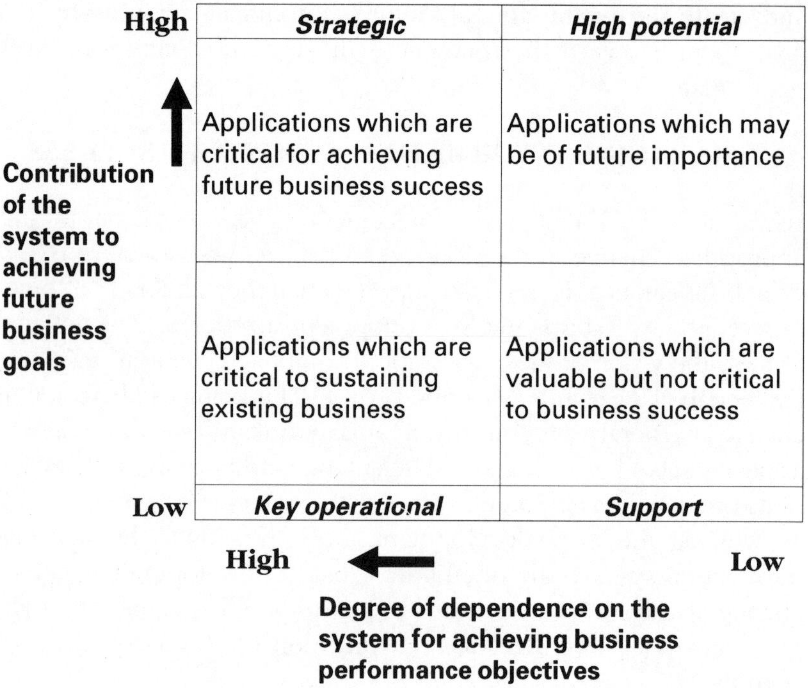


**Figure 11.2** An information systems portfolio: based on business contribution

## *Support applications*

This is where IS/IT is used to improve the performance of business activities, achieving productivity or efficiency improvements which deliver mainly economic benefits. Over time good support systems reduce business costs and enable people to be used more appropriately, but they are not critical to the business achieving its current or future objectives. Examples would be general accounting, personnel record keeping, expense reporting systems etc. Many of the uses of spread sheets and other PC based packages would fall into this category, as well as some major organisation-wide systems. Often 'package' solutions are available for such systems because the needs are very similar in many companies.

### *Key operational applications*

Here, IS/IT is embedded in the core activities of the business such that if the system fails the business has immediate and significant problems – orders or customers are lost, supplies cannot be purchased etc, leading to real loss of revenue or profitability in the short term. Problems and weaknesses in these systems lead to business disadvantages, since there is no realistic alternative way of running the business from day to day. Examples might be order management, inventory control, accounts receivable or production scheduling in a manufacturing company. The quality of the data and the degree of integration between these systems are critical to their success, if disadvantages due to errors, inconsistencies and delays are to be avoided.

### *Strategic applications*

Strategic applications are those which enable the organisation to achieve its future objectives and/or gain a competitive advantage – either because others do not have such systems or because the system is significantly better than those of competitors. Examples might be a sales forecasting system which reacts more quickly to market changes or a PC based system used by sales people to capture business from new customers or links to suppliers to achieve just-in-time (JIT) delivery of components and hence reduce inventory costs to virtually zero. The nature of strategic applications will depend on the stage of development of IS/IT in the industry and how well the organisation can link IS/IT investments to specific business objectives.

### *High potential applications*

These are not really systems at all, in that they are areas of R&D which may *lead to* new systems developments. New ideas for systems or new technologies are evaluated to determine what the potential benefits are and whether further developments are worthwhile. Many will prove to be worthless but a few may provide the basis for strategic investments. Examples might be the evaluation of image processing technology for document management or the feasibility of using expert systems to model the behaviour of competitors. The evaluation may be by means of a prototype, or by assessing market acceptance of an idea or by a purely 'paper' evaluation of the economics and capabilities of new technology.

The objective of such a classification is to determine the criticality of the relationship between the existing systems and new investments and business success and hence determine how the application should be managed. In any organisation it is important to establish an agreed view of the portfolio; a view which reconciles the different perspectives held by senior management, business users and the IT specialists on what is to be done, why and how. Otherwise some or all of the investments will be ineffective and fail to deliver the expected benefits.

The types of benefits which applications in each segment of the portfolio produce are different, hence the process for identifying the investments and how they are managed will also differ. Some of the key differences in terms of 'driving forces' and 'critical requirements' for successful delivery are described in Table 11.2.

In essence investments in support and key operational systems are aimed at avoiding business disadvantages by continual improvements in the productivity, accuracy and speed of business processes, in line with key competitors in the industry. This may require redevelopment or improvements to existing systems to avoid falling behind competitors, eg by adding electronic links to customers or suppliers to exchange orders, invoices and so on. The systems must be kept up to date in terms of how the industry operates, but in addition the quality of the key operational systems will be a factor in the enterprise's ability to build further strategic systems. Most organisations have a wide range of existing key operational and support systems, built up over many years. This normally results in two problems:

1. They are poorly integrated and the information resource is at best poorly structured and at worst incoherent, as stated earlier.
2. Much of the IT resource is tied up in maintaining this complex, ageing mix of systems and supporting technologies.

Over time these problems inhibit further development and the way key operational and support systems are managed affects the ability of the organisation to move forward. It is critical to replace this 'base' with more integrated, less resource intensive systems over time. Many companies are tackling this systematically with a combination of database driven systems and software packages. Others are resolving the resourcing issue by out-

**Table 11.2** Some key issues in the segments of the portfolio

| | *Driving forces* | Critical requirements |
|---|---|---|
| *High potential* | – New business idea or technological opportunity<br>– Individual inititative – owned by a 'product champion'<br>– Need to demonstrate the value or otherwise of the idea | – Rapid evaluation of prototype and avoid wasting effort/resources on failures<br>– Understand the potential (and the economics) in relation to business strategy<br>– Identify the best way to proceed – the next step |
| *Strategic* | – Market requirements, competitive pressures or other external forces<br>– Business objectives, success factors and vision of how to achieve them<br>– Obtaining an advantage and then sustaining it | – Rapid development to meet the business objective, and realise benefits within the window of opportunity<br>– Flexible system that can be adapted in the future as the business evolves<br>– Link to an associated business initiative to sustain commitment |
| *Key operational* | – Improving the performance of existing activities (speed, accuracy, economics)<br>– Integration of data and systems to avoid duplication, inconsistency and misinformation<br>– Avoiding a business disadvantage or allowing a business risk to become critical | – High quality, long life solutions and effective data management<br>– Balancing costs with benefits and business risks – identity the best solution<br>– Evaluation of options available by objective feasibility study |
| *Support* | – Improved productivity/efficiency of specific (often localised) business tasks<br>– Legal requirements<br>– Most cost effective use of IS/IT funds and resources available | – Low cost, long-term solutions – often packaged software to satisfy most needs<br>– Compromise the needs to the software available<br>– Objective cost/benefit analysis to reduce financial risk and then control costs carefully |

sourcing the support for such systems.

The strategic and high potential segments are aimed at gaining advantages for the business in much the same way as 'star' and 'wild cat' products are needed to deliver and sustain the enterprise's long-term success. In the applications portfolio they represent the ways in which the business can or could possibly use information systems to achieve advantage by out performing the competitors now and in the future. To achieve this they need to be linked closely to the business strategy and directly support the essential ingredients of that strategy – those ingredients that differentiate the company in some way from its competitors. That implies that these IS investments will be unique to the company in some way and will be part of a process of changing what the organisation does and how it does it to achieve the key differentiators. The organisation will need to use its own skills and resources not only to define what is to be done, but also to avoid the advantage being rapidly eroded by copying by competitors. Clearly retaining the 'secrets' of how it was achieved and having the vision of how to exploit the opportunities created will reduce the chances of losing the advantages too soon. The 'how' does not just refer to the 'system' but also to the changed relationships developed with trading partners and in the way the activities have been reorganised and people have changed the way they work.

## DEFINING THE COMPLETE PORTFOLIO: MANAGEMENT APPROACHES

Earl (1990)[11] has reviewed the ways in which organisations plan their IS/IT investments and describes a number of fundamentally different processes. It appears that 'traditional' approaches to IS/IT planning are appropriate to manage the key operational and support segments of the portfolio in a controlled way, with the objective of avoiding disadvantages. Further examination of these processes in research at Cranfield shows that three of Earl's approaches are used jointly by most organisations to tackle these segments of the application portfolio:

1. **Technology driven** – to provide an IT infrastructure as a foundation on which a variety of applications can be developed in a cost-effective and, where appropriate, integrated way. Whilst each system may not be done in an optimum way the approach produces the most effective overall architecture of information, systems and technology.
2. **Method driven** – uses highly structured techniques to analyse business processes and information flows in detail to identify the systems and data resources required and their relationships. Such

techniques are best applied to stable areas of the business, but can identify some process and organisation changes to improve business performance.

3. **Administrative led** – the objective is to ensure that all investments are budgeted for and approved formally so that the plan and the particular systems are endorsed by management. Particular managers are then accountable for their spend and for delivering benefits in their area of responsibility.

With a combination of these approaches a coherent, manageable suite of support and key operational systems can be developed and maintained. Most of the benefits result from cost displacement, linking specific activities together more effectively and accelerating some business processes, in the terms used by Parker et al.[12]

However, Earl and others have recognised that to identify potential strategic and high potential applications requires a different set of approaches. The three approaches above can, for the most part, be delegated by senior management to the business users and IT specialists, within a set of organisational policies. The two approaches suggested by Earl, to determine the opportunities for strategic and high potential investments and manage them to success, require senior management involvement in the planning.

## *Business led planning*

This is the term used by Earl to describe how business managers have to interpret, usually via a form of critical success factor (CSF) assessment, how information and systems are related to the achievement of overall or functional business objectives. This assessment can lead to the need for improvements to existing systems, and shows how information systems can be used to achieve the business changes implied by the CSFs. This process can be used both across and within functions, depending on whether the assessment process is orchestrated by senior management based on overall objectives and/or carried out by functional managers. Obviously the approach has more to offer if carried out at both levels in a structured, systematic way. It can produce both high potential ideas (what is needed can be defined, but how to do it needs further evaluation) or strategic opportunities (both the what and the how are known).

The potential weakness of this approach is that it takes a relatively short-term view based on the current business objectives, which may only relate to 12–18 months ahead, and many of the CSFs will reflect current or even historical problems.

Earl's last approach overcomes this weakness and provides a complementary process. From the empirical evidence it appears to provide the best way of defining how, in the longer term, strategic advantages can be gained from IS investments.

### *Organisation led planning*

This approach is based on 'themes' for the use of IS in supporting the long-term direction of the business, which may incorporate current objectives but considers the mission and longer-term strategy of the enterprise. The themes are developed by senior management to focus others on how IS could be used to bring about major changes in business performance. For instance, a major manufacturer of pharmaceuticals has developed two such key themes where excellence in IS is critical. First they wish to coordinate manufacturing worldwide, to rationalise and then optimise the manufacture and distribution of existing and future drugs. This will require a new approach to its systems, as will the second which is to reduce the lead time for drug development (a very information intense set of processes) by several years. In a similar vein, a major oil company is restructuring its exploration process to use prospecting teams to carry out all the activities associated with finding and evaluating major oil fields, rather than the traditional approach to appraising a set of prospects through each technical and business stage in different organisational functions. All these examples are 'themes' which imply major changes to the existing systems and the need for new systems to enable the enterprise to work in new ways. Each will take a number of years to achieve. Having established the direction the next stage is for the functional managers acting in concert to ascertain how this could be done, in the way that was described by the Butler Cox five stage approach, and by being able to recognise how options identified by the business led approach contribute to this longer-term vision for change.

Without both of these two approaches it is unlikely that an enterprise will be able to both identify and then achieve many IS applications of either a high potential or strategic nature. Traditional ways of determining IS investments cannot be neglected – they will continue to be essential in managing key operational and support investments. 'Business' and 'organisation' led approaches are complementary to that and are essential if business vision and objectives are to be translated into systems which bring about the types of change and benefits considered earlier in the chapter. As organisations by choice or otherwise seek the higher order benefits which IS can bring about in conjunction with business and organisational change, the benefits become less easy to quantify in relation to the IS project alone. They result from a combination of changes enabled in part by the IS investment and that investment cannot be assessed in isolation but has to be judged in the wider context of the business strategy. Hence senior management must not only establish that context but also ensure that the users and providers of the systems understand it.

## SUMMARY AND CONCLUSIONS

This chapter has attempted to provide greater understanding of the increasingly important interrelationships between information management and business and organisational strategies. Figure 11.3 summarises how the three key concepts of the chapter are related, i.e

- the nature of the benefits of IS/IT investments and how their achievement is related to business and organisational changes;
- the portfolio analysis for assessing the contribution of different IS/IT investments; and
- the management approaches required to enable the different types of investments to be identified.

Clearly, the diagram is an oversimplified view of the world but it is intended to show that there are some patterns – relationships between how an organisation plans its IS/IT investments, how it understands the contribution they make to business success and the types of changes needed to ensure that contribution can be realised. By ensuring that all these key aspects of information management are managed coherently, at least the business will not find itself at a disadvantage because of its information resources, and at best some specific business advantages may be obtained. A lack of recognition by management of these key relationships is likely to lead to many failed IS/IT investments, which will be less affordable in the 1990s since they are likely to lead very quickly to real business disadvantages. It is one of many management challenges of the 1990s: it is also a challenge which many managers have often declined to accept in the past. More understanding of the way information management and business success are linked and some insight as to how that interdependence can be dealt with, should enable more managers to accept the challenge in the future and succeed.

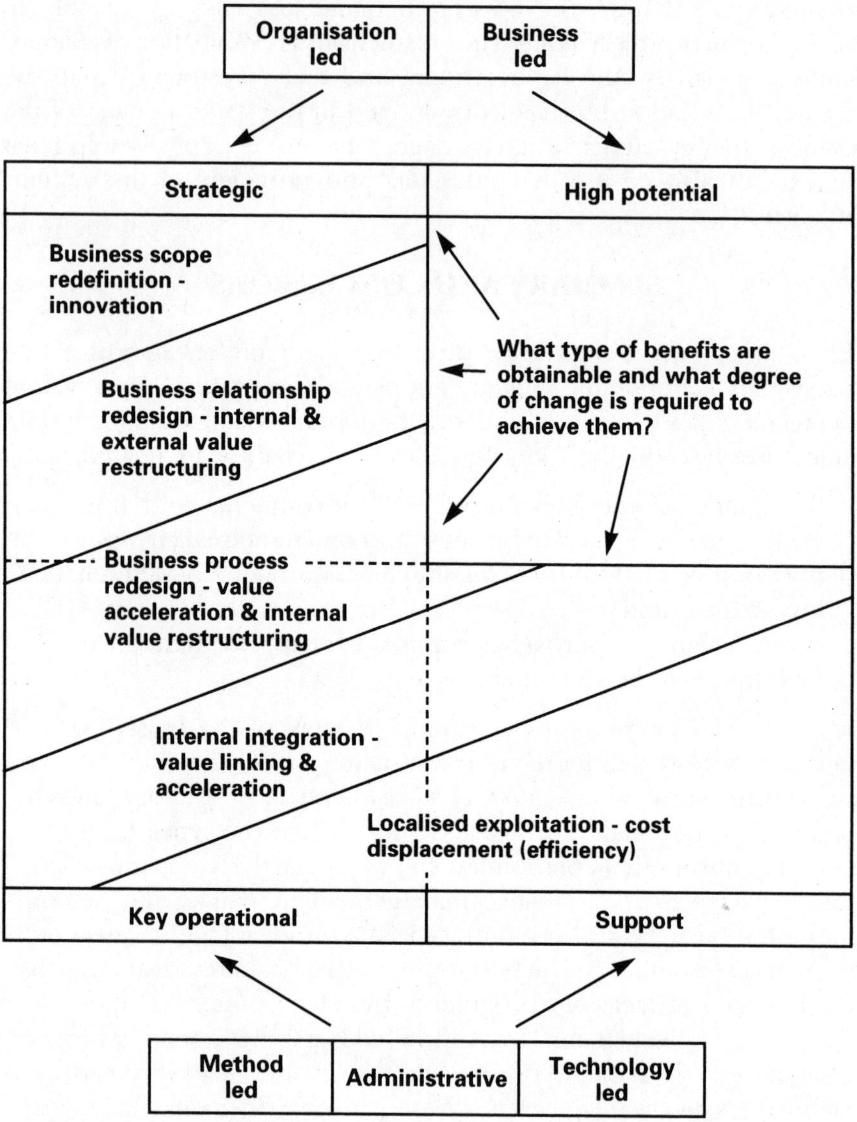


**Figure 11.3** Overall relationships between the applications portfolio, the benefits available and the planning approach required

## References

1. Scott Morton, M S (ed) (1991) *The Corporation of the 1990s*, Oxford University Press

2. Strassman, P A (1985) *Information Payoff*, The Free Press, Macmillan, New York
3. Davis, S and Davidson, W (1991) *2020 Vision*, Simon & Schuster, Hemel Hempstead
4. Drucker, P F (1988) 'The Coming of the new Organisation', *Harvard Business Review*, Jan-Feb
5. Zuboff, S (1989) *In the Age of the Smart Machine: The Future of Work and Power* Heinemann Professional, Oxford
6. Handy (1991) *The Age of Unreason*, Arrow, London
7. Venkatraman, N (1991) 'IT induced business reconfiguration' in *The Corporation of the 1990s*, Oxford University Press, pp 122–58
8. Parker, M M, Benson, R J, with Trainor, H E (1988) *Information Economics*, Prentice Hall, New Jersey, USA
9. Butler Cox Foundation (1991) *The Role of Information Technology in Transforming the Business*, Report no 79, Butler Cox plc
10. Ward, J M, Griffiths, P M, Whitmore P (1990) *Strategic Planning for Information Systems* Wiley, Chichester, pp 29–37, 246–79
11. Earl, M J (1990) 'Approaches to Strategic IS Planning in 21 UK Companies', *Proceedings of the International Conference on IS*, Copenhagen
12. Parker, M M et al (1988) *op cit*

12

# STRATEGIC CHANGE: THE ROLE OF THE TOP TEAM

*Siobhan Alderson and Andrew Kakabadse*

## INTRODUCTION

This chapter is based on research work conducted at Cranfield School of Management by the top executive research team. The research set out to answer questions like: What does vision mean at the top? What is required for consistent success as a top manager? What does the word 'team' really mean at the top? What does it take to perform well as a top team and as an individual in a top team?

Through intimate involvement, in a consultancy and research capacity, with 36 separate public and private industry and service sector organisations, throughout the UK, the US, Ireland, Greece, and France, and through the executive competencies questionnaire developed as a result of this in depth research, and distributed to thousands of executives all over Europe, the research programme has come up with some key findings in answer to its initial questions, and has been able to quantify and statistically prove many key relationships between top management team performance and personal, organisational, and business success. Several of these key relationships are shown in tables *in this work.

The research shows that:

- the quality of executive interactions can enhance or damage a business;

---

* Tables adapted and taken from Kakabadse, A P (1991) *The Wealth Creators*, Kogan Page, London

- the top team is crucial because it is the key forum for strategic dialogue;
- there are a number of key competencies associated with high individual, team, and organisational performance;
- the values which executives hold concerning how the business, organisation and people should be managed can profoundly affect top team interactions;
- there are clearly identifiable organisation, business, and people impacts associated with executive and team performance and behaviour.

From the findings of the research the great importance of the top team in strategic decision-making and strategic change becomes apparent, and suggestions for appropriate individual and team executive development are made.

## THE TOP TEAM AND STRATEGIC CHANGE

Within a business organisation, the top team is the key forum for strategic dialogue. Top managers have in common a high degree of discretion, that is, the ability to make strategic choices and decisions. It follows that both the performance and behaviour of individual top managers and the performance and behaviour of top teams has major implications for the strategic direction and ultimate success of the organisation.

In previous literature, the foundations for the belief that top management teams are crucial to strategic success are well set. Hambrick[1] notes that 'team qualities are the essential foundation for a successful strategic process within the firm', and lists 'open mindedness', 'perseverence', 'communication skills', and 'vision' as key competency areas. Hambrick concludes that 'the business with a top team whose qualities are well suited to emerging trends in the environment, as well as forming a complementary whole, will have the best chance of competitive success'. Mann[2] also espouses the notion that it is essential for top management to have clear vison and objectives, as well as the ability to clarify roles and direction. Mann acknowledges that these are areas which require very specific development. Westley and Mintzberg[3] discuss visionary leadership and conclude that it must encompass 'strategic content as well as the strategic contexts of product, market, issue, process, and organization'. The authors also conclude that 'how the vision is communicated . . . becomes as important as what is communicated'. The issue of shared top management vision and values is addressed by Bender, Murphy, and Redden[4] when they assert that 'different values placed on strategic planning and a lack of commitment to and ownership of the process will obstruct and limit the change process'. These authors further develop the notion of top management's role in strategic change by concluding that top management must communicate the goals of change clearly, allow time for change and initiatives, clearly define responsibilities, identify interim goals and resistance to them, while clearly defining long-term objectives.

The competence and performance of individual top managers and top management teams, then, is particularly important in times of strategic change, where strong, clear, and principled leadership is needed. At times of strategic change there is uncertainty in organisations and both business and people are vulnerable to confusion and demotivation. Clear vision, strong top management team cohesion and clear communication are particularly vital at this time.

From the research, a number of key competencies and behaviours were identified, along with clearly identifiable opportunity costs of low performance on these key areas. These competencies and behaviours are important in all circumstances for high individual team and organisational performance, but are particularly important for successfully and effectively managing change and transition.

## MANAGING THE PROCESSES INVOLVED IN GENERATING A VISION FOR THE FUTURE

### *Vision*

Once in a role of strategic responsibility, each manager needs to form a vision for the future of the organisation or function for which he is responsible and accountable. Individuals may foresee radical change, or they may wish to maintain the status quo. *Not* forming a vision for the future causes clearly identifiable problems:

- Organisation/function not focused to achieve objectives;
- Resources poorly utilised;
- Confusion and disarray concerning objectives and strategy;
- Demoralisation of personnel;
- Decline of the business.

Forming a sincerely held vision for his area of responsibility and accountability is based on the individual's *ability to manage discretion*, their *in depth knowledge of the business* and their *understanding of sales and marketing as far as the business is concerned.* In large organisations, the contribution of the corporate centre is also particularly important.

### Managing discretion

At the top level of management with which this research deals, one characteristic common to all role incumbents is discretion. Discretion is the choice available to managers to identify and pursue the policies, strategies and directions that are deemed appropriate. Managing discretion effectively demands an intimate understanding of the parts of the business other than those for which the manager is responsible, and an ability to manage functional objectives as integrated with corporate objectives.

Managerial maturity is the ability to invite, receive and handle feedback calmly and well; the discipline to practise an open, listening style; and the patience and tolerance to work through ambiguous and unclear issues and situations while maintaining cohesion in the team and sustaining morale among staff and management. These are all crucial personal qualities at the level of discretion which top management possess.

### In depth knowledge of the business

Forming a realistic and enhancing vision of the future mean having an intimate knowledge of the business and the markets in which operates. This means an intimate understanding of the different functior within the business and their contribution to overall corporate goals. It mns having a clear understanding of customers, suppliers, and competirs; of their needs and the best ways of managing and nurturing preserand future relationships with them. It also means having a coprehensive understanding of costs and revenue structures, the time need for sales, and the nature and life cycle of products/services. Being able recognise and concern oneself with relevant detail within the lits of one's discretion is what distinguishes the high performing execute.

### Understanding sales and marketing as far as th business is concerned

The key phrase here is 'as far as the business is concerneds part of the formation of a meaningful vision for the future, extives must understand and appreciate in depth what both sales and rketing mean for the business. Understanding the contribution of each ftion and part of the business towards the achievement of sales and marketing objectives; recognising whether members of the top team share an appreciation or are divided as to what sales and marketing practices are wanted; recognising whether debate has or has not taken place about any differences of view; and recognising when the top team are committed to decisions about the shape of sales and marketing for the business are all important parts of understanding the true nature of sales and marketing as far as the business is concerned and of forming a realistic vision for the future.

## EFFECTIVE SHARED VISION FOR THE FUTURE

Holding and enacting a vision for the future involves the whole team: it is not sufficient that each member holds a vision for the future. Vision must be *shard*. This means negotiation, consensus and a team commitment to the emergent view, so that strategies, structures, and cultures can be created, maintained, and managed to achieve the vision. Individual variations and inputs are still important, but must be managed within the context f achieving a shared team vision.

If visio is not shared, the top team will pull in different directions, each membe pursuing his own path, resulting in division and incompatible strategie Because, once a vision is formed, an individual may be reluctant o open to change, and long-term damage to the team, and hence to he organisation, can occur. Failure to share a vision for the future an failure to overcome the problems preventing shared vision are directly a clearly associated with poor management of the organisation, poor ma gement of change, declining business performance, low morale, a conflict and poor cohesion within the team. The effects of 'split visi can be summarised as follows:

- Obje es poorly defined and communicated;
- Poor derstanding/knowledge of the structure;
- Orga tion structure in need of improvement;
- Reorg sations viewed as poorly planned and implemented;
- Mann n which functions/departments are run viewed as requiring attenti
- Poor i rnal controls and wastage due to poor understanding of the structu
- Rules, cedures and guidelines not respected due to poor environment;
- Marke anges to products/services poorly managed;

- Frictions within top team communicated downwards and damage relationships down the line;
- Little pride in the organisation;
- Poor response to new initiatives;
- Problems exaggerated with larger organisations;
- Interpersonal problems;
- Identification with functions/departments rather than the corporate whole leading to diminished awareness of issues;
- Lack of trust in top management down the line;
- Lack of basic discipline;
- Poor follow through on commitments;
- Interdepartmental/interfunctional collaboration poor;
- Low job satisfaction leading to resignations;
- Declining business performance.

## MOULDING A TEAM IDENTITY FROM PEOPLE WHO HAVE DIFFERENT STYLES AND ATTITUDES

The mix of leadership styles, personalities and personal values within the top team can inhibit or facilitate discussion on strategic issues which are sensitive or difficult to discuss. The mix can also affect the ability of the team to decide upon and share a vision for the future. Understanding how to manage the top team, therefore, is crucial to generating an effective, shared vision and strategies that work.

Values are deep seated convictions which people hold about events, situations and processes. Business values refer to the 'what should be done' of business, for example quality of service, customer care, and 'right first time', and there is little dispute as to which values an executive or team should hold for optimising business performance. However there is another set of values or orientations which refer to 'how' things should be done. These 'process orientations' refer to style, philosophy of management, and fundamental approaches to managing situations. They strongly influence the interactions between executives, since they not only affect their approach to managing the business but also to managing and interacting with others. Most importantly, they influence whether or not, and to what depth, executives will be able to mutually understand and communicate with each other. These orientations affect the way in which managers make and implement decisions, and determine what business values are adopted, so they affect individual relationships, decision-making, and culture. In effect, they influence the whole organisation.

In the research, six orientations were identified. It is important to understand that no individual holds one exclusive orientation, but that all individuals hold varying mixes of these process values.

1. *Low disclosure oriented*: The individual communicates on an 'only what they need to know basis'. Such a manager may be insensitive to the needs of others, and believe strongly that they should do what is required of them. People and the organisation are seen as a system which requires instructions to perform. This individual does not appreciate that communication is something other than telling people what to do. This orientation may develop because of a failure to appreciate the need to develop other people to accept delegation, or because of an overly strong task orientation.
2. *Discipline oriented*: The discipline oriented individual has a high regard for the maintenance of structure, protocol and role boundaries within the organisation. Such highly disciplined individuals are effective at administration, and they will certainly run an 'efficient, tight ship'. However, they may be resistant to change, particularly change derived from external development initiatives.
3. *Specialist oriented*: An individual with this orientation identifies with the values of a functional discipline profession, or particular technical expertise. The person may exact and expect high standards which are professionally acceptable, but which may be inappropriate in particular individual or organisational situations. Communication may be easier with people from a similar discipline, and blockages may occur in communication with those who do not understand or identify with the professional values. They may have difficulty appreciating the demands of the general management aspects of their role and may find it difficult to see beyond their own discipline to broader issues.
4. *Independence oriented*: The independence oriented individual needs to be able to express and apply their own views. They have a high need for personal space, like to do things their own way, and view encroachments on this space quite negatively. Particular problems may arise when one or more executives hold independence oriented values within a team, making a cohesive and shared vision difficult to attain.
5. *Interpersonally oriented*: This individual judges people by their overall appearance and manner, their interpersonal skills, and their interpersonal behaviour. Others may be judged simply on whether they are comfortable to be with. Supportive, comfortable interactions are viewed positively, while negative interactions may be seen as threats. Such an individual may be blinded or blocked by their

emotions and thus fail to appreciate the skills, role, performance and contribution of the other party with whom they are dealing. As a result, their decision-making may also be emotionally driven.

6. *Intergration oriented*: The 'integrator' is sensitive to both the business and people dimensions of organisational life. They are sensitive to the problems and needs of their team colleagues, subordinates, external business, stakeholders, and the demands and constraints of internal organisational circumstances. The aim of such an individual is to help people to come to terms with their challenges and constraints, identify with the organisation, and face the future as a team. This person works closely with and through other people: he is able to judge the progress, and understand the challenges, of effective team interaction.

Moulding a team identity and shaping the team means managing and handling personalities and their values in such a way as to ensure that ownership and commitment in implementing vision and strategies for the future is shared. If team identity and composition are not managed properly poor performance is the result. Objective setting and communication poor and unclear. Morale and motivation are low. Trust within the top team, and of the top team at lower levels suffers. Particularly vulnerable to poor top team performance are general managers, for it is they who are the buffer between the top team and the levels below, and it is they who must field dissatisfaction from both directions. Sensitive but crucial issues are not addressed, initiatives and relationships are poorly managed, and eventually performance and the existence of the business may be threatened. The effects of a poor top team are:

- poor market responsiveness;
- poorly configured structure;
- low follow through;
- poor internal controls;
- low strategic insight;
- poor morale.

## SHAPING THE BUSINESS

It has been said already that executives must have an intimate understanding of the business in order to form a meaningful and workable vision for the future. In addition to this there are specific competencies required to shape and manage the business so as to fulfil the vision.

### *Understanding and identifying structure*

Executives need to understand and know the structure of the organisation. This means being able to clearly identify the structural type and appreciate its advantages and limitations as far as the business and its vision and strategies are concerned. Understanding how the structure facilitates or constrains individuals, functions, and business units in achieving their objectives is important, as well as being able to identify structural changes and adaptations that need to be made to further facilitate achievement of these objectives. The impact of organisational structure must be clearly recognised in business terms.

### *Clear identification of performance targets*

Executives must be able to identify and set individual, functional, and organisational performance targets so that they best contribute towards the achievement of overall organisational goals, objectives and strategies, in this way contributing towards the fulfilment of the vision.

Performance targets must be realistic. If targets are too high, damaging, overly competitive relationships may be established within the organisation, or individuals may be overstretched and demotivated. Likewise if targets are too low, peak performance will not be achieved and individuals may feel understretched.

### *Clearly identifying responsibilities*

In order to achieve their objectives, individuals and functions must clearly understand their role and their accountabilities, ie precisely what *is* expected of them and what their responsibilities are. Within the overall vision and strategies, executives must be able to identify, communicate and ensure that these individual roles and accountabilities are understood and recognised.

### *Knowing the job*

An understanding of the top management role happens with time. This research has shown that an executive must be at least five years in his role before peak performance is achieved. Performance continues to rise after

**Table 12.1** Effects of clearly and poorly defined responsibilities

| | |
|---|---|
| • Poor cash flow control | • Disciplined staff and management |
| • Poor meeting discipline | • Higher tolerance for people |
| • More time on administration than customers | • Higher Levels of feedback |
| • Internal controls and systems seen as synonymous with bureaucracy | • Positive attitude to change |
| • Lose track of new initiatives | • Ownership of the job |
| • Job dissatisfaction | • More supportive senior management |
| • Self rather than team orientation | • Job satisfaction |
| • Staff turnover | • Greater follow through |

five years until about ten years in the role. Within the role executives must understand their limitations and their competence at different stages so as to maximise their effectiveness. The following qualities all greater impact as an individual approaches ten years total in a particular job:

- Understanding and influencing organisation structure;
- Trust and tolerance;
- Follow through;
- Attention to detail and discipline;
- Outlook and awareness of issues;
- Understanding of customers, competition and improving profitability.

### *Individual qualities and skills*

Individual executives must also possess appropriate personal qualities and business and people skills so as to perform effectively in their role, manage their function, and manage internal and external relationships effectively.

## PRACTISING THE PERSONAL QUALITIES AND SKILLS REQUIRED FOR EFFECTIVE PERFORMANCE AT SENIOR MANAGEMENT LEVEL

So as to be sensitive to what is happening in the organisation, executives must communicate effectively *and* be open to communication.

**Table 12.2** Qualities and skills identified

| Skills | Qualities |
| --- | --- |
| • *Job related* | • *Personality* |
| Functional | Humour |
| Technical | Sympathy |
| | Patience |
| | Honesty |
| • *Personal related* | • *Dynamism* |
| Intelligence | Forward thinking |
| Creativity | Creativity |
| Articulate | Judgement |
| Motivation | Energy/drive |
| All round ability | Versatility |
| • *Business related* | • *Management style* |
| External issues | Motivating |
| Internal issues | Being open with people |
| | Leadership |
| | People oriented |
| | Customer oriented |
| • *People related* | • *Inner strength* |
| People management | Determination |
| Training development | Resilience |
| Interpersonal skills | Logic |
| Communication | Discipline |

## Communication

At top executive level, communication means identifying and transmitting key business values shared and agreed by the top team. Business values, as has been mentioned earlier, concern areas such as service quality, customer care, respect for people and ethical stances. All these are affected by the process orientations which top team members hold. However, if a strong and committed culture is to be created, executives must share and communicate, with a sense of unity and commitment, the key business values on which they want to base the organisation.

Executives must also provide *direction*. Of course they will lead and manage, by virtue of their role as managers, but they must do this so that, by their actions and statements, they show also what the organisation represents and the values it espouses. They must give clear signals that they hold a shared vision of where the organisation is going by identifying and projecting the organisational identity through the mission statement and objectives.

**Table 12.3** Effects of good communication of mission and objectives

| *Objectives* | *Mission* |
|---|---|
| • Improved understanding of the structure | • People better informed |
| • Greater job satisfaction | • Positive attitude to change |
| • Greater respect for discipline | • Greater need for challenge |
| • Greater respect for organisation | • Greater attention to details |
| • People better informed | • Supportive attitude to others |
| • More positive attitude to change | • Greater openness |
| • Greater need for challenge | • Higher tolerance to pressure |
| • Greater commitment to the organisation | |
| • Greater openness | |
| • More supportive attitude to others | |

Top executives must provide *example*. They must act as they wish others in the organisation to act, for they are example setters. They must show consistency in their follow through on initiatives, communicate trust from within the team, and always be exemplary in their ethical conduct.

Finally, executives must be able to nurture and manage key interfaces, both internal and external. They must understand how key interfaces operate within the structure and be aware of any constraints on individuals or groups, and must understand the organisation's relationship to external interfaces and stakeholders.

## *Hearing what's said*

Hearing what's said means more than simply listening: it means projecting a desire to be approached and communicated to; having an openness of style which invites communication and feedback. Such openness demands managerial maturity, the ability to accept feedback and criticism without internalising it and 'taking it personally'.

Hearing what's said also involves the ability to manage feedback, both giving and receiving. Managing feedback effectively means a) managing the relationships within which feedback is given and b) understanding the maturity levels of others and tailoring feedback and response accordingly. Self understanding and an understanding of others is an important element of effective feedback, and involves taking into account others views and opinions and setting ground rules, such as guaranteeing follow through and action before feedback is given or received.

## GENERATING A POSITIVE, SUCCESS ORIENTED CULTURE WITHIN THE ORGANISATION

With top performing executives and top performing teams a culture of success and high performance is established. Such a culture has a number of characteristics.

Firstly, the culture gives people within the organisation the confidence and freedom to act. Individuals perceive that in their role and in the objectives which they have to achieve they are supported by top management who are in touch with and who understand and appreciate the constraints and demands facing people in their role. Objectives and business values are clear and communicated so that people know what they have to do and how they are expected to do it. Responsibilities and accountabilities are clearly defined. There is an attitude of tolerance of mistakes as opportunities for learning. Feedback and communication are well managed and part of the culture.

Secondly, the right business values are expounded. Success cultures value quality of service and customer care and they follow it through. In success cultures people count and are the primary resource of the organisation, to be treated with integrity and respect.

## OPPORTUNITY COSTS

A success culture is associated with high individual and team performance. Opportunity and personal costs are associated with low individual and team performance. The research clearly identified several specific areas of impact.

- Poorly allocated or misallocated overhead;
- Poor internal motivation strategies;
- Failure to address competitor impact;
- Lack of trust at the top;
- Weak business push;
- Lack of stakeholder awareness;
- Poor time perspective.

All the above factors are strongly associated with poor executive performance. Vision is not formed or shared, the business and sales and marketing are not understood, structure is not managed adequately, objectives are not set or communicated clearly, relationships are poor, and communication is sporadic. All of these failures of competence and business management can induce opportunity costs.

Poor individual and team performance can also lead to personal costs for the individual in the form of stress, effects on home life, reduced confidence to act, loss of motivation and drive, and emotional vulnerability. Any of these costs further reduce an individual's performance, effectiveness and confidence.

## APPROPRIATE DEVELOPMENT

This chapter has concerned the crucial role top management teams play in organisational and business performance. Appropriate management development strategy, therefore, centres on the team.

*Feedback* is the most important development strategy for both individuals and teams. The importance of developing a culture of feedback within the organisation has already been highlighted. But feedback is also vital in management development. Because top managers operate at the highest strategic levels, their need for feedback is very great: the more feedback which they can invite and assimilate, the more conscious they will be of their impact on the mission, strategy, and structure of the organisation.

Developing executives so that they can participate in and manage the feedback process effectively, involves examining and if necessary, improving, their capacity for self understanding, and examining their ability to handle appraisals. Such development also involves assisting *teams* in responding well to team feedback. For top teams, just as for individuals, the need for feedback centres around the need to understand how the quality of interaction amongst the team members impacts on management and the business growth of the organisation. In team feedback it is important to link individual and team performance and behaviour (styles and competencies) with their concrete business, organisational and people impacts. The *team grid*, developed by the research team, is an instrument which attempts to do this.

The process of team feedback, whether with an internal or external consultant, must be managed carefully, giving attention to the strong individual and team challenges and emotions to which it gives rise. The process needs to be carefully managed also because of the high level strategic impacts and processes with which top team actions and interactions are associated.

## CONCLUSIONS

The research on which this chapter is based is unique in that it is conducted at executive level, and has allow quantification of the idea that the quality of executive interactions can enhance or damage a business. A number of key competencies are identified for high individual, team, and organisational performance, and the characteristics of a success culture can be clearly identified. Similarly, clear damages and opportunity costs can be correlated with poor performance.

Because the top management team is the key forum for strategic dialogue and high team performance is vital in strategic change, management development, while important at the individual level, must concentrate on the team.

### References

1. Hambrick, D C (1989) 'The Top Management Team: Key to Strategic Success'
2. Mann, R W (1990) 'A Building Blocks Approach to Strategic Change', *Training and Development Journal*, pp 23–5, August
3. Westley, F and Mintzberg, H (1989) 'Visionary Leadership and Strategic Management', *Strategic Management Journal* 10, pp 17–32
4. Bender, A D, Murphy, A W, and Redden, J P (1990) 'Managing Strategic Change', *Healthcare Supervisor* 9, 2, pp 27–31

# INDEX